Are You Dancing?

IRISH CULTURE, MEMORY, PLACE

Oona Frawley, Ray Cashman, and Guy Beiner, editors

Are You Dancing?

Showbands, Popular Music, and Memory in Modern Ireland

REBECCA S. MILLER

INDIANA UNIVERSITY PRESS

This book is a publication of

Indiana University Press
Office of Scholarly Publishing
Herman B Wells Library 350
1320 East 10th Street
Bloomington, Indiana 47405 USA

iupress.org

First Printing 2025

Cataloging information is available from the Library of Congress.

ISBN 978-0-253-07235-1 (hardback)
ISBN 978-0-253-07236-8 (paperback)
ISBN 978-0-253-07238-2 (ebook)
ISBN 978-0-253-07237-5 (web PDF)

To my family,
Tom, Sam, and Avi Randall

CONTENTS

ACKNOWLEDGMENTS

I am grateful for all the assistance and encouragement I have received in researching and writing this book. Various institutions supported over a decades' worth of my fieldwork, beginning with a 2006 summer fellowship from the Marion and Jasper Whiting Foundation. Subsequent research in Northern Ireland and Ireland was supported by annual awards from Hampshire College's Mellon Foundation Summer Faculty Development as well as by three grants from Hampshire College's President's Office (2007–2009). Finally, I am grateful to the Centre for Irish Studies at the University of Galway (formerly the National University of Ireland, Galway) and the Irish-American Cultural Institute for a generous and well-timed fellowship (2018–2019) that supported fieldwork and research on Irish dance bands and orchestras.

Many musicians, fans, managers, promoters, and others generously agreed to an interview with me; indeed, theirs are the voices and experiences that animate this study. I had the great good luck to interview some artists not once but twice, and I thank them for the additional time they spent with me: Brendan Bowyer, Paddy Cole, Jim McDermott, Gay McIntyre, Martin Mulhaire, Margo O'Donnell, and, lastly, Jimmy Higgins, whose advice and help has been much appreciated as well as his generosity in allowing me access to his archive of showband postcards, photos, ephemera, and recordings. I also want to thank the following musicians and their family members for their generous hospitality: Ian Henry Garber and Judy Ferguson (Isle of Wight, England); Tony and Winnie Killeen (Greystones, Co. Wicklow); Claudette Colbert McCarthy (Florham Park, New Jersey); Henry McCullough and Josie (Ballymoney, Co. Antrim); Johnny Quigley and family (Derry, Co. Derry); Jim Reynolds and his daughter, Orlagh (Longford, Co. Longford); and Billy Robinson (Ramelton, Co. Donegal).

Many colleagues have helped me move this book forward. I am grateful to the faculty, staff, and graduate students at the Irish Studies Centre, University of Galway, for their collegial assistance and collective good humor during my fellowship year there, and especially to Méabh Ní Fhuartháin, whose longtime friendship, advice, and encouragement is much appreciated. I also thank Paul Maguire of Omagh and Paul McIntyre of Derry for their help locating key musicians in Northern Ireland as well as their generosity with my questions and fact checking. Many thanks go to colleagues in Irish Studies and media: Sean Campbell, Anna Falkenau, Paddy Gillan, Sara Goek, Dave Laing, Noel McLaughlin, James Rogers, Tes Slominski, William H. A. Williams, and three anonymous readers whose questions and ideas have helped me craft (and recraft) this manuscript. Early versions of essays that inform chapters 5, 7, and 8 appeared, respectively, in *New Hibernia Review, A Quarterly Record of Irish Studies*, 18, no. 3 (Autumn 2014); *Ordinary Irish Life: Music, Sport and Culture* (Dublin: Irish Academic Press, 2013); and *Popular Music History* 9, no. 3 (2014/2016).

At Hampshire College in Amherst, Massachusetts, I thank Rachel Beckwith and Yaniris Fernandez for help with research resources as well as John Gunther and Josiah Erickson for much appreciated tech help over the years. Many thanks also to Sean Norton for help with coding interviews and to Caitlin Allen, who, for nearly a decade, has done yeoman duty with interview transcriptions and fact-checking. I thank Louise Colligan, Brown Kennedy, and Nicola Smith for their thoughtful editorial suggestions on early chapters of the manuscript.

I am indebted to those who helped me locate photographs and secure permission to use them, many of which are rare and archival: Francis K. Beirne (www.irishshowbands.net), T.J. Byrne, Monica Coade, Sharon Coade, Sheila Mulhaire Colbert, Deirdre Connolly, Robert Flately (Knock Shrine), Pamela Frawley, Máire Harris (Gael Linn Records), Shirley Jones, James Laffey (*Western People*), Conor Makem, Rory Makem, Don Meade, Brendan Mulhaire, Sean Quinn, Fionnuala T. Regan, Tom Reilly, Ray Rooney, and Mary Reynolds Tielve. Thanks also to James J. Bunyan for contacts and advice; Noelle Dowling of Dublin's Diocesan Archives, Drumcondra, Dublin; Michael Fanning and The Tipperary Museum of Hidden History, for the copy of the 2020 CD, *Mick Delahunty and his Orchestra: the Lost Recordings*; David Nathan, Jazz Research Archivist at the National Jazz Archive, Loughton, England; and the University College Dublin Archives for access to the T. K. Whitaker papers. Finally, I am grateful to my editors at Indiana University Press—Bethany Mowry and Jennika Baines and their assistant, Sophia Hebert—for advice and support along the way.

Enormous thanks go to my family. I am always deeply grateful to my late mother, Lillian B. Miller, an art historian who taught me how to write, and to my late father, Nathan Miller, an economic historian who, even into his ninety-ninth year, was reading through manuscript chapters and offering spot-on suggestions. Special thanks to my husband, Tom Randall, for his support, keen ear, and expansive knowledge of popular music and early jazz. Last but certainly not least, I thank our sons, Sam and Avi Randall, both of whom served as able fieldwork assistants and whose smart, good humor continues to buoy me.

Are You Dancing?

1

Introduction

Remembering the Showbands, Documenting Popular Music

At the time, see, when . . . you come into the music business like this, and you're part of a band with very nice fellows in it, and you take on the road, everything is a novelty. You're young, you're adventurous, you're on for trying anything.

Eileen Kelly, vocalist, Nevada Showband

I suppose it was the dream at the time, you know? The showband carried a lot of what appeared to be class about it, you know, the in-thing, it was in vogue. You did all the good things that go with music. You'd always be seen in the hotels and driving cars, and you would be looked up to in the village, you know? And it was a big thing to be in the showband.

John Kelly, vocalist, Niagara Showband

In 1955, the late guitarist Henry McCullough attended his first live music event at the age of twelve. His mother had often taken him with her to her job as a cloakroom attendant at the Palais de Dance in Portstewart, in County Derry, Northern Ireland, but because he was young, he hadn't been allowed away from the cloakroom. This time, McCullough paid no mind and sneaked his way toward the new and groundbreaking music by the Clipper Carlton Showband: "They were massive, you know! And I remember it vividly: early Bill Haley stuff. You know, the saxophone player on his back, [the bass player] on top of the bass. He stood astride it and he twirled it round and round. That was the first band I ever saw. It made a huge impression on me!" (interview, 2007).

McCullough would go on to play in several Irish showbands before embarking on a career as an internationally acclaimed rock guitarist with Paul McCartney and Wings. The Clipper Carlton themselves would go on to revolutionize the course of Irish popular music. By landing on a formula that combined familiar musical and performance elements with contemporary pop hits, the Clipper Carlton not only inspired the next generation of Irish pop and rock musicians like McCullough but also, along with other early showbands, forged a new, quintessentially Irish showband sound.

From the mid-1950s through the mid 1970s, showbands generated massive excitement among legions of young men and women who had chosen to remain in Ireland rather than emigrate like many of their peers. Former showband drummer Mildred Beirne of Castleduff, Carracastle, County Mayo, remembers the 1950s as someone who stayed behind:

> Life was very simple. The only thing we had to look forward to was maybe the dance at night or meeting the people at crossroads . . . or meet at somebody's gate and talk and chat and talk about what the dance last night or where are we going next week? . . . I'd go to the dance and see the showbands. It was wonderful. And I loved to go into the dance and be the first one out on the floor. It was a wonderful time to be alive and be young. (Interview, 2007)

On the evening of a showband dance, young Irish men came in from the fields or home from the factories, washed up, and dressed in a formal suit with tie and collar. Young Irish women who worked returned home from agricultural or service industry jobs, changed clothes, and packed up their crinoline underskirts and shoes. Getting to the dance, whether at a local parochial or commercial dance hall or further afield in a neighboring town, posed its own challenges, recalls Eileen Lavin and Mary Duffy, respectively, of Aghamore and Charlestown, County Mayo:

> EL: We'd thumb to get there . . . down the road. There weren't many cars that would be coming, you'd be hoping somebody would come along.
>
> MD: In my day, people would cycle from Charlestown to a dance. There was no transport, no, but people thought nothing. I would have cycled to places maybe nine or ten miles away to dances, and then cycled home. . . . Your crinoline and your cushion in a bag, and then your shoes, your stilettos. And you put them in the back of your bicycle on a carrier. And then when you got to wherever you were going, you packed up the bag, and you put on the crinoline, and you put on the silk— [*laughter*]. (Interview, 2009)

The showband booked for that night would arrive several hours earlier in a vehicle with the band's name emblazoned on its sides. These wagons could fit most if not all the musicians, their instruments, and rudimentary sound systems. Showband musicians routinely spent long and tedious hours traveling to the evening's venue and while many would rather forget this aspect of the life of a professional musician, Miami Showband vocalist Dickie Rock recalls taking it in stride:

> We loved it. I loved traveling and I loved going on stage. It was tough work now! We'd arrive at a place maybe at 7:00 in the evening and the dance would start at 9:00 or half eight. And we'd work from 9:00 sometimes to 2:00 in the morning. . . . And we'd have an interval break. I would go bang, bang, bang, song after song after song. No breaks. . . . I'm lucky that I have the stamina and I don't get tired; I'm lucky that way. I love it, you know? (Interview, 2006)

Upon arriving, the band took to the stage to set up sound systems and tune instruments. Audiences paid their admissions at the door and once in the dance hall, separated into men on one side, women on the other recalls Mildred Beirne:

> So when the dance was called, the men all the way went across the floor. They'd have you sized up like first to see, could you dance? And they all went across their floor, [asked] 'Are you dancing?', picked up their lady, and out to dance then. 'Twas lovely. (Interview, 2007)

Audiences danced to the showband's rendering of the most recent pop and rock 'n' roll hits imported from Britain and the United States as well as old-time waltzes and the occasional Irish popular song. At the start of the showband era in the mid- to late 1950s, dancers took a break halfway through the evening and clustered around the stage to watch the "show," which, depending on the mood of the band members, included comedic and sometimes dramatic skits, and was always a highlight of the evening. While these shows dwindled by the 1960s and then disappeared altogether, what stuck was the name ("showband") as well as the variety of pop music and song styles that showbands were known for. Audiences looked forward to watching musicians perform live on stage, the excitement of dancing to the newest, popular sounds, and being part of an instant social community that offered the potential to meet future spouses, recalls County Donegal bassist/producer Billy Robinson:

> Dance halls weren't really about the music. I think good showbands attracted people because they were good, firstly, but mainly . . . people went there because there would be a good crowd. And because dance halls were mainly for men meeting women and women meeting men, it was like almost code. . . . It was very easy to say to a girl, "Do you want to dance?" And then you would say: "Would you like a mineral?" or "Would you like to drink a soft drink?" And then you would say, "Would you like a lift home?" And you never had to actually say, "Would you go out?" It was almost like a code: it was very easy to meet people, to meet each other. (Interview, 2009)

Beginning in the mid-1950s, the showband phenomenon hurtled into Ireland's popular music and dance landscape, ultimately displacing within a few years the majority of sit-down dance bands and orchestras that had dominated the Irish dance halls and marquees for more than four decades. Created by Irish musicians for Irish audiences, showbands emerged first in Northern Ireland with the Clipper Carlton, followed by other bands from the border region, and, soon after, from throughout Ireland. Despite these origins, the showband industry, particularly during its heyday in the mid-1960s, was largely unbounded by the border: Northern Irish showbands routinely traveled south, and showbands from Ireland seamlessly crossed the border to perform in Northern Ireland. The emergence of this new popular music scene was more significantly an outgrowth of Ireland's changing economic and social landscape than a response to the intrinsic economic policies of Northern Ireland. And while religion and sectarian conflict certainly played a role in the politics of Northern Ireland, these tensions, until around 1975, were insignificant in the largely apolitical showband world. Leaving politics at the ballroom door also held true for most showband audiences, particularly those in Northern Ireland, where Protestants and Catholics routinely and comfortably danced together even during the years of sectarian violence and upheaval.

Showbands typically consisted of seven to ten musicians who aimed to keep their fans entertained and dancing. They did so by learning the weekly hits from British and American radio broadcasts and bringing these new sounds, provocative choreographies, and glimpses of pop culture from outside of Ireland to audiences of sometimes two thousand or more. These performances riveted Irish youth, dismayed many parish priests (but delighted others), and revolutionized Irish popular entertainment. By the early 1960s, the showband phenomenon had grown into its own industry with hundreds of showbands crisscrossing Ireland in their vans up to six nights a week to perform in venues that ranged from small parish halls to cavernous ballrooms.

Irish showbands were not so much a transitional music genre; rather, they grew out of a peculiar confluence of economic, political, and social circumstances in Ireland, filling an entertainment vacuum generated by changing aesthetics and social demands. The showband industry got its start in no small part as a result of the vision of young male—and less visible but equally important female—entrepreneurs who saw the potential and opportunity in the fledgling groups and who willingly shouldered the risks of creating what would ultimately emerge as a highly lucrative popular music circuit. Their efforts were informed by and well timed with Ireland's improving economy beginning in the late 1950s, creating the space for a new musical industry, which itself would contribute to the economic renewal and growth of Ireland at the time.

Figure 1.1 The Miami Showband, publicity postcard, ca. 1962.

In laying the foundation for Ireland's contemporary popular music and recording industries, the showband scene was central to the rapidly shifting sensibility of identity among the young Irish audiences with respect to the larger world outside of Ireland. Similarly, in creating an altogether new performance aesthetic, one of the long-lasting effects was the changing perception of the role of musicians in general—from strictly working players whose job it was to provide dance music, to a new, elevated status as "entertainers." Inspired, in part, from recordings and film footage of American and British popular performers, early showband musicians quickly grasped the importance of charismatic stage performance and forced the gaze of the audience from the dance floor to the action on stage, thereby turning many showband musicians into overnight celebrities.

While every aspect of the showband industry was unquestionably male dominated, increasing numbers of women found their way onto the stage during these years as vocalists and, occasionally, instrumentalists. In some instances, women were able to break down even more barriers to become bandleaders themselves and, in doing so, would arguably pave the way for women in Irish popular music for decades to come.

Remembering (and Forgetting) Irish Popular Music, 1925–75

There is a paucity of documentation and scholarship not only on showbands but also on Irish popular music in general in the twentieth century up to the emergence of Irish rock music beginning in the late 1960s. Of the documentation and scholarship that does exist, there is a wide range of how showband music in particular is remembered and why. Former musicians and their fans unsurprisingly recall the music that they played and danced to in celebratory and often nostalgic terms. These narratives have been countered over the years by often vociferous critiques of showbands by popular music critics and academics. In the case of the dance bands and orchestras that dominated Irish dance halls before the showband years, there has been near total silence.

The contradictions as to how showbands are remembered point to something deeper at play or, in fact, the presence of a problem. To untangle this, I draw on the methods and approach central to the field of memory studies. Vernacular narratives, such as the interviews and oral histories that I liberally put to use here, add much-needed nuance and perspective to "official" historical, media, and academic accounts while also illustrating how individuals make sense of their past. The field of memory studies also draws on the flip side of memory—that is, forgetting—to better demonstrate how both facilitate the construction of identity going forward, a concept cogently articulated by historian Guy Beiner (2013, 9), who points out that "forgetting is not the antithesis, but an integral component, of memory." The fact that over fifty years of Irish popular music have, until now, been largely overlooked and, at times, forgotten is as telling as the emotion and range of terminology used by music scholars, critics, and others to convey how these music genres and trends are remembered. This also plays out periodically with occasional bursts of revived interest in Ireland's showband era, moments that generate new narratives much in keeping with Beiner's (2013, 11) observation that "the marking of certain recollections for disregard paradoxically identifies them as an object of particular curiosity."[1]

Such has also been the case with how two eras of Irish popular music, from 1920 to the mid-1970s, have been remembered and forgotten. Most extreme is the near total absence of documentation of Irish sit-down dance bands and orchestras. Spanning over fifty years, these ensembles proliferated on both sides of the border, from the smallest villages to the largest cities, creating music and critical social spaces for their local communities. Despite their importance, sit-down dance bands and orchestras have received scant attention both in the popular media and by academics. What exists focuses negative but deserved attention on the Catholic Church's many decades

Figure 1.2 Melrose State Dance Band, Dublin, 1931. (Photo courtesy of Monica and Sharon Coade.)

of antipathy toward public dancing, dance halls, and on what the Church deemed the "evils of jazz." Works that do shed light on Irish dance bands include several parallel studies of British popular big band ensembles from the Interwar and postwar years and, closer to home, scholarship that focuses on jazz performance in Ireland and Northern Ireland.[2]

Given their repertoires of popular music ("jazz") from the United States and Britain, Irish dance bands and orchestras functioned in near-constant tension with state and cultural institutions as well as the Catholic Church. Presented by these institutions as a threat to Ireland's emerging identity as an independent state, the music played by dance bands and orchestras and happily consumed by untold numbers of dancing audiences was systematically condemned—often in barely concealed (and sometimes, by contemporary standards, explicitly) racist terms—as was the very act of attending a dance. At the same time, the Church and various arms of the state championed what was then a recently invented tradition—*céilí* dancing (group folk dancing done to traditional Irish instrumental music). To address this gap in scholarship, then, this study begins with an account of the Irish dance bands and orchestras alongside the near-simultaneous emergence and growth of céilí bands to parse the dynamics of Irish cultural nationalism in the first half of the twentieth century. This also conveniently sets the stage for understanding the early years of the showbands in the mid-1950s, groups that would all but replace dance bands and orchestras.

While the Catholic Church hierarchy maintained its staunch opposition to popular music and dance throughout the 1950s and into the 1960s, showbands were increasingly insulated from this critique thanks in part to larger reformulations of Catholic Church doctrine with Vatican II beginning in 1962. Further, individual parish priests recognized the social and significant financial benefits to their parishes as sponsors of dances that featured showbands. What started as a handful of bands quickly formed into an industry, driven by and contributing to Ireland's brightening economy starting in the late 1950s—an industry that could and largely did ignore concerns from the Church hierarchy. Indeed, the critique of Irish popular music shifted from the purview of Ireland's Catholic Church in the first half of the twentieth century to stinging condemnations by the popular media—primarily Irish music writers and critics—beginning in the 1970s.

For showband fans, the rose-tinted glasses of showband nostalgia recall the music, dance, and, indeed, general excitement of the era itself, particularly in comparison to the economic hardship, limited opportunities for young people, and high rates of emigration in the preceding years. Almost universally, fans equate showband music and dancing with a time of new possibility and opportunity. Ireland's improving economy beginning in the 1960s offered better employment opportunities and disposable income, which, in turn, allowed young Irish to flock to showband dances. In addition to these happier memories, audiences recall the era also as a time of relative innocence and fun that offered a taste of the world beyond Ireland as well as the delight offered by these new sounds and dance styles. Even the most cynical recognized the aesthetic sea change brought on with the showband era. Irish novelist Patrick McCabe, somewhat grudgingly, recalls how refreshing the showband world was to him as a teenager in Ireland in the 1960s: "I suppose [showbands] were kind of a curious phenomenon. Like they wore these daft suits and everything else. But I suppose the only reason I liked them was that they added a bit of color to an otherwise drab kind of village life" (quoted in Heffernan 2001).

Showband musicians themselves recall the prestige of performance, the sheer pleasure of playing music, their fleeting moments of fame, and the excitement of being on tour and seeing other parts of Ireland, Britain, Germany, and, for some, the United States. For many, being part of this new industry provided a crucial recognition of their own potential. At the same time, many temper their narrative with memories of the destructive effects of alcoholism associated with the showband scene; the dangers of late-night travel and fatal car accidents; the repercussions of marital infidelity; and the grind and exhaustion of constant road travel. Women showband artists almost universally have starkly ambivalent memories of the very real challenges of working in a male-dominated, sometimes hostile, and often misogynistic music industry.

Almost universally, everybody with a connection to the showband world—musicians, managers, agents, dance hall owners—recalls its meteoric ascent into a highly lucrative industry, one that put considerable money into the pockets of musicians, promoters, dance hall owners, support industries, and many a parish coffer. It was (and, for some, remains) this relationship between musical performance and unapologetic commercialism that taints showbands and their music as "inauthentic," given the convoluted logic that equates profit with diminished artistry. This assumption has clearly vexed Irish popular music critics, producers, and academics: music critic Mark Prendergast (1987, 11), for example, writes that showbands were merely commercial and therefore utterly lacking "artistic integrity and creativity."

Fueling this retrospective critique was the related assumption that because showbands covered American and British hits, neither they nor their music were "Irish," a central concern given the strong currents of nationalism that permeated Ireland beginning in the 1960s. Amplifying the non-Irishness of showbands was the near simultaneous revival of traditional Irish music and song—genres that eventually functioned in Ireland as both "official" (high culture) as well as "popular" or folk culture (the "music of the people"). In fact, while showbands did centrally cover songs from outside of Ireland, their performance practice was uniquely Irish as was their inclusion of Irish popular songs and the occasional céilí dance and old-time waltzes. In drawing on familiar Irish performative and musical elements while they covered the most recent American and British hits, showbands essentially translated modern sounds from abroad for their Irish audiences.

Irish pop music critics and academics often recall the era with reference to what came after the showbands. Beginning with the Beat groups in the late 1960s and early 1970s, Irish rock swept Ireland with lyrics and sounds that specifically located Irishness but wrapped in the popular sounds of rock music. Artists such as Van Morrison, Rory Gallagher, Horslips, Thin Lizzy, U2, and others underscored this shift with original material that brought it home by incorporating elements of Irish music and song as well as Irish locality into their lyrics.[3] The recollection of the showbands became further stained by the trends that rendered them obsolete in the first place.

Another critique stems from the perception that showbands were primarily rural (this, despite the existence of many urban showbands, renowned and otherwise) and, by extension, unsophisticated. Some felt that people who played in showbands were uniformly weak musicians—an exaggeration given the wide range of musical skills among showband players and, indeed, among musicians of every stripe worldwide. This notion was informed by yet another critique of showbands as strictly imitative—"live jukeboxes" and "copycat bands"—groups that lacked the creativity or willingness to compose and perform new material. Indeed, the work of showbands was to cater to their audience for exacting replications of the American and British hits as heard on radio broadcasts. For many in the Irish rock fraternity, this indicated a lack of musical skill and imagination and was damaging to other musicians in Ireland. Niall Stokes, longtime editor of the Dublin-based *Hot Press*, famously argued that because they played strictly covers, showbands "stifled people's creative instincts" and, because they dominated the popular music scene, stymied the development of "real" Irish popular music (Stokes, quoted in McLaughlin and McLoone 2012, 24). Musician/producer Phil Lynott seconded Stokes, arguing that "showbands have destroyed some of the finest musicians in the country" (Clayton-Lea and Taylor, 1992, 9). Given this perspective, the showband era was often remembered in pejorative terms ("Frankenstein creatures");[4] and perhaps most famously, by Irish rock singer/activist Sir Bob Geldof who observed that the era was a "musical desert" and concluded that "the showbands were crap" (interview in Heffernan 2001).

Geldof's assessment is heard in the widely viewed 2001 television documentary series, *From a Whisper to a Scream: The Living History of Irish Rock*. Devoting six minutes to the showband era out of a total of two and half hours of programming, the documentary reiterates that showbands were centrally imitative, not creative; damaging to the genesis of popular Irish music; and a veiled rejection of things Irish, an observation articulated in the documentary by Irish filmmaker Jim Sheridan: "It wasn't as if [the showbands] were confined in where they got their inspiration. It was just that their inspiration stopped short of believing there was any worth in their own particular culture" (interview in Heffernan 2001). The sole voice of reason here is that of Van Morrison, himself a former member of the Belfast-based Monarchs Showband. He notes that successful showband musicianship demanded high levels of professionalism and the mastery of an array of diverse musical skills. For him and other young players, showbands offered an opportunity to develop their musical chops and stage presence: "They weren't just doing covers. It was like a whole show. They did comedy, they did Top 10. They did jazz, you know, they did impersonations. And it was something they could have done in Las Vegas. It was a very professional show. It wasn't just a matter of, like, guys doing steps and wearing suits. It was a couple of levels above that" (interview in Heffernan 2001). Van Morrison's perspective notwithstanding, the final thoughts on showbands in *From a Whisper to a Scream* are cinematically bounced between U2 vocalist Bono and Sir Bob Geldof. Presented in a neatly edited montage, Bono's and Geldof's views are intercut with performance footage of Miami Showband vocalist Dickie Rock—unquestionably one of the most successful yet often criticized showband singers:

> BONO: Showband music was just, it was the enemy! . . . These people were from an Ireland that we had *no* interest in being a part of.
>
> GELDOF: I just thought that they were an appalling travesty. It was just typical 'Paddydom.'[5]

Only a handful of books in the general press focus on showbands. One of the earliest was Vincent Power's 1990 book, *Send 'em Home Sweatin': The Showband Story,* which presented the showband phenomenon from the perspective of the best known groups. Indeed, most accounts of the showband era focus on the stars to the exclusion of the vast majority of semiprofessional and amateur showbands that dominated dance halls throughout Ireland and Northern Ireland. This imbalance was mitigated to a certain extent beginning in the early 2000s with a spate of memoirs penned by former showband musicians that capture the excitement of the era from an insider's perspective; a folio publication of photographs that offers remarkable visual documentation of artists, venues, and fans from these years; and informative websites devoted to showband archives, ephemera, and updates to document this bygone era.[6]

In the hands of academics, showbands have also not done well and the genre has largely been ignored, aside from the occasional reference and, by the 2000s, entries in music encyclopedias.[7] In 2000, Noel McLaughlin and Martin McLoone (2000, 188) wrote that showbands were "pale imitations . . . with local heroes aping the American originals" while also acknowledging that these groups "brought to the youth of rural and provincial Ireland the same kind of liberating hedonism that was associated with other imported forms of popular culture." Twelve years later, they revised this perspective, pointing out that with regards to showbands, "great mimics . . . can also be great innovators" (McLaughlin and McLoone 2012, 28–29). Music critic John Waters (1994) writes in similarly tart terms about showbands but notes that this scene did, in fact, provide "distillation of the options of modern pop music and gave the emerging generation a glimpse of the possibility that they might not otherwise have been given for another decade" (96). Somewhat later, popular music scholar Gerry Smyth (2005, 15) recognizes the significance of the localized nature of the showbands, also in mixed terms: "The best showbands played your favourite songs, they played them well, and they played them on your own doorstep. In a very real sense, these groups were more important than the hopelessly remote originals they were aping."

New York City, 1986: Discovering the Showbands

As a longtime traditional fiddler, I first came across Irish showbands when I was the Director of Folk Arts Programs at the Irish Arts Center in New York City. I was initially hired to produce the annual Irish Traditional Music Festival at Snug Harbor, Staten Island, as well as other festivals and concert series that focused on Irish traditional music, song, and dance throughout New York City's five boroughs. One evening in 1986, I was on the phone, planning a series of evening céilís at a parish hall in the Bronx. My task that night was to line up musicians to play for this dance, and I started by calling the late Matty Connolly, an outstanding Irish uilleann piper, originally from County Monaghan. He told me that he was not available for the céilí as he was already booked that night to play at the Tower View, a popular ballroom in Queens, New York. Always curious to know about the competition, I asked him about this gig, but he assured me that I wouldn't be interested because it wasn't traditional music.

I was, in fact, very interested. As it turned out, the flip side of Matty's musical personality was as an electric bass player in the Majestic Showband, one of the longtime ensembles of its type in New York's Irish immigrant community. The electric guitarist in the Majestic Showband was the late Martin Mulhaire, of Queens, New York (formerly of Eyrecourt, County Galway), whom I knew as a renowned traditional button accordionist and composer. I subsequently conducted several interviews with both Mulhaire and Connolly and others in the Irish immigrant community who were connected to this music scene from the 1950s through the 1960s. From this, I developed a nationally distributed public radio series entitled *Old Traditions—New Sounds*.[8]

A few years later, in August 1992, I was writing as a freelancer for the *Irish Echo* in New York City. I was assigned a profile piece on a visiting Irish singer based in Las Vegas who was booked to perform at the Irish Center in Mineola, Long Island (Miller 1992). That singer was none other than Brendan Bowyer, the celebrated vocalist and founding member of the Royal Showband. I had never heard of Bowyer or the Royal Showband, but I went out to Mineola, had a delightful interview, and, later, attended his show, which also featured the well-known Kerry Blues Showband vocalist, D. J. Curtin.

Figure 1.3 The author with Brendan Bowyer, July 30, 2006, Cork City, County Cork.

The Irish Center that night was packed with middle-aged Irish women and men, most of whom, I gathered, had immigrated to New York between the late 1940s and mid-1960s. Dancing as couples counterclockwise around the hall pretty much continuously, they sang along to the songs, watched the charismatic stage performances, and laughed and socialized over drinks and snacks at the tables that lined the hall's periphery. I recall despondently comparing the impressive size of this dancing audience with the much smaller attendance garnered at those traditional céilís that I was organizing for the Irish Arts Center. Clearly showbands, particularly those fronted by the likes of Brendan Bowyer and D. J. Curtin, were far more popular among this age group even by the early 1990s.

What also struck me was not necessarily the repertoire (mostly covers of songs I associated with "oldies" radio stations) or the performance itself (although Brendan Bowyer's and D.J. Curtin's gyrating stage moves were certainly fun to watch). What I remember most was the energy generated by the audience and by the performers and, most importantly, the synergy between the two. From the first downbeat of the evening, there was instant community, both the temporary sort that one would expect during an evening of music and dance but also a sense of long-shared belonging among Irish immigrants, brought together through the remembered pleasures of popular music and dance, despite dislocations of time and distance.

On Ethnography, Oral History, and Archives

Because so little has been published on the eras of Irish popular music before the 1970s, this book relies on primary sources, including archival documents, newspaper articles, and, centrally, nearly eighty recorded interviews and oral histories I conducted between 1988 and 2019. Far from being anecdotal, oral histories and interviews offer a deep multiplicity of perspectives from those who have had direct, lived experience; as such, these accounts provide valuable primary data and complement other research methods.[9] In challenging the "official" narratives and histories as recorded by religious, governmental, and other formal institutions, oral histories and interviews complicate standard methods of historical interpretation, widen perspectives of how people recall history, and, crucially, pose the question of whose version of the past gets recorded and why. Moreover, conducting and working with oral histories and interviews bring much deserved recognition and attention to those whose experiences and viewpoints would otherwise be ignored or buried. As historians Paul Thompson and Joanna Bornat put it, "History becomes, to put it simply, more democratic" (Thompson and Bornat, 2017, 17).[10]

Because of this and given the dearth of scholarship on showbands in general, I sought out and interviewed, beginning in 2006, former showband musicians, managers, and agents; dance hall promoters and their families; priests who ran parish hall dances; fans and roadies; and the few remaining musicians from the previous era of sit-down dance bands and orchestras. Some of the people I interviewed had gone on to achieve international fame as musicians well beyond the showband scene; others had become national politicians or moved into other positions of leadership. Most of my interviews, though, were with those whose fame was fleeting and limited to their locality—working men and women whose considerable contributions have essentially gone unsung but whose labors, unquestionably, were central to the growth of the showband industry. Welcoming me into their homes or meeting with me in the lobbies of hotels, pubs, and other public spaces throughout Ireland and Northern Ireland as well as locations elsewhere in Britain and the United States, these interviewees, who ranged in age from their early sixties to early nineties, generously gave their hospitality and time, recalling their lives and these eras in deeply thoughtful, always colorful, and often emotional terms.

Because popular music in Ireland during most of the twentieth century was male-dominated, I also searched for women showband musicians and

Figure 1.4 Tony Killeen (Mexicans Showband) and granddaughter, Nadine, July 11, 2008, Greystones, County Wicklow. (Photo by author.)

Figure 1.5 Sonny Knowles, June 5, 2009, Westbury Hotel, Dublin. (Photo by author.)

Figure 1.6 Seamus Gallagher, July 18, 2008, Falcarragh, County Donegal. (Photo by author.)

fans in an effort to include their voices and experiences. Ultimately, I was able to interview quite a few women showband artists—Margo O'Donnell, Philomena Begley, Maxi McCoubrey, Muriel Day, Eileen Reid, Eileen Kelly, Sandy Kelly, Mildred Beirne, and others.

Far more challenging was locating women musicians who had been active in the sit-down dance bands and orchestras. Ultimately, I found and interviewed just one, Claudette Colbert McCarthy, who, at age eighty-six, retained sharp memories and delightful insights of her years as a pianist in a sit-down dance band in County Tipperary in the 1950s. I am very grateful to her and to all these women who so willingly shared their memories—good and bad—and, in doing so, contribute to an increasingly balanced reframing of gender and popular Irish musical performance in the twentieth century.

Figure 1.7 Philomena Begley, Pomeroy, County Tyrone, July 14, 2008. (Photo by author.)

Figure 1.8 Eileen Kelly, July 8, 2008, Dublin. (Photo by author.)

Figure 1.9 Sandy Kelly and Avi Randall (author's son), July 9, 2008, Oldtown, Dublin. (Photo by author.)

This study also draws on archival news accounts, interviews, reviews and previews, and advertisements published in Irish newspapers from 1920 through 1980, from the smallest villages to the largest cities on both sides of the border. I made solid use of personal remembrances contained in booklets and pamphlets that commemorate local celebrations and community events, historical documents online and those located in libraries, and those housed in physical archives.[11] Most valuable, however, are the memories and informal accounts of showbands and venues, initially penned by enthusiastic fans and former musicians, in response to radio interviews in 2008 with me about this project on the BBC as well as on the radio arts program, "Rattlebag," on RTÉ (Raidió Teilifís Éireann). In an effort to move beyond the handful of the best-known showbands and include the experiences of less famous players, I gave my email address during an on-air interview (a very successful fieldwork strategy, as it turns out). I received over one hundred responses and eventually interviewed more than half of these individuals. This study benefits hugely from these accounts as they provide a much-widened perspective, one that focuses on the relatively unknown showband musicians who played

Figure 1.10 Claudette Colbert McCarthy, January 8, 2019, Florham Park, NJ. (Photo by author.)

semiprofessionally and in amateur showbands as well as those whose names and accomplishments are well known.

With the exception of that 1992 Mineola, New York, show featuring Brendan Bowyer and D. J. Curtin, what I missed out on was the opportunity to attend live performances of both showbands and sit-down dance bands and orchestras because these musics are no longer performed.[12] Further complicating this is the fact that few recordings of live performances exist of either of these genres. This is particularly true of the music of sit-down dance bands and orchestras because, aside from the traditional music label, Gael Linn, Ireland's recording industry simply did not exist prior to the early 1960s. As a result, there are almost no audio recordings of over four decades of Ireland's dance bands and orchestras.[13] That said, I was delighted when, in 2018, Jimmy Higgins, former showband trumpeter/bandleader and Galway radio DJ, presented me with a copy of the informally titled and unreleased "Mick Dell Tribute CD 2002," a twenty-track recording of a live performance on

Figure 1.11 Jimmy Higgins, October, 2018, Renmore, County Galway. (Photo by author.)

September 10, 1958, by Mick Delahunty and His Orchestra. Simultaneously broadcast over radio from the Hangar Ballroom in Galway, this recording captures Delahunty's pristine arrangements and skillful musicianship by orchestra members as well as the ambience and excitement on the dance floor.[14]

Also missing from the record is archival footage of RTÉ's (then Telefís Éireann) enormously popular television program *The Showband Show,* which aired weekly beginning on June 13, 1963, through 1968. Additional missing materials are copies of RTÉ's Sunday night radio broadcast *The Seventeen Club,* which began in 1965. Showband fan John Doyle notes that despite the huge number of fans for both of these shows at the time, there exists in the RTÉ archives only one complete program of *The Seventeen Club* and none of the broadcasts of *The Showband Show.* These shows were apparently erased in the interest of economizing by reusing the tape on which they were originally recorded. Doyle's reaction is typical of many showband fans:[15] "I have had bouts of futile anger towards RTÉ, over the erasing of the entire series of *The*

Showband Show. . . . A whole era of a uniquely Irish idiom was erased. Showbands were as important to Ireland as rock 'n' roll was to the United States, and the Beat groups were to Britain (pers. comm., 2006).

By all accounts, showband music was centrally about the moment and something to be experienced live, in person, rather than on recordings. While many studio recordings of showband music were produced in the 1960s and 1970s, few, if any, capture the excitement of live performance. Since then, there have been occasional releases of compilation albums and remixes of showband hits and new studio productions by surviving band members. In addressing the nostalgia from this era, these albums more than adequately serve their purpose, albeit with a very different energy from live performance.

"Let's Do the Hucklebuck!"

This book aims to fill in the gap of knowledge surrounding Irish popular music from roughly 1925 to 1975 and, in doing so, balance the often unquestioned assumptions that Irish dance bands and the later showbands were "musical deserts"—aesthetically and culturally valueless and, indeed, worthy of forgetting. This lacunae has obscured not only a critical understanding of the relationship of popular music to mid-twentieth-century Ireland—an era of change and growth—but also of the energies, agencies, and aesthetics of musicians and their fans, whose lives were deeply impacted by the popular music industry. Shedding light on why an entire era of popular music has been summarily ignored also raises questions about the changing historical nature of Irish identity in response to pressure from local and national government, cultural institutions, and Ireland's Catholic Church. It brings into focus people's deeply entrenched reactions over generations to a legacy of colonial and postcolonial domination as well what once was endemic poverty and neglect—humiliating and painful conditions that, for those who experienced them directly as well as residually among subsequent generations, were best left behind as distant memories.

This account also presents the wide range of showband musicians—from those who were nationally known to those whose fame was strictly local—who learned to play and how to perform and, in doing so, saw their potential for growth move well beyond standard expectations at the time. In weaving together these memories and experiences, along with those of their fans, this account sheds light not only on the dynamics of cultural rejection and forgetting but also on memory, celebration, and the visceral joy of musical performance and dance through the embrace of the popular.

Notes

1. In part a sentimental response to a bygone era, occasional revivals of interest in the showbands are indicative of a collective willingness to engage with this period of Irish cultural history. The early 2000s saw the first of these revivals, including productions of playwright Enda Walsh's 2004 *The New Electric Ballroom*, in Ireland, Britain, and the United States. In 2007, the Waterford Treasures Museum curated the traveling exhibition *Hucklebuck Time: A Celebration of the Generation That Danced Their Way into History*, and the following year, RTÉ produced two series of documentaries on showbands.

In 2010, commemorative showband stamps were issued by An Post, followed in 2013 with the opening of the Rainbow Ballroom and Showband Memorabilia Museum in Glenfarne, County Leitrim. This event was accompanied by several reunions of long-retired showbands and reissues of showband recordings. Several internet sites also celebrate this bygone era. In March 2017, Van Morrison and the Monarchs Showband from Belfast made headlines when they reunited to play for a charity fundraiser.

2. Studies of British popular big band ensembles from the Interwar and postwar years include James Nott's *Music for the People: Popular Music and Dance in Interwar Britain* (2002); Christina Baade's "'The Battle of the Saxes': Gender, Dance Bands, and British Nationalism in the Second World War" (2008); and Helen Southall's 2015 doctoral dissertation, "Dance Bands in Chester: An Evolving Professional Network." Scholarship that focuses on the same era of popular music in Ireland includes Damian Evans's (2019) research on jazz in Ireland between 1918 and 1960; Ruth Stanley's (2018) chapter on Irish jazz performance during the Interwar years; and Sean Shanagher's (2014) doctoral dissertation on dance halls and dancing in County Roscommon between 1940 and 1960.

3. Thin Lizzy's 1973 rock remake of the well-known Irish song "Whiskey in the Jar" is iconic.

4. Smyth and Campbell 2005, 2–3.

5. In response to Geldof's assertion of showbands being "typical Paddydom," *Irish Times* critic Eddie Holt tartly writes that Geldof is "accurate but unduly accusing" and pushes back: "In a poor country, emerging from repressive political colonisation and gripped by an intensely inhibiting religious substitute, the abject 'paddydom' might have been understood a little better. Times were hard, Bob, and sometimes a lack of self-confidence is more attractive than a surplus of it, if you can imagine that" (E. Holt 2000).

6. Memoirs from the showband era include Finbar O'Keefe, *Goodnight, God Bless, and Safe Home: The Golden Showband Era* (2002); Jimmy Higgins, *Are Ye the Band? A Memoir of the Showband Era* (2007); Stephen Travers with Neil Fetherstonhaugh, *The Miami Showband Massacre: A Survivor's Search for the Truth* (2007); Dickie Rock, *Dickie Rock: Always Me* (2007); Gerry Anderson, *Heads: A Day in the Life* (2008); and Tom Gilmore, *Larry Cunningham: A Showband Legend* (2009).

Other media that documents the world of showbands include Michael O'Reilly's 2015 folio of photographs entitled *Dancehall Days: When Showbands Ruled the Stage* and several internet resources: in particular, Irish-Showbands.com, https://www.irish-showbands.com/, and Album of Irish Showbands, http://www.irishshowbandalbum.com/.

7. In 1996, musicologist Harry White made oblique reference to showband music in the context of demonstrating Ireland's musical diversity: "And if it is a country of the mind (and of the media) it is marvellously plural, value-free, unembarrassed: one can hear *sean nós* singing in its archival purity, the virtuoso brilliance of The Chieftains or a tepid admixture of ethnic and commercial traditions, and all of it thrives happily under the mantle of Irish music" (126).

Following that, White, in 2013, together with co-editor Barra Boydell and popular music subject editors Mel Mercier and Méabh Ní Fhuartháin, oversaw the inclusion of a number of entries on showbands and the genre's cousin, Country and Irish music, in the two-volume *Encyclopaedia of Music in Ireland*, eleven of which were contributed by the author (Miller 2013a–k).

8. From this chance encounter emerged *Old Traditions—New Sounds*, an award-winning, thirteen-part series of one-hour public radio documentaries that was aired nationally between 1991 and 1994. Hosted by folk singer Judy Collins, each episode of *Old Traditions—New Sounds* focused on outstanding traditional musicians from throughout the world who immigrated to the United States and who, like Matty Connolly and Martin Mulhaire, performed both traditional music and a related contemporary, popular style (Miller 1991).

9. Regarding the research methodology most often used by memory studies scholars, Guy Beiner writes, "As opposed to the more prominent works of canonical history, this is a vernacular historiography, which needs to be pieced together through inspection of less familiar, unconventional sources rooted in local traditions." Among these sources are travelogues, folk poetry, personal reminiscences, memoirs ("recollections"), autobiographical literature, stories and songs, traditions, and, crucially, oral history (Beiner 2013, 16; see also Beiner 2014).

10. The oral historian, Alessandro Portelli (1991, 52) writes, "What is really important is that memory is not a passive depository of facts, but an active process of creation of meanings." Similarly, Thompson and Bornat (2017, 17) argue that the process by which people create meaning from historical memory as captured in oral history "provides a more realistic and fair reconstruction of the past, a challenge to the established account."

11. These include, among others, the National Library of Ireland in Dublin; the archives of University College–Dublin (which houses the unpublished papers of Dr. T. K. Whitaker, former secretary of the Department of Finance); the (then) unpublished papers of Archbishop John McQuaid, stored in boxes at the Dublin Diocesan Archives, in Drumcondra, Dublin; and the papers of Monsignor James Horan, located in the archives at Knock Shrine, County Mayo.

12. As Sean Shanagher (2014, 9) discovered in his own work on recreational dancing in County Roscommon in the 1940s and 1950s, participant observation and "an extended 'live' engagement in participants' worlds is largely meaningless when that world has vanished."

13. Some dance orchestra leaders have recorded retrospective albums of their music well after the end of the dance band era. In 1994, for example, County Mayo saxophonist/dance orchestra leader Brose Walsh recorded *The Best of the Brose Walsh Band*, and in 2000, Derry-based Johnny Quigley released his CD, *Johnny Quigley and The Allstars*.

14. In 2020, the Tipperary Museum of Hidden History released an album of Mick Delahunty's music entitled *Mick Delahunty and His Orchestra: The Lost Recordings*.

15. I had a similar experience at a conference of the International Council for Traditional Music, held in Lisbon, Portugal, in July 2022. In a presentation on Siamsa Tíre (The National Folk Theatre of Ireland), Susan Motherway and Daithí Kearney presented film footage from RTÉ's archives of this traditional music and dance troupe from the 1960s. At the end of the tape, the visuals/audio jarringly shifted from traditional Irish music and step dancing to a few seconds of boisterous rock 'n' roll as played by an unidentified showband. Motherway said that her source at RTÉ had explained that back in the day, workers routinely recorded over existing taped footage in order to save money; this footage of Siamsa Tíre was a case in point.

2

"The Archbishop's Quadrille"

The Church, the State, Dance Bands, and Céilís, 1925 to 1955

Page eight of the *Meath Chronicle* from October 7, 1950, featured no fewer than twenty-eight advertisements, large and small. As one of the many hundreds of local newspapers published throughout Ireland and Northern Ireland at the time, the *Chronicle* ran ads that reflected the primarily rural and agrarian interests of the community it served. There are notices for classes in butter and cheese making and fruit growing, requests for bids from electricians for wiring jobs, ads from grain purchasers who promise to pay only the highest prices, announcements from margarine and cheese purveyors, and at least one offering from a service that removes "dead or disabled horses and cattle," among others.

Of these twenty-eight ads, fully sixteen announce upcoming dances at a number of commercial ballrooms and parish halls. Some publicize dances to be held under marquee tents at upcoming carnivals; others list the performance schedules of local and visiting dance bands. Taken individually and together, these advertisements reveal much about popular culture in Ireland at the time. One advertisement, for example, references a then-popular 1935 British musical comedy as it reminds readers that "'Music Hath Charms' especially if played by The O'Growney Céilídhe Band." Another neatly conflates the global anxieties of the time with the excitement of dancing to the very popular Mick Delahunty Orchestra: "Hear the band which is more powerful than the atom bomb!"

Virtually all Irish newspapers—rural and urban and on both sides of the border—between the mid-1920s and the 1960s regularly filled several pages of each issue with ads that attested to the enormous popularity of social dancing over these four decades. The ads offer no particular hierarchy: céilí dances receive equal billing with the dance bands and orchestras that specialized in the imported, popular ballroom dance music—foxtrots, quicksteps, big band standards, and, somewhat later, Latin styles, such as sambas and rumbas—from the United States and Britain. Some dances advertise both céilí and popular dance music as part of an evening's entertainment, reflecting a healthy range of audience interest. In some instances, dance hall owners hired two bands—a céilí band and a "modern" dance band—to play in the same evening, while others promoted a single band with versatile musicians who could perform both styles and, for that reason, attract large audiences. Judging from the proliferation of these events—céilí and ballroom dancing or both—Ireland was awash in music and social dance for much of the early and mid-twentieth century.

Beyond the differences in repertoire, playing style, and instrumentation, dance bands and céilí bands had much in common: they shared the same venues, touring circuits, and often, the same audiences. Both performed at local dances; at life cycle events, such as weddings and anniversary parties; and for political and parish fundraisers and other charitable activities. Aside from a handful of nationally known groups, the majority were mainly locally or regionally known; most are now largely unheralded and forgotten. Despite this lack of documentation, musicians and dancers today recall that local ensembles of both types filled the crucial role of reinforcing bonds of community as they created entertainment spaces for people to socialize and, for single people, to meet a future spouse.

In spite of the enormous demand for popular dance bands and orchestras, the hierarchy of Ireland's Catholic Church was strenuously invested in their rejection while equally invested in promoting Irish céilí dancing. For over four decades, the archbishops and bishops of Ireland routinely published columns in local Irish newspapers that warned of the evils of popular dance music and American jazz. In the same breath, the Church hierarchy praised Irish music and ceílí dances and instructed parish priests to regularly remind parishioners of these concerns: "Irish dances do not make degenerates. . . . Irish dances may not be the fashion in London or Paris. They should be the fashion in Ireland. Owing to the growing dangers attendant on the importation of foreign dances and lax methods of control of dancing halls, the statement will be read until further notice on the first Sunday of each Quarter of the Ecclesiastical year" (*Longford Leader*, September 25, 1926, 3).

Figure 2.1 Noel Coade, compère/vocalist (front, center), with unidentified musicians and dancers, ca. 1955, Dublin. (Photo courtesy of Monica and Sharon Coade.)

In pitting Irish music and dance against popular dance music, the Church pushed back, perhaps with futility, against the proliferation of the popular sounds of dance music (often termed "jazz") from abroad. Over the years, this tension between the Church's push to control and regulate leisure time versus a growing secularism and the sheer popularity of ballroom dancing and music would ultimately (and perhaps ironically) result in the Church itself becoming invested in the very activities that it condemned. These efforts were reinforced in the mid-1930s by the passage of regulatory policies that governed where and when public dancing could and could not take place. At the same time, the Catholic Church worked closely with the Gaelic League (Conradh na Gaeilge), an influential national institution that centrally promoted the Irish language and culture and, beginning in the late 1800s, was instrumental in the development of ceílí dancing.

Despite these tensions, the parallel growth and popularity of both ceílí bands and modern dance bands and orchestras continued unabated for decades until the 1960s. The result was not only an ongoing, vibrant music and dance scene throughout Ireland but also the emergence of a distinctive musical hybridity that, in the best of instances, seized and delighted the imaginations of musicians and their audiences.

Irish Sit-Down Dance Bands and Orchestras

Unquestionably, popular music from the United States and Britain was a source of entertainment for Irish dancing audiences of all ages. This imported repertoire was most often performed by so-called sit-down (or "sitting down") dance bands and orchestras. (The moniker "sit-down" was earned retrospectively with the 1960s showband era, to indicate that the musicians read from sheet music arrangements on music stands and therefore sat as they played in contrast to the later era of showband musicians, who stood.) While the terms "band" and "orchestra" were often used interchangeably, generally dance bands were smaller groups of six to eight musicians, whereas an orchestra could be a larger ensemble (eight to fifteen or more players). Dance bands often served as opening or warm-up acts for the larger, professional touring orchestras. That said, a dance band could instantly become an orchestra upon being hired to be in residence in one of the larger ballrooms. In these instances, recalls Dublin-born jazz pianist Ian Henry Garber, advertising a group as an orchestra conferred a certain amount of prestige, given the term's association with high art and culture (personal communication, 2017).

Whether a dance band or an orchestra, instrumentation consisted of reed and brass sections, including trombone, trumpets, clarinet, and various saxophones, and a rhythm section (typically piano, drums, and upright bass). In pre–World War II bands, tenor banjo was also a featured instrument but was replaced, in the postwar years, by electric guitar. Vocalists were important and bands had one or two singers. The vast majority of sit-down dance band musicians were men with the exception of "girl singers" or, rarely, a woman pianist.

It is impossible to know precisely how many dance bands and orchestras existed at any given time in both Ireland and Northern Ireland, although one online archive lists at least 213 Irish orchestras that were active beginning in the mid-1930s until the 1960s.[1] Among the best known were the Mick Delahunty Orchestra (Clonmel), the Maurice Mulcahy Orchestra (Mitchelstown), the Gay McIntyre Orchestra (Derry), Chick Smith Orchestra (Dublin), the Johnny Quigley All-Stars (Derry), Jack Flahive and His Orchestra (Dublin), Jack Ruane Orchestra (Ballina, County Mayo), Syd Shine

Figure 2.2 Rick Morgan (guitar), Jack Daly (drums), Ian Henry (piano), and Jimmy McKay (bass), ca. 1953. (Photo courtesy of Ian Henry Garber.)

and His Crescent Dance Orchestra (Athlone), Brose Walsh and His International Orchestra (County Mayo), Kevin Woods and His Royal Dance Band/Orchestra (Drumshanbo), William Bradley's Woodchoppers Orchestra (Derry), and others.

Aside from these better-known ensembles, there were untold numbers of less popular groups that proliferated during these years. Among other community-based bands and dance orchestras include the Blue Haven Dance Band (County Leitrim), the Brideside Serenaders (Tallow, County Waterford), the Red Shadows Dance Band (County Meath), Jimmy Wiley and His Eleven Piece Orchestra (Mitchelstown), the Emerald Valley Dance Band (County Leitrim), Billy Gerrard and His Dance Orchestra (Dublin), Jackie Harvey and His Crotchets (County Meath), Jack Silver and His Famous Band, the Hugh Tourish Dance Band (Strabane, County Tyrone), and many others. Aside from the memories of those who once danced to these bands, mentions in advertisements in local papers, and perhaps a listing in the annual Irish Federation of Dance Musicians roster, documentation of these and other dance bands is scant if not altogether nonexistent.

Figure 2.3 Johnny Butler Orchestra, Dublin, ca. 1945. Photo credit: Philip G. Elliott, Dublin. (Photo courtesy of Monica and Sharon Coade.)

Dance bands performed a variety of American and British popular music from written arrangements; for this reason, band musicians often referred to their groups as "reading bands." Dixieland jazz tunes, swing numbers, selections from the Great American Songbook, big band ballads, popular Irish songs, and old-time waltzes constituted much of their repertoire. While some of the larger dance orchestras cut back on variety and emphasized American ballroom dance standards, waltzes, and British popular tunes and songs, most included a céilí dance set or two, Irish popular songs, and old-time Irish waltzes—markers of Irishness that were embedded both explicitly and subtly in their repertoire.

There was no lack of access to American popular music on both sides of the border. For those who could afford them, imported recordings on the Decca, Columbia, and Brunswick labels supplied the contemporary sounds of big band music, jazz, and popular singers such as Frank Sinatra and Bing Crosby, among others. These recordings were also heard in people's homes via radio: the BBC regularly programmed broadcasts of American and British popular music, as did the American Armed Forces Network, which

Figure 2.4 The Metropole Dance Band, Dublin, ca. 1929. (Photo courtesy of Monica and Sharon Coade.)

broadcast via shortwave radio from Germany. By the late 1930s, Radio Luxembourg captured the musical imaginations of large audiences throughout Ireland with similar programming. Irish audiences were also exposed to American musical culture via imported Hollywood films and newsreels, many of which included performances by the popular musicians of the day.

"TO-DAY, JAZZ IS MORE A SUBJECT FOR THE PATHOLOGIST THAN THE MUSICIAN"

—Mr. Arthur Bliss, the composer.
(*Evening Herald*, Dublin, August 10, 1935, 2)

As in neighboring Britain, the Interwar Years ushered in Ireland's jazz era in concept if not in actual practice. The line between dance bands and jazz bands was blurred owing to the frequent use of the term "jazz" to describe ballroom dance standards such as foxtrots, quicksteps, and the like, while steering clear of more old-fashioned sounding genres, such as the valetta (waltz) and the polka. Notes cultural historian James Nott (2002, 129), "There were few if any real 'jazz' bands on the American model, but lots who called themselves such."

The same blurred musical categorizations held true in Ireland. Missives from the Catholic Church warned against the "evils of jazz" but, in the main, were referring to popular music as played by dance bands and orchestras. While some bands did include a set or two of bona fide jazz tunes with improvised solos over chord changes, most musicians recognized that what they were playing was not American jazz (Paddy Geary, Mick Delahunty Jr., interviews, 2018). Rather, much of the "jazz" played by Irish dance bands was akin to what in Britain was termed "sweet" music—that is, popular dance tunes without soloistic improvisation, otherwise known as "hot" music. Sweet music emphasized melody, whereas hot music, according to a 1934 article in the British magazine, *Radio Pictorial,* "distort[s] the original melody" and makes it "difficult for most people to follow." The article continues, "The Britisher must have a song to sing—something simple and easy to learn. Even the errand boy must have something to whistle. It is characteristic of the race . . . the masses, highbrow and lowbrow, representative of all classes, are not interested in the highly involved patterns of ultra-modern dance music. . . . What they want is a simple, appealing tune (*Radio Pictorial,* March 2, 1934, 7, as cited in Nott 2002, 201).

Jazz was considerably more popular in Northern Ireland, particularly in Belfast and Derry, than in the Republic, thanks to frequent broadcasts of American jazz recordings over the BBC and the presence of a large American naval base in Derry in the years surrounding World War II.[2] In contrast to musicians from the Republic, Northern Irish musicians often distinguished between jazz and "cabaret jazz," the latter of which included, for example, tunes from the Great American Songbook (Jim McDermott, interview, 2008). For many Northern Irish jazz musicians, exposure to the legendary American jazz greats began at an early age. Gay McIntyre, a well-known clarinetist and saxophonist from Derry, recalls an American sailor visiting his family's home in 1943 when he was ten years old. The sailor had with him a 78 recording of jazz legend Artie Shaw; upon hearing this record, McIntyre recalls being so moved by the music that he cried. Shortly thereafter, his parents acquired a clarinet for him to learn (McIntyre, interview, 2018).

Many young musicians on both sides of the border were introduced to jazz and popular music through live performances by local dance bands. The late composer/multi-instrumentalist Charlie Lennon was born in 1938 in Kiltyclogher, County Leitrim. He started out with both piano lessons and learning traditional music on the fiddle. He recalls, as a child, enjoying the popular music he heard on the radio and then reproducing these tunes on his fiddle. Lennon's interest in popular music and jazz was reinforced by stealth visits to the small commercial dance hall in Kiltyclogher to hear performances by the Blue Haven Dance Band, a group that he would eventually join as a violinist at the age of twelve: "I would sneak in to hear the music live. I loved the sound. It was a big sound. . . . [The] combination was always interesting, because our tradition at home and generally in the area was for solo playing. [So] . . . I liked different sounds, like of the saxophone or the trumpet or the drums or whatever was being played" (Lennon, interview, 2019).

Remembering the Dance Bands

If they are remembered at all, Irish sit-down dance bands and orchestras are often recalled in narratives, newspaper articles, and memoirs by both musicians and audiences as dreary and unimaginative. Some of this may have had to do with the fact that their heyday coincided with an Ireland that, from the 1930s through the 1950s, struggled with a stagnating economy, high unemployment, and, for many, grinding poverty. Capitol Showband bass player/vocalist Desmond ("Des") Kelly was born in 1936 on a small farm in North Galway. He recalls the Ireland of his youth as a "dour place" with few opportunities: "There was no money around in those days. . . . It was quite simple. You finished your primary school education. The eldest son would automatically take over the farm, small as it was. And the others would just emigrate" (interview, 2006).

In the post–World War II years, these increasingly dire conditions became "push" factors as postwar emigration spiked (Delaney 2002, 25). Between 1946 and 1971, an estimated one in every three men and women under the age of thirty had left the Republic; in 1957 alone, nearly sixty thousand people left (Donal Garvey, as cited in Delaney 2002, 5–6). For many, the era of sit-down bands and dance orchestras became synonymous with and reminders of these decades of hardship and dislocation.

Another factor contributing to the semi-erasure from cultural memory of the sit-down dance bands is the paucity of recordings—audio and film—that might otherwise have captured the sounds, images, and sheer energy of the era. While there exist rare radio broadcasts of some of the larger orchestras, many if not most of the smaller dance bands are entirely undocumented.[3] Also, Ireland's popular music recording industry did not exist until the early 1960s, which coincided with the end of the sit-down dance band era. With few, if any, sonic or visual records of this music and dance, these ensembles soon faded from popular memory.

This narrative became further entrenched thanks to the next generation of Irish popular musicians—those who played in the showbands that all but eclipsed the earlier dance band era. For example, in his memoir, *Goodnight,*

Figure 2.5 Jim McDermott, July 17, 2008, Derry City. (Photo by author.)

God Bless, and Safe Home: The Golden Showband Era, Finbar O'Keefe (2002) of the Saints Showband, recalls the Ireland of the 1940s and 1950s as a "drab and stagnant place, still suffering some of the privations and rationing of the war. . . . Nothing seemed to change and this was equally true of the music scene—what there was of one (13)." O'Keefe depicts the dance band era as one where a "few dozen established orchestras" enjoyed an "unassailable position in a time that had no competition to offer" (14). While underscoring the economic and social challenges of that era, O'Keefe's summary privileges the larger, well-known sit-down orchestras to the neglect of the smaller, less popular dance bands. While it was certainly the case that the professional orchestras garnered most of the publicity and excitement, it was, in fact, the smaller bands that fueled local dances and did the work of providing music for weddings and other life cycle and social events. As such, the local dance bands served as the largely unheralded social and musical backbones in their communities.

The contrast between the dynamism of the 1960s Irish showbands and the more sedate sit-down dance bands all but eclipsed the popular memory of the latter. With their eyes trained on the music in front of them, sit-down dance band musicians wore dark suits and white shirts and often had little interaction with their audiences. Showband musicians, in contrast, played by ear and had no need for sheet music or music stands. They could thus stand up and dance light choreographies in their brightly colored mohair suits. In doing so, they radiated charisma and showmanship, in contrast to the physically staid dance band musicians, recalls Derry-based clarinetist/saxophonist Jim McDermott, who played in both: "Oh, God. I think the difference would've been like working for a morgue and working in a circus!" (interview, 2018).

"Playable from Three to Twenty": The Transnational Sheet Music Industry

Irish dance band musicians and bandleaders focused centrally on imported dance music; their audiences, in turn, followed and learned the accompanying dance steps from the United States and Britain. Because of this, the dance band genre is often recalled as imitative or derivative and, crucially, not Irish. Contributing to this perception was the large pool of common repertoire shared among most dance bands thanks to the widespread availability of imported, inexpensive sheet music of American hits. Some of these arrangements were imported directly from New York City; the majority arrived by way of England.

In the years leading up to World War I, London music publishers cornered the market for sheet music arrangements of well-known dance band standards and popular hits of the day with an estimated 20 million pieces with 40,000 new titles. London's "Tin Pan Alley," a name borrowed from the parallel New York City music publishing industry, was located on Denmark Street off Charing Cross Road, and, by 1938, employed—all in one block—nearly three hundred workers (Nott 2002, 105). Catering to the many dance bands in Britain and Ireland, British music arrangers crafted dance music orchestrations that were versatile and flexible and could be performed by bands of various sizes. Exported to Irish bandleaders on both sides of the border, these arrangements allowed for some level of interpretation and variation with their performance dependent on ensemble size, skill level, and, ultimately, the creativity of the musicians and bandleaders.

In a 2006 radio interview with RTÉ presenter Brendan Balfe, compère and former president of the Irish Federation of Musicians Noel Coade, pianist/arranger Noel Kelehan, and bandleader/vocalist Johnny Devlin reminisced about these band arrangements:

Noel Kelehan: You could buy the orchestrations from England.

Brendan Balfe (BB): Where did the orchestrations come from? Did bands make up their own charts?

Figure 2.6 The Johnny Devlin Band, ca. 1952. (Photo courtesy of Monica and Sharon Coade.)

JOHNNY DEVLIN (JD): Well, in some cases. But in most cases, a lot of the bands were playing the same printed music which you could get from London, you know.

BB: Well, I presume the entire Glenn Miller book was available. . . .

NOEL COADE: 'Playable from three to twenty [band members]!' (*General laughter*).

JD: The arrangements were made in such a way that . . . a small band could play them, except that you couldn't get the Glenn Miller sound for obvious reasons. But the audience could hear the same lines that they heard on the original disc. . . .

BB: Would they reproduce, were they written in, the solos?

JD: Oh, absolutely, yes. The solos that were on the records . . . were written in. The bandleaders would buy them in. Do you remember, Noel, you joined a club and you paid something, quarterly or a six monthly subscription and they sent you the hits? If you remember, they were kind of adaptable. They could be played, well more or less, with a trio or a 10 or 11 piece band, whatever number you had. (*Brendan Balfe's Dance Band Days,* 2006)

It is hard to know whether widespread interest in American popular music contributed to the growth of the British music publishing industry or whether this burgeoning industry itself was a catalyst that focused the public's fascination on American sounds. In all probability, it was a combination of both factors. The sheet music industry itself was dominated by several influential Denmark Street music publishers, one of which was the Lawrence Wright Music Company. Well known for its magazine, *Melody Maker*—a publication that, for decades, informed the tastes of many popular musicians, bandleaders, and music aficionados in Britain and Ireland—the Lawrence Wright Music Company recognized early on the potential of big American hits and spent more than any other British music publisher in buying up the British rights to songs from the United States (Nott 2002, 111).

In direct competition were the ever-popular arrangements by the British orchestrator, Jimmy Lally, whose work was initially distributed by another London-based music publisher, Chappelle and Co. Beginning in 1933 until the end of the 1960s, Jimmy Lally arrangements were ubiquitous among dance bands and orchestras throughout Britain, Ireland, and Australia. Inexpensive and adaptable for any size dance, Jimmy Lally arrangements were simple enough that even a marginally musically literate player could reliably contribute to the band sound. In a June 1966 interview with the British jazz magazine *Crescendo*, Lally describes his populist approach to providing music for the average working musician: "I've got the formula, a couple of standard choruses, make it so any band can play it, no matter what the size. . . . I have to please mainly the small bands, and I also have to please the publishers. . . . But when you write printed stuff, it's got to be playable by anyone" (Jimmy Lally, quoted in Staples 1966, 9–11).

In creating highly accessible scores, Jimmy Lally arrangements catered to working musicians rather than to virtuosic performers. For many, playing in a "reading" band was a point of pride as it demarcated true musicianship in contrast to musicians who played exclusively "by ear."[4] Indeed, musical literacy on both sides of the border was not easily acquired during these decades, because, with few exceptions, music education was largely or entirely absent from the curricula of Irish and Northern Irish schools. Most often, young people learned to read music from a family member or from a local piano teacher—many of whom, incidentally, were women. Some, such as Derry saxophonist William Bradley (b. 1929), learned to read music upon joining the Foyle Flute Band (interview 2018)[5] while others learned these skills by joining other ensembles, such as the Dublin-based St. James Brass and Reed Band, the Police Bands, the Transport and General Workers' Union Band, and the Artane Boys Band, among others.[6] The late vocalist/saxophonist Sonny Knowles recalled the start of his music education as a boy when he joined the Irish Post Office Workers' Union Band in Dublin: "[I learned] how to read and sight read and how to read while you were walking [marching], which wasn't an easy thing to do, but that was all in the training" (interview, 2009). In addition to the personal satisfaction that came with this acquired skill set, there was also the pleasure derived from mastering a musical instrument and learning repertoire. Knowles, for example, recalls with pride his developing expertise with the more challenging jazz arrangements: "And then Duke Ellington's stuff would come in and Count Basie. We thought we were big shots, playing all that stuff!"

The Brotherhood of Musicians

Becoming musically literate opened up work opportunities well beyond what many young people in Ireland could imagine during these years. By the mid-1930s, the dance craze that had taken hold in Ireland a decade earlier was generating an enormous increase in demand for both full- and part-time musicians. Performing music could provide a reasonable and concrete means of earning a living. William ("Willie") McIntyre was a well-known, self-taught musician in Derry, Northern Ireland. Beginning in the late 1920s, McIntyre taught his two brothers, Jimmy and Josie McIntyre, as well as Jack Ayling and Freddie Robinson how to play, and together they formed the Melville Dance Band. His son, Gay McIntyre, a jazz saxophonist and clarinetist, recalls that his father saw the possibility of earning a living through music as a solution to his family's poverty, which was endemic in Derry at the time:

> It would be very hard to explain Derry City in those days because most people, including my family, don't believe me when I tell them how poor things were. The woman next door would borrow a spoonful of sugar from my mother, and my mother would say, "Well, do you have a drop of milk?" And this is the way they lived, because the area was very, very poor, you know?
>
> Now [my father's] band was . . . quite unique because they knew nothing about music, yet my father was able to pick it up, teach his next brother saxophone, clarinet and flute; teach his next brother trumpet, accordion, and violin. And they got the parts and the tune and all that sort of Glenn Miller things and different pretty good arrangements that you could buy at that time. So they were very good readers. They were extraordinary, actually.
>
> Well, [my father saw music] as a way out of the impoverished situation that existed. He got twenty-seven shillings . . . for working for three nights. It wasn't good, but it kept the wolf from the door. (Interview, 2008)

Sit-down dance band musicians identified centrally as laborers who were hired to do a job. Recalls bandleader Johnny Quigley: "Well, we were workers. It was to make a living. You know, it was the main purpose, and we had to work hard to make a living at it. You had to draw crowds. If you had a band that was drawing a crowd, no problem getting bookings, you know" (interview, 2018). Saxophonist/clarinetist Paddy Cole got his start as a musician in 1951, at the age of twelve, when he joined the County Monaghan–based

Figure 2.7 The Melville Dance Band at the Melville Hotel, Derry, 1935. *Left to right*: Jimmy, Willie, and Josie McIntyre; Jack Ayling; and Freddie Robinson. (Photo courtesy of Paul McIntyre.)

Maurice Lynch Band. Two things immediately drew him to the life of a performing musician at the time—the money and the pleasure of playing music: "During school holidays, I would play with the band all the time, because it was a great way of making money. . . . Plus the fact that the band was what I liked; the music was what I liked" (Cole, interview, 2007). Derry multi-instrumentalist John Trotter similarly views his lifelong involvement as a professional musician as a career but also emphasizes that for him and for his fellow musicians, it was more than just a job: "I saw them as artists really, and friends. There is a fraternity among musicians, as you being one would probably know. *Them and us*. And that's the way it was, that's the way it always was. It was a brotherhood, really" (interview, 2018).

Mirroring larger trends in Irish organized labor, the proliferation of dance musicians in the Republic generated a spate of attempts to unionize players, culminating in 1936 with the successful formation of the Irish Federation of Dance Musicians (Swift 2012). That said, in the post–World War II years, union membership was variable at best: the union reportedly had little power, and most musicians saw little benefit to joining. The exception to this were those who lived or wished to work in Dublin where union membership

Figure 2.8 Maurice Lynch Band, 1951. *Back row, left to right*: Tommy Toal, Charlie Lynch, and Eileen Lambe; *front row, left to right*: Pat Donahue, Peter Hickey, Paddy Cole (age twelve), and Francie Leonard. (Photo courtesy of Paddy Cole.)

was mandatory for both radio work and for playing in the unionized dance halls (Garber, interview, 2018). The other exception was the Northern Ireland Musicians Association, established in 1939, and arguably more powerful than the Irish Federation of Dance Musicians, given the larger percentages of musicians who were members. Johnny Quigley recalls that union membership was particularly important for bands from Northern Ireland like his that toured south of the border:

> QUIGLEY: We used to go to Dublin too, they had a union down there and if you weren't in the union, they made it hard for you. . . .
>
> MILLER: Could you play if you didn't belong to the union? Would you be allowed to play?
>
> QUIGLEY: Well, you weren't supposed to. You felt you had to be in the union to be safe. (Interview, 2018)

In the years following World War II, professional dance musicians found regular work in a range of venues, rural and urban, from the smallest of parochial halls to the largest ballrooms. The less well-known dance bands could play one or two nights a week, while the larger orchestras as often as six and even seven nights a week, with the exception in the Republic of the Lenten season, when the Catholic Church forbid dancing. The best-known orchestras occasionally toured internationally in Britain and, rarely, the United States, to entertain Irish diasporic communities.

Figure 2.9 Publicity postcard for Johnny Quigley All Stars, ca. 1959. (Photo courtesy of Johnny Quigley.)

Musicians universally recall the discomfort of traveling, squashed together in band vehicles for long hours on poorly paved rural roads as well as the challenges of transporting equipment and instruments. In 1943, Gay McIntyre was ten years old when he was hired to play clarinet in a small dance band in Bundoran, County Donegal, every Sunday evening:

> McIntyre: Anybody that had a car, didn't matter how bad it was, but the fact that [the bandleader] had a car, that was something else, you know? And the conditions were very bad. We used to lift the piano onto the back of a lorry, put a tarpaulin over it and then the melodeon player and myself, we got under the tarpaulin and we'd travel maybe twenty miles to the gig on a Sunday. Rain, hail or snow, it'd be the same thing. Lift the piano on, get on underneath.
>
> Miller: What did the piano sound like when you got it there? Did you have to tune it?
>
> McIntyre: No! It wouldn't matter (*laughs*).

Upon arrival, the band might have been offered a hot meal, although plenty of musicians recall suppers consisting of a half-hearted ham sandwich

Figure 2.10 Paddy Cole (right) with the Stradella Dance Band, Castleblaney, County Monaghan, ca. 1950. (Photo courtesy of Paddy Cole.)

and tea. Working conditions are nearly always remembered as basic to the point of primitive. Gay McIntyre recalls that at the Bundoran dance, there was "an old hurricane lamp hanging over the stage and a battery amplification that broke down every two minutes" (interview, 2008). There were many other routine discomforts, recalls Claudette Colbert McCarthy, pianist in the Brideside Serenaders: "One hall, it was so cold, that when Frank [Prendergast] blew the trumpet, a piece of ice came out. [The hall had] a corrugated roof on it. Yes, think of it! . . . Ice came out of his trumpet as he was trying to shake the moisture out. The things that would happen to you!" (interview, 2019). As a touring dance band player in the 1950s, Paddy Cole remembers how basic these dance halls were: "A lot of those ballrooms, we used to joke that they put up four walls, a huge floor and a telephone box as a changing room for the bands. And they didn't worry about heat, or anything like that. They put a few radiators about the place, and if you complained about the ballrooms being cold, sort of a stock answer was that if you're drawing enough people, then the ballroom wouldn't be cold" (interview, 2018).

And drawing crowds was the point. Even the smallest parish hall could accommodate one hundred or more of dancers; larger ballrooms often saw up to two thousand dancers. Audiences arrived at the dance halls on foot, wagon, and by bicycle, often traveling eight to ten miles from neighboring towns. Dances typically began at 9:00 p.m. and ended at 1:00 a.m. or later and consisted of two long sets with a short break at the interval (intermission). It was common for a smaller ensemble—a trio, for example—to perform during the interval so as to provide continuous dance music. Bandleaders grouped the dance tunes in sets of three: three foxtrots were followed by three old-time waltzes and then three quicksteps, for example. Admission for the more popular sit-down dance orchestras was in the range of four to six shillings; entry fees were less for the smaller dance bands. Part-time players recall that income earned from even one music job a week was a welcome supplement to their family's income; full-time players often enjoyed quite a nice standard of living. Michael McEvoy, vocalist and guitarist with the Maurice Mulcahy Orchestra, recalls earning twenty-five pounds a week in the mid-1950s, a fortune by most working people's standards at the time: "Anyone who got ten, twelve, or fifteen pounds a week in those days [was] doing well. Because you could get a good plenty for that pound then" (interview, 2018).

Propelled by the new sounds and dance styles as well as the widespread availability of sheet music, dance bands of all stripes were kept busy. The dances themselves generated handsome profits for private dance hall owners and parish coffers. These profits were not limited to dance evenings that featured popular music: céilí dances also often generated excellent earnings, and, as demand grew, dance hall owners and parish priests were quick to offer entire evenings devoted to this type of social dancing. Some enterprising ballroom owners saw opportunity here too and advertised dance evenings that featured both popular dancing and céilí dancing in the same night. Nimble musicians with the musical skills to play both types of music could double their performance opportunities and income.

Despite this, the two genres received very different treatment by Ireland's leading cultural, state, and religious institutions. As a relatively new genre, the popularity of céilí dancing reflected the growing Irish nationalist discourse in the years leading up to and especially following Irish independence in 1922. Officially embraced by the Gaelic League and the Catholic Church, ceílí dancing was promoted as an important symbol of Irish cultural heritage and autonomy. In contrast, imported popular American and British dance music—"jazz"—was routinely demonized by the Church with the support of Irish cultural and political institutions, culminating in the Public Dance Halls Act of 1935, which impacted public dancing of all sorts. The dynamics of Irish popular music and dance from the 1920s to the 1960s are therefore best understood alongside the popularity of céilí dancing because, despite their inherent differences of substance, style, and tradition, they shared a touring circuit, venues, musicians, and, especially, the delight of dancing audiences.

Céilí Bands and Dances: Origins/Inventions

The term "céilí" originally referred to informal and unplanned gatherings in Ireland that featured storytelling, instrumental tune playing, singing, and dancing. Céilís traditionally took place in the homes of families that were known for their musicality—or, at least, for their love of music—and the gatherings served as a social space that centered on participatory performance. Charlie Lennon's family frequently hosted céilís or, more colloquially, a "céilí in house," whereby "céilí-ers" visited unannounced and might stay for a few hours. Lennon recalls that "[people would] go around the room and [tell] a story or a poem or sing a song or whatever. And then the fiddle would be passed round if there were a number of people there" (interview, 2019).

While this community-based understanding of the céilí persisted at least into the early 1950s, the term itself had been appropriated and recontextualized decades earlier by members of the Gaelic League. Established in 1893 by Eoin McNeill, Douglas Hyde (its first president), and others, the central mission of the Gaelic League was to counteract what was seen as the Anglicization of Ireland through an embrace and widening of the Irish language, sport, music, song, and dance.

With this in mind, the Gaelic League organized the first céilí on October 30, 1897, in Bloomsbury Hall, London. The brainchild of Fionán MacColuim, the secretary of the London Branch of the Gaelic League, the evening was modeled on MacColuim's experience at Scottish *céilídhs*. The evening opened with tunes played by piper Tomás O Gearacháin, followed by songs and music by Irish, Scottish, and Welsh performers and instruction in group Irish step dancing by Professor P. D. Reidy, an emigrant from Castleisland, County Kerry. Because the organizers, writes Fintan Vallely, were conscious of "breaking new ground and the need to create a good image," the céilí was by invitation only, designed to be participatory, and tightly controlled: the tune "Phil the Fluter's Ball," for example, was deemed "stage Irish" and therefore unacceptable (Vallely 2011, 116). Constructed in no small part as a nationalist project, the organizers ultimately settled on the word *céilí* to distinguish the event from the English connotations of "concert" and "ball" (Scahill 2018, 185).

As a sort of invented tradition, céilí dancing took hold in Ireland and steadily gained popularity in the early decades of the twentieth century.[7] So strong was the Gaelic League's influence at the time in codifying and crafting Irish traditional dance as purely Irish that quadrilles and other presumed "foreign" set dances were excluded altogether from the developing canon of céilí dances (Lawler and Scahill 2013, 181). By the early 1930s, céilí dancing was systematized with the documentation of thirty or so choreographies "chosen for ideological purposes" to the marginalization and neglect of older, regional styles of Irish group folk and set dancing (Foley 2001, 36; see also Shanagher 2014, 79).

The earliest documentation of a céilí band is from 1918 and featured a group of musicians who played at a St. Patrick's night céilí in London. In the years that followed, céilí bands played for Gaelic League–sponsored events and then eventually in communities to supply music for crossroads and in-home dances. As their popularity grew, céilís moved from smaller venues to the larger commercial and parochial halls that could accommodate larger crowds. Because amplification equipment at the time was rudimentary and often non-existent, ceílí bands expanded from some combination of fiddles, flutes, accordions, melodeons, tenor banjo, and other traditional instruments to larger groups in order to be heard across these larger halls. To do so, céilí bands added two instruments: piano and drum kit.

The piano had figured prominently in earlier Gaelic League events to accompany singers during the Gaelic Revival and, by 1926, was adopted into céilí bands, notably the Ballinakill Traditional Dance Players (later known as the Ballinakill Céilí Band). With steady chords and added bass line, the piano added volume as well as a definitive harmonic accompaniment.[8] Around the same time, in 1927, the Kilfenora Céilí Band became the first group to include drums (including the iconic woodblock); their first drummer was Jimmy Leyden (Danaher 1988). With the added volume and a stricter rhythmic feel, céilí drummers stressed down- and offbeats, thereby obscuring the subtle pulse typical of traditional Irish dance music. Like the piano, drums were central to the modern, sit-down dance band sound but, up to that point, not commonly heard in Irish traditional music. With the addition of both piano and drums to céilí bands, the musical textures and rhythmic feel shifted from a more traditional Irish instrumental style and, ironically, embraced a sound more consistent with that of popular sit-down dance bands. What the

Figure 2.11 The Douglas Céilí Band, Cork City, 1958. (Photo courtesy of Bob Kearney.)

Gaelic League had originally envisaged as an expression of "authentic" Irish culture, céilí bands paradoxically appropriated some of the same musical aesthetics, instrumentation, and textures that drove the non-Irish popular dance music.

By the 1950s, céilí bands had taken on other characteristics of sit-down dance bands. Some groups added saxophones and other nontraditional instruments to the mix. While most céilí bands focused their repertoire on a range of instrumental dance tunes (reels, jigs, hornpipes, set pieces, and the like), some incorporated popular songs into an evening's program. Charlie Lennon played fiddle in the Liverpool Céilí Band from 1960 to 1968. He recalls that this band, like the sit-down dance bands at the time, featured a vocalist who sang Irish songs and ballads that were sometimes rearranged into waltz time so that people could dance to these well-known songs. Lennon recalls, 'Twasn't for listening. Well, it was [for] listening, but it wasn't 'stood there' listening. They were always dancing" (interview, 2019).

The Liverpool Céilí Band members added another level of professionalism to their music. Aiming for a seamless blend of the instruments, the band emphasized a front line of melody provided by four fiddles, flute, and accordion. This was supported by a solid interlocking beat produced by the piano and drums that, according to Lennon, "stabilized everything." The members

Figure 2.12 The Liverpool Céilí Band, 1964. *Back row*: Kevin Finnegan, Sean Murphy, and Frank Horan; *front row*: Sean McNamara, Eamon Coyne, Pat Finn, Albert ("Cruiky") Cruikshank, Charlie Lennon, Kit Hodge, and Peggy Atkins. (Photo courtesy of Ray Rooney.)

of the Liverpool Céilí Band were also known for their showmanship as well as their ability to read and respond to their audiences:

> Among ourselves, we'd be lively and we'd be kind of playing little tricks on ourselves, [and] very much communicating with the audience. So we were all sitting down, but we would kind of tend to move around on our seats. Or have a nice good change from one piece of music to the next one, you know, that would raise them. . . . Maybe pick a tune that would give you a boost! So we were very conscious of our audience.
>
> [Our aim] was to get cohesion and to get rhythm, but most of all, to have enjoyment. And we did really enjoy, and we were very popular because of that. And the dancers would be delighted to see because we'd have fun onstage among ourselves as we went along. (Lennon, interview, 2019)

This understanding of musical professionalism and entertainment mirrored that of the dance bands in which Charlie Lennon also played. As the guitarist/pianist in the Leitrim-based Blue Haven Dance Band and, later, the

Emerald Valley Dance Band, Lennon saw the similarities between playing in a céilí band and a sit-down dance band:

> [For both], you had to put on a show for the night: you brought all your amplification which you had all that packed into your car or van or whatever. And you had put it up yourself and took it down afterwards. You hoped that the crowd would come and you hoped that the band would rebook for the month's time or whatever it was. And you know, you did your best to entertain the people that came there, make them happy, go home happy. (Interview, 2019)

The Church: Sounding Irishness, Silencing the Popular

There persisted a profound disconnect between the hierarchy of Ireland's Catholic Church and many of Ireland's working musicians, audiences, and dance hall owners. While audiences delighted in dancing of all sorts and musicians were often inspired by the new sounds from outside of Ireland, Church leaders doggedly promoted céilí dancing for an array of moral and pragmatic reasons while disparaging popular music and dance. Much of this discourse was explicit in its alignment with the Gaelic League. Historian Kieran Waldron (2008, 104) writes that Dr. Thomas Patrick Gilmartin, archbishop of Tuam from 1918 to 1939, was a strong proponent of the Gaelic League and balanced his dislike of "'foreign dances' and the new rave of jazz" with his appreciation of Irish music and dance and the belief that "Irish dances, or Céilís, were permitted and could be promoted by priests under proper conditions." Indeed, like other members of the Church hierarchy, Archbishop Gilmartin was blunt in his public condemnations of American jazz. In 1930, he addressed the audience at the opening of Tuam's annual Feis (an Irish traditional dance competition). Juxtaposing praise for the day's "rich feast of Irish music and Irish dances," Gilmartin opined that "Irish culture is at present in as much danger of perishing as it was at any time in the past" and, using a racist slur, made his views clear on Irish dances versus those imported from the United States: "Must we admit, I ask you, that Irish dances have been discarded for what has been described as 'mere sensuous contortions of the body timed to n— music, a semi-barbaric music?' If that is so, and I fear it is to a very great extent, there is a serious rift in our Irish culture" (Archbishop Gilmartin, quoted in *Connacht Sentinel*, May 27, 1930, 2).

Local newspapers routinely published editorials similarly describing jazz in both explicit and semiveiled racist terms, such as "apish and heathenish inventions," and the Gaelic League critiqued the behavior of politicians as "anti-national," given their fostering of jazz on Radio Éireann

(Chan 2005, 21). Most insidiously, blackness was often equated with evil, such as in this column from a 1927 article in the *Leinster Leader*:

> "N— music comes from the devil," said Dr. Farnell, Rector of Exeter College . . . "Vulgar music might not be so criminal as murder, but it was far more degrading. Our civilisation was threatened by our own inventions, by our dreadful noises, our horrible motor traffic, our Americanism, and 'jazz' music. Don't take your music from America or from the N—s," he said: "Take it from God, the source of all good music." (*Leinster Leader*, August 13, 1927, 2)

Neatly fusing conservative nationalist ideologies with Catholicism, this discourse was released in edicts issued by the archbishops and bishops of Ireland and widely published in local papers: "There is danger of losing the name which the chivalrous honour of Irish boys and Christian reserve of Irish maidens had won for Ireland. If our people part with the character that gave rise to that name, we lose with it much of our national strength and still more of the high rank we have held in the Kingdom of Christ" (*Longford Leader*, September 25, 1926, 3). Other dangers, such as the potential for sin, were frequently mentioned: "Purity is strength, and purity and faith go together. Both virtues are in danger these times, but purity is more directly assaulted than faith. The danger comes from pictures and papers and drink. It comes more from the keeping of improper company than from any other cause; and there is no worse fomenter of this great evil than the dancing hall" (ibid.).

The Church leadership noted that these concerns did not hold true for céilí dancing, which was seen as healthier in both body and spirit and which required only minimal contact in contrast to the more physical nature of couple dancing to popular music. Céilí dancing was also presented in practical terms as aerobically challenging and thus tiring: "Our young people can have plenty of worthy dancing with proper supervision and return home at a reasonable hour. . . . It is no small commendation of Irish dances that they cannot be danced for long hours" (*Longford Leader*, September 25, 1926, 3).

Aside from the narrative of what constituted appropriate entertainment for young people was another that relied on fear to dissuade them from attending popular dances in commercial dance halls. One perspective focused on the assumed wickedness of the individual should they decide to go "dancing on the hobs of hell" (Ó hAllmhuráin 2005), a choice that might result in dire consequences. For example, in a 1925 newspaper column, the Most Reverend Dr. O'Donaell of Dundalk warned that he "would excommunicate people frequenting those places if the evils continued" (*Liberator* [Tralee], August 18, 1925, 1). Another perspective shifted the burden of sin from the individual to the external dangers an innocent might encounter in a dance hall. One of the most common was the frightening possibility of evil individuals who attended dances halls with the express aim of taking advantage of young people: "Given a few frivolous young people in a locality and a few careless parents, and the agents of the wicked one will come there to do the rest, once a dance is announced without proper control. They may lower or destroy the moral tone of the whole countryside" (*Longford Leader*, September 25, 1926, 3).

The Public Dance Halls Act of 1935

These national anxieties came to a head in 1934 when the Gaelic League launched a "war against jazz" with the support of the Catholic Church, some county councils, and Taoiseach (Prime Minister) Éamon de Valera, who soundly condemned jazz music and dance as "denationalizing" and, ultimately, "instrument[s] of social degradation" (Gaelic League, quoted by J. Smyth 1993, 53). The following year, the Dáil passed without debate the Public Dance Halls Act of 1935, which placed strict limitations on public dancing. Both the Church and the Fianna Fáil government supported passage of the Act for moral reasons, while other governmental agencies expressed concern about large crowds in unregulated small spaces and required explicit oversight: "Any member of the Gárda Síochána in uniform may enter any [licensed public dancing] place . . . at any time . . . and there make such inspection, examination, and inquiry as he shall think proper" (Public Acts Records of 1935).[9] While public dancing was now subject to regulatory sanctions by the police, judiciary, and clergy, the Public Dance Halls Act was, as Jim Smyth notes, "probably honoured more in the breach than in the observance" (Smyth 1993, 53).

The Public Dance Halls Act of 1935 required that all public dances obtain licensing to operate, thereby allowing the state to generate revenue through fees collected from these licenses as well as from the imposition of a ticket tax on each entrance fee. Admission fees went into the pockets of individual commercial owners as well as local priests, who put revenues toward the upkeep of parish buildings and programs. This collaboration between the Church and state allowed for shared financial gain, one strengthened through moral justification and upheld through the influence of the local *Garda* (police) with the oversight by parish priests (Austin 1993, 11, 16).

Dance hall owners also enjoyed handsome profits. Born in 1925 in Woodford, County Galway, flutist Jack Coen recalls that dance halls often charged more than many members of the community could afford:

> Things were changing as I was growing up and [traditional Irish music] was going out. Even to the point that in the smaller little town halls right around through the country, they used to up the price so high that the poor people couldn't afford to go to the dance.

Back then, nobody seemed to care. The only people that cared back then were the people who wanted to make money on it, the people who ran the dances or the people who owned the dance halls. They were entrepreneurs who wanted to make music and they couldn't care less what you played in there, so long as it bought in the crowd and they make money off of it. They weren't interested in concerts, they weren't interested in the arts, or anything like that. It was strictly commercial. (Interview, 1992)

Coen's contemporary, the late County Clare fiddler Junior Crehan, similarly recalls the far-reaching effect of the Public Dance Halls Act on traditional Irish music in general:

> The clergy started to build the parochial halls to which all were expected to go and the Government collected 25 per cent of the ticket tax. In these halls modern dance bands played a different type of dancing—foxtrot, one step, and Shimmy Shake. . . . The dance halls were not natural places of enjoyment; they were not places for traditional music, story-telling and dancing; they were unsuitable for passing on traditional arts. The Dance Hall Act had closed our schools of tradition and left us a poorer people. (Junior Crehan, quoted in Austin 1993, 16)

While the Public Dance Halls Act of 1935 was not intended to regulate public crossroads dances or house dances, the net effect was that it drove all dancing—popular and céilí—indoors. In doing so, it shifted social dance from what had been a community-based activity to one that could be contained and controlled. Indeed, the immediate aftermath of the Act also saw the construction of a spate of new commercial dance halls, which, perhaps ironically, served as a provocation to local clergy. Writing in the January 1953 issue of *The Furrow,* an Irish church publication that aimed to assist young priests with "problems not envisaged in the official text-books," Reverend Michael T. Mooney argued that the Act "should have been a great boon" but "in practice, it had one very undesirable effect": "The rigid enforcement of the new act put an abrupt end to [house dances] and young people had to look elsewhere for dancing facilities. Keen *entrepreneurs* were quick to see—and seize—the business opportunity afforded by the situation. It was thus that the era of the 'commercial' dancehall began. . . . As a result of this, many priests decided that they would build halls which they could effectively control" (Mooney 1953, 3–4, emphasis in original).

Aside from the potential to generate revenue from parish dances, some clergy, such as the Right Reverend Monsignor Dargan of Drimnagh, saw parochial halls as important to the life and health of the parish: "The Church [is] the centre of the religious life of the community, and the hall [is] the centre of the social life . . . to be used for dramatic and choral performances, dancing and other social activities" (*Irish Press*, October 31, 1955, 7). Other clergy took a dimmer view: Fr. F. J. Fehily (1953, 22), of Crosshaven, County Cork, argued that the cost of running a parochial hall could only be met through the sponsorship of dances and that "when it comes to organized dances . . . there is no difference, from the Catholic point of view, between the dance in the parish hall and the one in the commercial hall." In addition to concerns about whether priests should be seen by young people as frequenting parochial hall clubs given their greater spiritual duties, Fr. Fehily also argued that contrary to popular understanding, parochial halls and their programs do not "stem the constant flow of the young people from the rural areas," noting that young Irish wished to emigrate for solely economic reasons, not as a result of the paucity of entertainment (16). Finally, Fr. Fehily drew on his colleague Fr. Heenan, who was similarly unimpressed by the argument that parochial halls fill a crucial role as social centers: "We deceive ourselves if we imagine that club work is mainly spiritual. There is no Catholic way of playing billiards" (Heenan, quoted in Fehily 1951, 22).

These debates aside, what is clear is that the Public Dance Halls Act of 1935 opened the doors wide for the commercialization of social dancing in Ireland of all stripes. In doing so, the Act created incentives for entrepreneurs—both commercial and clergy—to build an infrastructure that ultimately created the cornerstones of Ireland's emerging popular music and dance industry.

"The Archbishop's Quickstep"

Along with the regulations imposed by the Public Dance Halls Act of 1935, the Church hierarchy's campaign against popular music and dance intensified after December 1940 with the ascendance of John Charles McQuaid as Catholic Primate of Ireland and Archbishop of Dublin.[10] In solidifying the Church's position regarding popular culture, Archbishop McQuaid routinely denounced a wide range of ideologies, behaviors, and practices, ranging from the dangers of Communism to dog, horse, and pony racing. Archbishop McQuaid warned followers about sending children to non-Catholic schools and aspiring toward the "acquisition of wealth with the power that wealth brings of satisfying lust." He routinely condemned cinemas and theaters "where paganism is subtly insinuated" and urged followers to ward "off the insensitive vulgarity of mind, dress, and gesture . . . in Catholic homes and schools" (*Fermanagh Herald*, March 4, 1944, 4).

Archbishop McQuaid had a particularly strong abhorrence of dance halls and popular music because of, as he saw it, their potential to incite sin. A column in the *Evening Herald* reports on Archbishop McQuaid's 1941 New

Year's Eve sermon in which he articulated concerns about the Irish "craze for pleasure" and the disintegration of Irish home life owing to "the dance hall, the pictures, drink, and sinful company keeping" (Archbishop McQuaid, *Evening Herald,* January 1, 1942, 4). Many of the archbishop's columns replicate, word-for-word, his concerns as published in years past. For example, both a 1951 column in the *Irish Examiner* and one four years later in the *Irish Press* warn parents to "supervise their children," especially with regard to the "adequate control of the place and circumstances of dancing" (*Irish Examiner,* May 2, 1951, 5; *Irish Press,* February 21, 1955, 8).

Archbishop McQuaid's edicts were embraced by other members of the Church hierarchy and clergy—concerns and opinions that were articulated both from the pulpit and published in local papers. A February 1941 *Irish Independent* article entitled "Dance Hall Dangers," for example, presents the argument of Most Reverend Dr. MacNamee, Bishop of Ardagh and Clonmacnoise, that dance halls should, like pubs, be closed by 11:00 p.m. to mitigate "the evils attendant on them" and so that children could return home and the day closed with "family prayer" and "obtaining rest needful for the work of the morrow."

Archbishop McQuaid's influence filtered down into the dance halls themselves. The late Fr. Micheál Mac Gréil of Westport recalls that at some parish dances, the last dance of an evening had to be a fast two-step: "It was known among my pals as the 'Archbishop's Quickstep.' . . . A slow dance would [be] too intimate. Well, I mean, in a quickstep you don't go body to body. So that was the rule anyhow. You [then] heard the national anthem and you went home" (Fr. Micheál Mac Gréil, interview, 2008).

Playing for All Dancers

While the Catholic Church pursued these concerns of moral purity and the national good, in practice, Irish audiences from the 1940s to the 1960s just liked to dance, recalls Charlie Lennon: "Well, they did both, yeah. They'd go to a céilí one night and they'd go to a dance hall the next night" (interview, 2019). Ballroom owners also took note, according to a 1956 article in the *Irish Press*:

> The ballroom owners, in adapting themselves to the demands of the public for modern dancing, did not allow themselves to neglect two other forms: Irish dancing and "old time" dancing. Provincial ballrooms, in particular, are as readily available to those who want to hold a ceildhe as a modern dance. In Dublin, as a rule, the ceildhe are held only in special halls, but both in city and country, the "modern" bands continue to include *Irish* dances in their repertoire, and these often bring the largest crowds on to the floor. . . . In the holiday

camps, where the gaiety of old-time is very much at home, the veleta and the "Gay Gordon" compete for popularity with the slow waltz and the mambo. (March 30/31, 1956, 10, emphasis in original.)

To this end, bands of all sizes throughout Ireland developed strategies to remain marketable over the course of four decades by combining in various ways popular and Irish dance music. Some, like Des Kelly's first dance band in 1954, played a distinct mix of traditional music for céilí dancing on the one hand and popular dance music on the other:

> We had a couple of good traditional players in the band . . . so we'd play a couple of "Siege of Ennises" during the night and we'd play a couple of barn dances. And we'd play the pop songs of the day, which might be Joe Stafford or Guy Mitchell or whoever else there was. And a lot of old time waltzes. And you played old Irish ballads. It was the only opportunity for boy meets girl, and we were the catalyst in the formula! (D. Kelly, interview, 2006)

While some bands like Des Kelly's could handle an equal mix of popular and Irish repertoire, others hired specific instrumentalists as needed to provide this dual repertoire. Some groups, particularly the large dance orchestras, limited their repertoire to popular dance tunes and songs from the United States and Britain and skipped céilí music altogether but nevertheless incorporated recognizable Irish stylistic practices into their performances. The sheer range of musical strategies put to use by dance bands and orchestras between 1930 and 1970 speaks to the flexibility and skill sets of the musicians as much as the ingenious direction by band and orchestra leaders, who read their audiences and responded with humor, creativity, and musicality. For dance bands and orchestras both, crafting new musical strategies that referenced Irishness while also remaining open to aesthetic change was rewarded by steady and well-paid work and, for some groups, an impressive longevity of nearly forty years of professional performance. Three diverse dance bands succeeded admirably in this regard: Thomas Mulhaire's dance bands, beginning in 1930, in County Galway; the Brideside Serenaders from Tallow, County Waterford, starting in 1951; and arguably the best-known dance orchestra, the Mick Delahunty Orchestra of Clonmel, County Tipperary, beginning in 1940.

Thomas Mulhaire: "Less Talk, More Music!"

Thomas ("Tommy") Mulhaire was born in 1906 in Eyrecourt, County Galway, into a family and community steeped in traditional music. The son of an accomplished Irish traditional flutist, Mulhaire was an award-winning multi-instrumentalist and a highly respected local music teacher, composer,

Figure 2.13 *Left to right*: Pat Joe Farrell, Martin Mulhaire, and Tommy Mulhaire, ca. 1939. (Photo courtesy of family of Martin Mulhaire.)

and bandleader. In an interview, his son, the late Martin Mulhaire, recalled that his father was a prolific instrumentalist: "He played the accordion, he learned the fiddle, played the flute, played the whistle, played drums" (interview, 1988). An ardent exponent of Irish traditional music, Mulhaire was one of the first traditional musicians to perform on Radio Éireann in 1936 and was a founder of the East Galway chapter of Comhaltas Ceoltóirí Éireann (a nonprofit organization, founded in 1951, to preserve and promote Irish traditional music).

According to Martin Mulhaire, Thomas Mulhaire was unlike most traditional musicians at the time: "He was different in that he liked all kinds of music. He listened to every kind of music from popular to jazz to American Latin bands. He just loved music in general" (Mulhaire, interview, 1985).[11] Beginning in the early 1930s, Mulhaire put together a versatile band that drew on and reflected his diverse musical interests:

> He had what was considered a dance band in them days where he played traditional music, but he also played some of the more popular songs of the day. And he played piano accordion as well as button key accordion. So he used the piano accordion for the more popular tunes because it had the bass, it has the chords, stuff that he could utilize more. It was a combination then of traditional music with more popular music of the day. (M. Mulhaire, interview, 1988)

Figure 2.14 Mulhaire's Eyrecourt Céilí Band, ca. 1938. (Photo courtesy of family of Martin Mulhaire.)

Figure 2.15 Lough Lurgan Céilí Band, ca. 1960: *Back row, from left*: Tommy Coen, Paddy Farrell, Micheál O'hEidhin, Tom Mulhaire, and Michael Hession; *front row, from left*: Brendan Mulhaire, Eddie Maloney, Eamonn Ryan, and Jimmy Commins. (Photo courtesy of family of Martin Mulhaire.)

Mulhaire's band was nimble and easily adaptable to all dance occasions, recalled Martin: "In them days, it was just drums. If there was a piano in the place, they would use piano. Fiddles and flutes [were] the dominant instruments. Later on, they got a saxophone player. . . . [My father] just went back and forth depending on what the call was for: you know, if they wanted a céilí, then the céilí band. If a modern band, he'd get the saxophone for the night" (interview, 1988). Depending on the nature of the engagement, Thomas Mulhaire's band was variously advertised as the Mulhaire Céilí Band, the Mulhaire Dance Band, or the Mulhaire Dance Orchestra with Thomas Mulhaire as the conductor. That said, even when his band was advertised as a modern dance band, Mulhaire always included traditional repertoire and dances, much to his audiences' delight, recalls Martin:

> It was their version of big band sounds . . . and people danced to that. Foxtrots, quicksteps, slow waltzes, slow foxtrots. And then they would dance to the Irish "Siege of Ennis" and so forth, and reel sets and barn dances.
>
> Both styles were popular. People didn't differentiate between music that much. They liked any kind of music. They would dance both interchangeably and there was no distinction made . . . they just liked both types of music and they were happy to hear both types of music." (Mulhaire, interview, 1988)

"You Wasn't in It If You Didn't Play Irish": The Brideside Serenaders

Like Thomas Mulhaire's, the Brideside Serenaders from Tallow, County Waterford, was a nimble dance band that easily pivoted to provide diverse dance music for their audiences. The Brideside Serenaders got its start in 1951 as a six-piece band under the leadership of saxophonist David Doyle. The band included Claudette Colbert McCarthy on piano, one of the rare women dance band musicians from these years, who was dubbed "Queen of the Ivories." In 1954, the band expanded to a seven piece with the inclusion of Paddy Geary first on upright bass and then drums. Paddy learned to play the bass from Claudette Colbert McCarthy, who also taught him how to read music. All the members of the band were part-time players—semi-professionals who typically had day jobs. Paddy Geary, for example, worked as a handyman and gardener in Tallow; Claudette Colbert McCarthy worked as an office clerk.

For thirty-four years, the Brideside Serenaders played in dance halls and marquees across the province of Munster, and most frequently in Tallow at the Regal Ballroom and at the larger Arch Ballroom. They performed four or more times a week, often as a relief band when a touring orchestra came through. This meant that they were often in the position of opening for

Figure 2.16 Brideside Serenaders, Arch Ballroom, Tallow, ca. 1955. (Photo courtesy of Paddy Geary.)

a better-known group, a status that resulted in plenty of work but that sometimes stung, recalls Paddy Geary:

> We never had to look for jobs, we took the jobs that came [and] we always had a job, we always came home [after] the job. But they had to have a relief band, we often played [relief]. Now, it wasn't looked on as very good, like you know, people thought you knew only shite, playing second fiddle. But you know, it gave us a lot of work. . . . People got to know us. (Paddy Geary, interview, 2018)

Central to the Brideside Serenaders' performance was their emphasis on variety with an eye toward marketability. Initially learning popular dance numbers by ear, by the late 1950s, the band increasingly turned to purchased Jimmy Lally arrangements to keep up with the newest songs and dance tunes. Geary recalls that the Brideside Serenaders also enjoyed playing jazz as it offered them an opportunity to stretch themselves with improvised solos and move away from the constraints of the written arrangement. During an evening's performance, the band always played familiar Irish songs and several céilí sets. According to Geary, this variety appealed as much to the musicians as it did to their audiences and was typical of Irish audiences generally at the time: "The variety was great! You know, it's monotonous sitting down playing, same old thing all the time! . . . You wasn't in it if you didn't [play Irish]. Like, the crowd were mixed. Half the people wouldn't go to you if you only played one type of music. That's Irish, I'd say!" (Paddy Geary, interview, 2018).

The Mick Delahunty Orchestra: "More Powerful Than the Atom Bomb!"

Like many dance bands and orchestras throughout Ireland, the Brideside Serenaders were inspired by the music and performance style of the Mick Delahunty Orchestra from nearby Clonmel, County Tipperary. Ranging between nine and fifteen musicians, the group was at least double the size of the Brideside Serenaders. Claudette Colbert McCarthy recalls the variety of musical textures and harmonies that the Mick Delahunty Orchestra produced in their music thanks to their size and versatility: "When you knew Mick Delahunty, you would often think 'Oh, wouldn't it be great to sound like that! It was unique!" (interview, 2019).

Well known for its members' musicianship and professionalism, the Mick Delahunty Orchestra was one of the most accomplished and best-known groups during Ireland's dance band era. Performing often seven nights a week, the orchestra enjoyed national and international renown, touring constantly on both sides of the border and occasionally abroad in Britain and the United States. The orchestra was well known for its exactingly reproduced arrangements of dance numbers by the Glenn Miller Orchestra, the renowned American big band that was enormously popular throughout Ireland at the time. That said, as an astute bandleader and businessman, Mick Delahunty (b. 1915) was well aware that his orchestra was playing not for American but for Irish audiences. Beginning in 1952, Delahunty locked into his widely sought-after style when his saxophonist, Brendan Ward of Foxford, County Mayo, turned his talents to writing arrangements of Glenn Miller tunes. In doing so, Ward singlehandedly created the Mick Delahunty trademark sound, one that was clearly indebted to Glenn Miller, but also appealed broadly to a specifically Irish aesthetic. Brendan Ward recalls his work during these years:

> Nobody [in Ireland] seemed to know how to write, to get that sound that [Glenn] Miller got . . . And the moment I heard it, I knew exactly how he was getting it. He was using a lead clarinet on top playing the melody . . . and a tenor saxophone one octave below, playing the same melody. In between there were three instruments playing very close harmony.
>
> It's very easy to understand—even a person who is not a musician can clearly hear the melody there. One problem, I think, that there was with the American music . . . was that you didn't hear a melody and the average person

Figure 2.17 Mick Delahunty Orchestra, ca. 1960. (Photo courtesy of Mick Delahunty Jr.)

on the street has to hear a melody, particularly an Irish person has to hear a melody." (Brendan Ward, interview, 1992)

Ward's arrangements proved to be on target, as noted by columnist Ann Daly in a 1959 issue of New York City's *Irish Echo*: "With a stroke of sheer genius, his orchestra opened up with a simple, old time waltz, beautifully played, with emphasis on the melody. The kind of familiar, well-loved lyrics [the audience] could sing as they danced" (Daly 1959).

Mick Delahunty routinely opened an evening of dancing with his signature tune—the Glenn Miller classic "American Patrol."[12] As heard on one of the rare existing recordings of Mick Delahunty's Orchestra, their rendition of "American Patrol" almost exactly replicates Glenn Miller Orchestra's 1942 recording, although the latter features a fuller sound given the sheer size of the ensemble. Mick Delahunty's version of the tune includes more melodic doubling, thereby emphasizing melody over harmonic accompaniment. Both Glenn Miller's and Mick Delahunty's recordings of "American Patrol" follow the same formulaic structure: the presentation of the main melodic themes (a modified AABA form), followed by a fanfare interlude and then a sixteen-bar drum solo. A "shout" chorus (call and response) follows and then

Figure 2.18 Mick Delahunty Orchestra: Mick Delahunty (*front center*); Brendan Ward (*front, second from right*), ca. 1952. (Photo courtesy of Fionnuala Regan.)

an eight-bar overlay of the Irish traditional tune "The Girl I Left Behind Me." First appearing as printed text in the 1791 Dublin song collection *The Charms of Melody,* "The Girl I Left Behind Me" has long been played in Ireland as a traditional two-part, thirty-two-measure polka. The tune migrated to the United States possibly as early as the American Revolution and was played as a march, one often associated with warfare. Sung by both sides during the American War of 1812, "The Girl I Left Behind Me" was heard in military contexts through at least World War I.[13] Glenn Miller's inclusion of this snippet of "The Girl I Left Behind Me" in "American Patrol" was a clear signifier of the times, given that he recorded this version of the piece just four months after the United States' declaration of war on Germany and Japan in 1941.

That "The Girl I Left Behind Me" appears in Mick Delahunty's version of "American Patrol" is unsurprising as his arrangements generally aimed to exactly replicate the original Glenn Miller sources. However, Mick Delahunty had other reasons for retaining the overlay of "The Girl I Left Behind Me." Not only did it emulate Miller's version and the American big band sound, but it also added a familiar layer of Irishness. Delahunty knew that his audiences enjoyed hearing a quotation from a well-known Irish dance tune, and particularly in the context of American big band music.

Perhaps just as important, so did he. Growing up in a household steeped in Irish traditional music and song, Delahunty learned the tin whistle and harmonica as a youngster, and by age ten, was a champion Irish step dancer. As a bandleader, he enjoyed finding ways of presenting elements of Irish music in the context of the American big band sound, according to his son, Mick Delahunty Jr., who played guitar in his father's orchestra for six years:

> My father wanted to incorporate the Irish "diddely diddely" music, as we call it, but played with the Glenn Miller [sound]. . . . People would come up to him in the ballrooms and say "Hey Mick, can you play this, can you play that?" That's the way it was in Ireland. He was able to do all the Irish music on the saxophone. And he was getting so many requests from so many people. And that's when he got in touch with Brendan [Ward], and he said, "Yeah, we'll have a go at it." (Interview, 2018)

To this end, Brendan Ward applied the same Glenn Miller orchestration techniques, this time to popular Irish songs. In doing so, he updated familiar Irish tunes into a contemporary big band sound, recalls Ward: "And I start to write for Mick, not Miller stuff now, but Irish music. . . . That's one thing that Mick became very famous for even after I left him. He was able to play Moore's Melodies, 'Love's Roses,' 'Believe Me If All Those Endearing Young Charms,' 'The Harp That Once Through Tara's Halls'" (interview, 1992).

Apart from Ward's innovative Irish big band arrangements, another way that Mick Delahunty was able to embed Irishness into an evening of dance music was through his carefully selected repertoire, some of which combined contemporary songs with Irish signifiers. One such piece was "Rooney," which, according to Mick Delahunty Jr., quickly became an integral part of his father's orchestral repertoire:

> Miller: Do you know the song, "Rooney?"
>
> MD Jr.: Yes I do. . . . It's an Irish tune, yes [he hums it]. Brendan [Ward] was able to do a Glenn Miller on that.
>
> Miller: It's a traditional Irish tune?
>
> MD Jr.: I think so, yeah.

In fact, "Rooney" was then a recently composed theme song from a 1958 British comedy film of the same name, itself based on Catherine Cookson's 1957 novel, *Rooney*. Produced in London and directed by George Pollock with a screenplay by Patrick Kirwan, the film chronicles the life of a Dublin rubbish collector and Gaelic football player, James Ignatius Rooney. The film got mixed reviews, but the song, composed by Philip Green with lyrics by Tommy Connor, enjoyed a measure of popularity, with a number of versions recorded by the early 1960s.

Mick Delahunty Jr.'s misidentification of the genesis of "Rooney" is entirely understandable, given that it certainly sounds like a traditional Irish instrumental tune. It starts with a low A part (eight bars repeated), followed by a higher contrasting B section, also eight bars repeated. The melody is much like a medium paced, Irish hornpipe, complete with the predictable internal melodic repetition that one hears in traditional tunes. Mick Delahunty's version begins with a short introduction and then plays through the entire tune twice before abruptly modulating up a sixth, a common technique in popular music that adds variation and excitement. For Mick Delahunty's audiences, "Rooney" was a perfect song: it sounded familiarly Irish while, at the same time, offered the cachet of the contemporary British film and music industries. Much like Ward's Irish big band arrangements, "Rooney" located Irishness in the context of popular culture and media from outside of Ireland while engaging the sensibilities of Irish audiences.

The Brideside Serenaders, Thomas Mulhaire's bands, and the Mick Delahunty Orchestra engaged different strategies to accomplish the same goal of accommodating their audiences' dual tastes in music. Mulhaire did this through his own nimble musicianship and ability to provide modern dance music and Irish music as demanded by each job. The Brideside Serenaders accomplished the same thing through sheer variety, presenting the old with the new, the American with the Irish. And the Mick Delahunty Orchestra couched elements of Irish music in both the choice of repertoire and through the skillful arrangements of Brendan Ward, to ultimately create a hybrid sound that resonated deeply with vast audiences. All three bands mastered the art of continually reading their audiences and developing performance skills that pivoted along with changing tastes. And they did this very well: they enjoyed varying degrees of popularity and success and all three survived in one form or another for upward of forty years.

The Last Dance: The End of the Sit-Down Dance Bands

By the 1960s, sit-down dance bands and orchestras went into a steady decline on both sides of the border. (Céilí bands and dances, on the other hand, flourished, particularly from the late 1970s on with the revival of interest in Irish traditional music and dance that swept the Irish diaspora and Ireland.) Residencies for sit-down dance bands at venues dried up, requiring more travel by the larger orchestras from performance to performance. For larger ensembles, the logistics of this type of continuous travel quickly became unwieldy and unprofitable. The Mick Delahunty Orchestra, arguably the longest-lasting ensemble from the dance band era, survived into the early 1990s thanks to a decades-long residency at the Greenwood Inn in Ardpatrick, County Limerick.

Delahunty's retirement performance was scheduled for February 29, 1992. Suffering from congestive heart failure, Delahunty was not well enough to perform that night with the orchestra, recalls family friend Denis O'Sullivan, who drove him to the Greenwood Inn that evening:

> [Mick] explained to [the audience] that unfortunately he wasn't well enough to play that night. And he thanked the members of his band and he thanked the former members of his band and he thanked the ballroom owners. . . .
>
> And, as he was leaving, "Look," he said, "we'll get together again, right?" They were his exact words: "We'll get together again," him and his dancers would get together. There was a huge cheer from several hundred people who were at the dance. And he walked off the bandstand, down onto the floor . . . went up there about ten yards and dropped. Gone like that. (Interview, 2018)

While Delahunty's death may have symbolically marked the definitive end of the sit-down dance orchestras, the end of the era happened some decades earlier. Beginning in the late 1950s, young people in Ireland were captivated by the sounds of American and British rock 'n' roll and popular music. Their tastes quickly moved beyond the big band music long associated with their parents and grandparents. While they flocked to the same parish halls, ballrooms, and marquees, they were excited not by foxtrots and quicksteps but by the newest popular music that was sweeping Ireland—the showbands.

Sit-down dance band musicians had two choices: they could adapt or they could retire. Some, like Brendan Ward, found showband music loud and unsophisticated in comparison to big band music that involved creative arrangements, musical literacy, and, to his ear, required a more refined and nuanced approach to performance:

> You could tell right away that [showband musicians] were fellows that certainly didn't sit down and study music. Their harmonies were not mine. Their choice of chords would not be mine. . . . It was extremely loud and to me, music is something that's very pleasant that you might even sometime have to strain your ears to listen, to hear what's coming. [With showbands], you covered your ears because it was so terribly loud. It kind of bothered me, in a way, because

Figure 2.19 Sonny Knowles (*rear, center*) and the Pacific Showband, ca. 1960, publicity postcard. (Collection of Jimmy Higgins.)

> I had spent so much of my lifetime taking music so seriously, and I find that it was just being torn asunder.
>
> [Showbands] would sometimes [put] on a bit of an act. . . . I had a baby grand piano on the stage there for my [orchestra] and they would stand on the seat to stand up on the keyboard to stand up on the top of the piano to perform on top of the piano and that to me was . . . absolute sacrilege. (Interview, 1992)[14]

The other choice was to adapt, learn the new style, and be hired into a showband lineup. Many sit-down dance band players did just that and, in the process, embraced a new music genre and playing technique. Sonny Knowles, for example, welcomed the opportunity to continue to make his living from music and joined the Pacific Showband:

> At first it took me quite a while to adjust [to the showband] because I thought it wasn't musical; we were musical snobs. . . . But the reading bands I love; I enjoyed it. When it ended, I had no regrets because if I hadn't have moved, my career, musically, would have been over. But as we went on, [the sit-down bands] just faded out: if you didn't get in [to the showbands], you got left on the outskirts. So we made sure to be in the race and that is how it changed. (Interview, 2009)

For more than two generations, dance bands and orchestras provided a soundtrack for Irish men and women to experience contemporary sounds and popular culture from outside of Ireland while also reinforcing Irish identity and belonging. During the same years, ceílí bands similarly offered dancing audiences a way to express Irishness, initially with an explicitly nationalist narrative supplied by the state, the Church, and cultural institutions. The net result was that dancers on both sides of the border and across four decades sought out and enjoyed either or both of these genres, facilitated by the legions of dance hall owners and some parish priests who accommodated the demand for dancing. Whether a foxtrot or a "Siege of Ennis," musicians, promoters, and audiences together created an ongoing dialogue about modernity, locality, and Irishness, all in the context of a rapidly changing world.

Notes

1. Irish Showbands.com, accessed February 28, 2019, https://www.irish-showbands.com/orchestras.htm.

2. In addition to jazz, these resources introduced Northern Irish listeners to a variety of American popular sounds, including R&B and, later, soul.

3. See, for example, *Brendan Balfe's Danceband Days*, a series of three RTÉ Radio One programs produced in 2006.

4. The exception to this were drummers, who, in theory, learned how to read staff notation for drums but who mostly played by ear, according to Brideside Serenaders drummer Paddy Geary: "I don't think I ever got used to [reading music], to tell you the truth. But I got used to the basics. . . . You get [through the first] ten or twelve [measures]you know, it's grand, you know what I mean. But when you get into the middle of it, a load of black dots! . . . Well, you always had to mind the stops" (interview, 2018).

5. Like Willie Bradley, many wind instrument players—particularly those from Northern Ireland—learned to play and read music by joining a flute band (aka fife and drum band). World-renowned flutist James Galway, for example, learned to read music from his uncle who was a member of his grandfather's Belfast-based band, the Apprentice Boys Flute Band (McCormack 2015).

6. Beginning in 1872, the Artane Boys Band was a renowned ensemble made up of boys who lived at the Artane Industrial School, Ireland's largest institution for orphaned, neglected, or impoverished boys or simply boys who were truants. While the Artane Boys Band developed a reputation for musical excellence and served as a training ground for many of Ireland's future orchestra and band musicians, the school itself was notorious for massive child abuse, neglect, and sexual assault and, by 1969, was closed.

7. The origins of céilí dancing resonate with Eric Hobsbawm and Terence Ranger's classic notion of the "invented tradition," that is, a practice "which seek[s] to inculcate certain values and norms of behavior by repetition . . . often not because old ways are no longer available or viable, but because they are deliberately not used or adapted" (Hobsbawm 1992, 1, 8). As such, invented traditions serve as "important symptoms and therefore indicators of problems. . . . They are evidence" (12). In the early years of the twentieth century, céilí dancing as a new genre was seen by the Gaelic League as a means to reinforce Irishness and Irish traditional culture in the face of what was perceived as the encroaching Anglicization of Ireland.

8. See Scahill (2018) for a history of pianos in céilí bands during the pre– and post–Gaelic Revival.

Ó hAllmhuráin (2005, 17) argues that the inclusion of the piano in céilí bands "butchered" the older, modal-based tunes "before disappearing forever into the black hole of fixed major and minor chords that were the stock-in-trade of convent-trained pianists." Despite the piano's role in céilí bands in general, some groups eschewed it and adhered to the older sound of a strictly melody-driven texture long associated with Irish traditional music. In 1952, Charlie Lennon joined the County Leitrim–based Sean McDermott Céilí Band at age fourteen. Featuring only fiddles, whistle, accordion, and drums, the band emphasized melody and rhythm with no harmonic accompaniment. Lennon recalls that this was common (interview, 2019).

9. "Public Dance Halls Act, 1935," Irish Statute Book, accessed February 4, 2019, http://www.irishstatutebook.ie/eli/1935/act/2/section/13/enacted/en/html. For a detailed analysis, see Austin 1993.

10. There is a range of scholarly perspective regarding Archbishop McQuaid's contributions as church leader, his impact on successive Irish governments, and his orthodox views and resultant strictures on Irish social life and behavior. Describing Catholic Ireland in the mid-twentieth century as "a grim, inward-looking and deeply repressive society," John Cooney (1999, 278–79) writes, "Presiding over and controlling that society was [Archbishop] McQuaid, now firmly established . . . as the arbiter of public morality in all spheres of human behaviours, particularly sexual misconduct."

Dermot Keogh (1998) argues for more nuanced and vigorous scholarship that pushes against this interpretation, given the complexities of McQuaid's leadership. The late Fr. Micheál Mac Gréil of Westport similarly notes that Archbishop McQuaid's legacy is complicated. As a theology student in the mid-1960s in Dublin, Mac Gréil recalls that like other leaders in the Church at the time, McQuaid operated "a very authoritarian system . . . [with] a lot of awful censorship." While he was, in Mac Gréil's view, "a prisoner of the protocol of the norm," he was, as well, "a very socially conscious man" (interview, 2008).

11. Thomas Mulhaire's diverse musical tastes and skills were passed down to his two sons, Martin—who, like his father, was also a well-known composer and button accordionist—and Brendan, a Galway-based, award-winning button accordionist. Like their father, both Martin and Brendan also went on to have illustrious careers as bandleaders and electric guitarists in the 1960s Irish showband world, in Ireland for Brendan (Raindrops Showband) and in New York City for Martin (Majestic Showband).

12. "American Patrol" was written in 1885 by Tin Pan Alley composer Frank Meacham. Glenn Miller's version includes the overlay of "The Girl I Left Behind Me."

13. Library of Congress, "Playlist for War and Conflict," Songs of America, http://www.loc.gov/static/collections/songs-of-america/articles-and-essays/historical-topics/war-and-conflict.html, accessed August 12, 2024.

14. Brendan Ward ultimately left City Center and opened Ward Travel, a very successful agency in New York City that catered specifically to Irish travel.

3

Origins

"The Band That Does the Show"

[The Clipper Carlton] became known as this strange band from the north who put on a show. They went, one night, to the Imperial Ballroom in Dundalk. And on the side of the wall, they saw for the first time "The Clipper Carlton Showband." And they said, "What the hell is a showband?"

(Fr. Brian D'Arcy, interview, 2007)

One day in 1950, pianist Hugh Toorish, the leader of a five-piece dance band, found himself in the uncomfortable position of having to fire the other members of his group. His reportedly unremarkable sit-down dance band performed regularly at the Palindrome, a dance hall in Strabane, County Tyrone. Like most dance band members at the time, the musicians wore dark suits, sat when they played, and read from music on the music stands that contained imported, written arrangements of dance standards. Apparently, his bandmates were thinking of replacing the sixty-year old Toorish with a younger pianist; what they failed to take into consideration was that he, as bandleader, held the contract for the jobs at the Palindrome. Turning the tables, Toorish sacked the musicians, leaving him in the unenviable position of having to quickly hire players to reassemble a band and cover the remaining jobs.

Hugh Toorish probably had no inkling of what he was getting into when he hired the four young replacements, none of whom had much musical training or were even remarkable instrumentalists at the time. One of these musicians was drummer Mick O'Hanlon, who recalls that first job: "I hadn't a clue. I hadn't even a good drum kit. . . . We went into the Palindrome on a Saturday night without a rehearsal. And to this day, I don't know how we got through two hours. I hardly knew Hugo and I don't know one of the tunes we played that night" (quoted in Maguire 2012, 64). In addition to

Toorish on piano, O'Hanlon on drums, and Art O'Hagan on bass, the group included Hugo (Hugh) Quinn on trumpet and Terry Logue on saxophone and clarinet. The Clippers expanded in 1953 to include Art O'Hagan's brother, Fergus (who was initially hired as a driver and eventually became a vocalist and MC), followed by trombonist/arranger Victor Fleming in 1954 and, two years later, in 1956, vocalist Dominic Shearer.[1] Playing largely Dixieland music and popular dance standards, the reconstructed band—then known as the Hugh Toorish Carlton Band—quickly developed a following and was in high demand for local and regional dances. At one of these shows, a priest in Fintona, County Tyrone, sponsored a competition—more or less as a gimmick—to rename the group. In a 1960 article in the *Irish Independent* that retrospectively celebrates a decade of the band's existence, trumpeter Hugo Quinn explains that three potential names were put forward:

> It was a tough year [for local farmers], 1950. Somebody suggested the "Bad Harvest Band." A critic put in "The Woodbine Orchestra" [after a low-quality cigarette called Woodbine], not a player in the lot. . . . Frankly, we were an amateurish bunch.
>
> Somebody suggested "Clipper Carlton"—a barman from Fintona, it was—and somebody else, taking words right out of the mouth of the late W.C. Fields, said, "What a euphonious appellation," and that was that. What's it mean? We don't know. It just sounded neat. (As quoted in *Irish Independent*, September 6, 1960, 6)

The barman's winning suggestion won him a prize of two shillings, six pence. The name itself captured the excitement of the era of the new sea planes—called Clippers—which were flying in and out of Lough Erne in Enniskillen. Fr. Brian D'Arcy, also of Enniskillen, is known as "the Showband Priest" and followed the Clipper Carlton since he was a teenager in the late 1950s. He recalls that the name "had this wonderful magic of being a new world and a new era and a different place," not to mention the potential for impressive visual marketing: "And the guys [in the band] said, 'You know—'CC,' Clipper Carlton, there's a lot in it!' Hugh Quinn was a sign writer and he saw this good idea—two Cs, Clipper Carlton" (Fr. D'Arcy, interview, 2007). Nicknamed "the Clippers," the band would go on to establish the model for the showband phenomenon, a quintessentially Irish genre that, from the start, came to redefine Irish popular music and entertainment. The Clipper Carlton not only were innovators in their own right but also served as a bridge between the sit-down dance bands and the emerging showband era.

While the Clippers might not have initially been the most seasoned musicians, the individual band members brought a variety of dramatic and stage experience to their early shows, performance skills learned from local

Figure 3.1 The Clipper Carlton, ca. 1969. *From left*: Terry Duffy, Neil McMahon, Hugo Quinn, Art O'Hagan, Mick O'Hanlon, Dom Shearer, and Jim Gunner. (Photo courtesy of www.irishshowbands.net.)

dramatic productions, visiting drama troupes, and the ubiquitous fit-up traveling shows. The members of the Clipper Carlton were also keen fans of and inspired by the American and British popular music of the time as well as African American doo-wop and jazz. A large part of their success was that they were able to frame these new imported sounds and dynamic performances styles alongside elements of Irish stage performance. It was here, sandwiched between the old and the new, the familiar and the emergent, that nuanced and changing meanings of popular Irish music and modern Irish identity arose.

Local Roots of Showband Stage Performance

The years surrounding World War II saw a spike of interest in dramatic productions primarily in rural villages and towns throughout Ireland and Northern Ireland. These events were often organized by parish priests, many of whom believed that local drama was morally healthier than the popular imported Hollywood films regularly screened in "picture houses" (Terence Brown, as cited in Ó hAllmhuráin 2016, 152). At the same time, a lively amateur theater movement was sweeping rural and urban areas on both sides of the border as early as the mid-1940s. Local drama festivals regularly brought theater to rural locations, notably the An Tóstal festival from 1953 to 1958;

the All-Ireland Drama Festival in 1953; and, in 1957, the Dublin Drama Festival. Irish theater historian Mary Trotter writes that while audiences for these types of productions tended to be rowdy, "they were also intelligent, informed theatregoers whose impact on Irish theatre mid-century was profound" (Trotter 2008, 130–131).

Unlike most dance bands at the time, the Clippers drew on comedic and dramatic material that they had seen and appreciated when drama troupes came through Strabane. As was typical of their generation, the members of the Clippers also had frequently participated in local, amateur dramatic productions. Art and Fergie O'Hagan, for example, both had experience singing and performing in locally produced, Christmastime pantomimes. Dating back to at least the sixteenth century, pantomimes, or "pantos," were a popular form of theater developed, in part, from the commedia dell'arte tradition and, somewhat later, from the British music hall tradition. Pantos rely on variety and dramatic narrative and variously include song, dance, slapstick comedy, topical references, mild sexual innuendo, and audience participation. In pantomimes, it is assumed that the audience is somewhat if not wholly familiar with the depicted original story. Plot lines and characters are frequently adapted for comic or satirical effect while situations not specific to the story are often integrated into the storyline. Pantomimes were also geared to the specific strengths of the performers, recalls Sonny Knowles, vocalist/clarinetist with the Pacific Showband. He remembers adapting a popular Christmastime pantomime into more of a musical format in the 1960s in partnership with showband vocalist Eileen Reid:

> [Eileen] did a pantomime on the road. . . . It is a comedy version of a story. And there was a villain in this, and dancers, fancy costumes. And the villain would always be the baron; he was the bad piece of the village. But it was all a musical thing. She took one of those on the road and we had a good stint with it around the Christmas period because the kids would be brought to it. (Interview, 2009)

Derry-born guitarist/vocalist Dáithí Sproule's extended family was also involved with Christmastime pantomimes. He recalls that pantomimes typically followed specific sets of performance and narrative conventions, including gender role reversal. Many pantomime narratives, for example, feature a young male lead performed by a young woman; likewise, the comic dame is frequently played by a man, oftentimes a well-known comedian (Sproule, interview, 2009).

The members of the Clipper Carlton seized on this theme of gender fluidity, a concept that was both familiar to audiences and translated easily to the showband stage. One example was of the Clipper Carlton's impersonation of Cork-born folk singer/banjo player, Margaret Barry, and her musical partner, fiddler Michael Gorman, both of whom were quite well known and recognizable to Irish audiences at the time (Irwin 2017). Because Margaret Barry self-identified as a member of the traveling community in Ireland, the skit became known as "The Gypsy and Wee Small Man with a Fiddle."[2] Embracing gender fluidity and the longtime trope of men dressing as women (and vice versa), the result was as entertaining to their audiences as it apparently was to the Clipper Carlton themselves, recalls Art O'Hagan:

> We were playing at The George Hotel in the center of Limerick. . . . Fergus and Mickey O'Hanlon, they were doing the show, "[The] Gypsy and Wee Small Man with a Fiddle." . . . And Fergus and Mickey took him off [impersonated them]. Fergus put on a wig and a big woman's dress, like. Mickey was playing the fiddle—scrape it out, you know. That was all right. And Fergus sang. That was on stage and great craic and everybody laughed.
>
> For a dare . . . someone said, "You wouldn't do that in Limerick!" And he bet him £20! Next thing, Fergus put on the dress and [they went] out into the street on a Saturday. And Mickey's standing and people were throwing money! (Laughing.) They were collecting money and Fergus and Mickey, they just loved the part, you know! (Interview, 2007)

"Everything Was Fresh Again": Fit-Ups

Irish audiences were also familiar with dramatic performances that relied on the variety format, thanks to the ubiquitous presence of "fit-up" troupes. Traveling shows had been a fixture throughout the Irish countryside from at least the late 1700s. Fit-ups, as they came to be known, emerged in the early 1920s, constantly traveling across Ireland and Northern Ireland and drawing large audiences, particularly in towns that were too small to have their own theatrical companies. The term "fit-up" is British slang that refers to providing needed equipment or furniture into a room or building. Michael McEvoy from Drumcondra, Dublin, joined a fit-up at age sixteen as a tenor singer in 1950. He remembers that Irish fit-ups got their name "because they used to uproot and pack their stuff away and go to another town. And then they fit up another stage, and . . . they'd start again in every place they were in" (interview, 2018).[3] Carrying literally every item they needed for their performances, fit-up troupes were mobile and self-sufficient, traveling in caravans with scenery, tents, marquees, upright pianos, and the like. Upon arriving in town, they set up their marquees and tents or booked the local parish hall and advertised their performances.

Figure 3.2 Michael McAvoy with the Billy Carter Band, National Ballroom, Dublin, 1958. (Photo courtesy of Michael McAvoy.)

McEvoy performed with the Vic Loving Show, a well-known troupe whose members, like many fit-ups at the time, consisted primarily of a large extended family:

> Vic Loving . . . she was a great singer, the old time music hall stuff. Her son was Chic Kay, that was his stage name. . . . And his wife, Nancy, and eventually their family. He did everything. He was the manager of the show, he [was] a very good guitar player, he wrote songs, and he was a comedian on stage. There was a whole group of five or six caravans. And everyone in the show did some bit of work. It was a family thing: there were an old couple [Dolly and Jimmy Stone] and the woman was well in her sixties and she played piano and she did all the accompaniments. She was a marvelous musician! They were nice people, they were lovely! (McEvoy, interview, 2018)

Sandy Kelly, vocalist with Fairways Showband, started out as a child in her family's well-known fit-up, the Duskey Road Show:

> I was born on the twenty-seventh of February 1954, in Sligo. And it was almost coincidental that I was born there. Because my father and his family were in a fit-up road show. You know, it was pre-television. So they traveled from town to town, and entertained people with the Dusky Road Show.

Figure 3.3 Vic Loving, ca. 1954. (Photo courtesy of Michael McAvoy.)

> And my father . . . was an actor and a comedian, and in the show, his brothers and sisters, everybody, did everything. His brother was a magician, and my grandmother was a phenomenal singer and yodeler, and my grandfather was "Dusky Dan." He blacked his face and did shuffle and sand shuffle and played the ukulele. (Interview, 2008)

Fit-ups such as the Dusky Road Show played to the strengths of individual troupe members, each of whom developed expertise in a specific style or genre, including drama, comedy, magic, and music and dance performances. County Cork–born piano accordionist Paddy Noonan performed in a similar fit-up before immigrating to the United States in the 1940s. He likens the approach of fit-ups to the variety format of American vaudeville: "They usually

Figure 3.4 Chic and Nancy Kay, the Vic Loving Show, ca. 1955. (Photo courtesy of Michael McAvoy.)

Figure 3.5 Dolly and Jimmy Stone of the Vic Loving Show, ca. 1955. (Photo courtesy of Michael McAvoy.)

had a pianist that accompanied the singers. I played accordion. I'd do a little spot. In my case, it was Irish music. I saw accordion players doing 'The Flight of the Bumblebee.' In many cases, it was like watching an early Ted Mack Show. You had a little raffle. It was very, very parochial" (Noonan, interview, 1992).

Fit-ups drew on entertainment strategies common to pantomimes, such as gender fluidity and role reversal. Michael McEvoy recalls, for example, that for the English music hall songs, Vic Loving sometimes dressed as a man in top hat and tails (interview, 2018). Crucially, however, fit-ups depended on the versatility of each performer to continually engage audiences in a variety show format; part of their success was this ability to offer something for every audience member. If spectators weren't interested in one part of the show, all they had to do was wait a few minutes for the next act. In this way, every member of the audience was assured of being entertained, and entertainers were assured of an audience. As such, performers in traveling fit-ups were, by definition, improvisers because, as Frank Bruce and Artie Foley (2000, 6) note, "they had to follow the opportunities and adapt to constant change and innovation" with "much of the excitement of the whole experience [being] the uncertainty. As one showman put it 'Everything was fresh again, fresh again.'"

Until it wasn't. Fit-up performances were largely eclipsed in late 1961 when television arrived in Ireland. At the same time, performance expectations and styles were also changing. Despite the variety format having been so strong for so many years, it too inevitably ran its course and became a practice to eventually reject. Among other factors was the enormous success of the Clancy Brothers and Tommy Makem, who achieved international acclaim starting in the late 1950s and into the early 1960s for their sing-along renditions of rousing Irish ballads and folk songs. Having immigrated to New York City, the three Clancy brothers and Tommy Makem ironically were looking to establish themselves as actors but fell into a band formation almost by accident. In 1963, they returned to Ireland for the first time to high acclaim and there gained traction in part by their move away from what had become the predictable and all too familiar variety format, according to Tommy Makem: "Any concert there ever was [in Ireland] would have eight or ten acts on it. You know, there'd be a tenor [singer], and they had dancers and there'd be a fiddle player and there'd be various other things on it. When we went back [to Ireland] in '63, there were the four of us and we did the entire two hours. It had been unheard of" (interview, 1992).

Makem could easily have been referring to the early showbands and in particular, the Clipper Carlton. Borrowing from the familiar and time-tested local performance practices of pantomimes and fit-up troupes, the Clippers similarly built variety into an evening's performance through the iconic "show" that featured dramatic skits, comedy routines, and impersonations. They also emphasized variety in their presentation of diverse music and song styles as well as light stage choreographies. And like the fit-up performers who paved the way, early showbands constantly adapted to and accommodated the changing tastes of their audiences, thereby keeping their show material novel and fresh.

Showbands Take the Stage: Standing Up and Moving On

While new music styles are often the result of incremental aesthetic change over time, just as often they are the product—either intentional or accidental—of the creativity of a single individual or group driven by artistic challenges, in response to audience demand, motivated by the pleasure of performance, and, more often than not, fueled by commercial potential. Such was the genesis of showband music. Young Irish audiences were ready for a new sound beyond the sit-down dance bands and orchestras, and while the Clipper Carlton did not necessarily set out to create a new genre, theirs was a very well timed and successful combination of innovation and stage experience. Hugh Toorish, a seasoned pianist and leader, was the musical glue that at least initially held together the more inexperienced band members, who themselves came to the group with stage skills learned from community dramatic productions. Thus equipped to take to the stage, but largely unconstrained by years of assumptions as to how musical performance should work, the members of the Clipper Carlton freely experimented with what they had, including an abundance of youthful energy and good humor.

Unlike the sit-down dance orchestras whose musicians relied on written parts, the new members of the Clipper Carlton did not know how to read musical notation and therefore had no need for sheet music. Joked Clipper Carlton vocalist Fergus O'Hagan, "We may not have been great [music] readers in those days, but we had good ears: two apiece. We studied the records. We studied the records as if our income depended on the outcome" (*Irish Independent*, June 9, 1960, 6). And because the Clippers used no sheet music, they also had no need for music stands, recalls bassist Art O'Hagan: "This is what actually put us to the fore because we learned everything as we went along.... We just knew what to play like, by ear. And we had *our* 'music stand': 'Right, what are we playing next?' *That* was our music stand!': 'What are we playing next?'" (interview, 2007)

Thus liberated, the members of the band jettisoned their chairs and stood when they played: "So that meant that you were looking at the crowd . . . instead of looking at the music, not bothering. We were practically waving!

Do things to the crowd that no one else could do because they were reading away!" (O'Hagan, interview, 2007).

The Clipper Carlton effectively redirected the attention of their audiences from the dance floor to the musicians on stage, possibly the most revolutionary shift in Irish popular entertainment. Standing, rather than sitting, changes the dynamics of performance as it conveys a stronger sense of ownership of the music and the stage to musicians and audiences both. And by standing, the Clippers were free to add a kinesthetic dimension to their performance. Their delight was not lost on audiences, as one anonymous *Irish Independent* reviewer noted: they "moved around the bandstand, snapped their fingers, clapped their hands. They had fun" (*Irish Independent*, September 6, 1960, 6). These light choreographies would come to redefine the role of the popular musician on both sides of the border. No longer were they laborers who only produced dance music; indeed, by virtue of looking out to their audience and making eye contact, the musicians became "entertainers." Mirroring the changing nature of pop music production in both the United States and Britain, this twist on performance would reconfigure what it meant to be an Irish working musician.

International Influences: African American Music and Stage Performance

Part of the inspiration for the members of the Clipper Carlton to move on stage came from the performances of well-known African American stage artists who they saw in imported films and newsreels from the United States. Fueling the Clippers' imaginations, these presentations offered a rich source from which to mine new performance ideas, recalls Mick O'Hanlon:

> We seen some old movie[s]. I don't know if it was the Mills Brothers or The Inkspots, some of those coloured guys and they . . . were all standing up and moving around . . . it was very effective. And I remember saying to the boys "Jayse, we better get rid of them bloody [music stands] altogether!" . . . And the attitude [among other bands] was, about the standing up, "Jesus Christ, how are you going to stand up all night, sure you'd be wrecked!" (Quoted in Maguire 2012, 71)

The Mills Brothers and the Inkspots, among other popular African American vocal groups of the 1930s, would come to define two of the precursors to rock 'n' roll: doo-wop and early rhythm and blues. Gaining widespread popularity among American audiences, both the Inkspots and the Mills Brothers were widely recorded and featured on American radio broadcasts. In Ireland

and Northern Ireland, they could be heard on the BBC starting in the mid-1930s and, by the 1940s, via the American Armed Forces Network.

The Inkspots and the Mills Brothers were well known for the dramatic elements they wove into their renditions of popular songs. They also added choreographies that had them stepping and clapping together in time to add percussive and dramatic effect. Rather than having one lead vocalist, both groups swapped the vocals among the different band members, a strategy that added varying textures to the music, not to mention sheer interest and entertainment value.

Musically, the Mills Brothers created their early signature sound through close vocal harmonies and scat singing. They are perhaps best known for their excellent vocal imitations of musical instruments commonly found in the dance orchestras of the era—first and second trumpet parts, tuba, trombone, and others. The Inkspots were similarly known for their scat singing and instrumental imitations as well as entertaining their audiences with lightly choreographed dance steps and stage movements. Performing on three tenor guitars and a cello played as an upright bass, the Inkspots were innovative with their integration of "talking choruses" into their arrangements—that is, speaking over the music and between sung verses to underscore the drama of the lyrics. The Inkspots added light dramatizations to their song lyrics, swapping verses with each other in a sort of highly staged sung conversation. Instantly appealing to large audiences throughout the United States, both the Inkspots and the Mills Brothers projected a creative and playful edge that inspired countless performers, including a handful of young dance musicians in Strabane in the early 1950s.

Mohair Suits and Miniskirts

The members of the Clipper Carlton were also hugely impressed by the visual impact of the Inkspots, Mills Brothers, and other African American doo-wop and jazz artists. Most immediately, the Clippers were captivated by the sharp and occasionally colorful matching suits worn by the members of these bands. They quickly traded in their conventional white shirts and dark suits and, in doing so, unwittingly established a completely new standard for showband attire:

> We seen all these Black boys colourfully dressed, even the Count Basie Band, they were all dressed in really loud suits. We went up to a shop in Strabane to get a powder blue suit and . . . the [clerk] said, "The only thing I could suggest is that you could get women's material. There would be plenty of bright colours in that," and I think that's what we did. We got light blue suits made and the first time we wore them, the rest of the bands that were about, they were laughing

> their heads off, a bright blue suit in Ireland! . . . But it caught on, it just caught on like that there. (O'Hanlon, quoted in Maguire 2012, 71)

Henry McCullough recalls being deeply impressed with the Clipper Carlton's suits when he first saw them perform in 1955. Five years later, McCullough joined the Skyrocket Showband from Enniskillen, County Fermanagh, who also were so inspired by the Clipper Carlton's stage dress that they went through several suit changes in an evening's performance. McCullough recalls that they began by wearing dress jackets for the first two hours, then changed into royal blue jackets midway through the evening, and, finally, into McCullough's absolute favorite: "The tartan jacket! When I got my tartan jacket on, I must tell you, I was really flying then, you know. All tartan with black shawl collar and stuff, you know. I used to love clothes and stuff and get suits made. So, to go onstage with a tartan jacket in the middle of, anywhere, was such a thrill like!" (interview, 2007).

Derry bandleader, Johnny Quigley, was similarly inspired by the stage attire of American popular musicians and instituted suit jacket changes for his band several times over the course of an evening performance. Quigley got the idea from his brother, Mickey, who, in the 1940s, was playing with the big band, the Day Brothers, in the United States: "They were down doing six months in Florida in a club. And they used to change their coats [suit jackets] every [set]: on three quarters of an hour and off for fifteen, you know, for three or four hours. And [Mickey] came home and we adapted that, the change in coats. We had bright, very bright yellow and . . . at the start, we wore bows and stuff" (Quigley, interview, 2018).

Matching, colorful suits—mohair was particularly favored for its light weight and shine—quickly became a trend among showband musicians and one that would come to visually define the showband era. As the showband market grew increasingly lucrative, professional, semiprofessional, and even amateur showbands invested in matching suits, often made to specification by tailors. Band members aimed to look polished and sophisticated. Brendan O'Brien, lead singer in the Cork-based showband the Dixies, recalled that their suits matched the energy of the showband: "We were up there with guitars and mohair suits playing rock 'n' roll and no music stands. Nice haircuts, clean-cut image. White jerked collar and tie, Ray Vaughn and, oh, boy! We all dressed! We'd be getting our tailor[ed] suits in Dublin; they were really expensive. . . . [Drummer] Joe [McCarthy] and [I] would always get two if not three of the jackets because we'd be sweating so much" (interview, 2006).

These stage outfits bore the mark of contemporary fashion and underscored the difference between the showbands and the increasingly outdated sit-down orchestras, recalls Sonny Knowles. "It was not until the showbands

Figure 3.6 The Johnny Quigley All Stars, ca. 1960. (Photo courtesy of Johnny Quigley.)

Figure 3.7 The Dixies, ca. 1965, publicity photo. *Left to right*: Theo Cahill, Steve Lynch, Joe McCarthy, Brendan O'Brien, Chris O'Mahoney, Sean Lucey, and Finbar O'Leary. (Photo courtesy of www.irishshowbands.net.)

started that people began to see the likes of us standing up with flashy jackets and flashy black pants, high heels—Cuban-heeled shoes and boots. We went in for style as well!" (Knowles, interview, 2009). For many showband musicians, their stage dress was a source of pride that centrally denoted an intentional professionalism, writes Finbar O'Keefe of the Saints Showband. "The showband was an academy all of its own. You turned out smartly, cleanly, punctually, and uniformly. On stage you had to project, to sell yourself—and in so doing sell the band. That sort of grounding is what honed and groomed The Saints into the outfit we were and earned us the right to stand with the best at that time" (O'Keefe 2002, 8–9).

Like their male colleagues, the handful of women showband performers also lavished attention on their stage attire, often changing their outfits several times during an evening's performance. But unlike the men, who wore matching suits, women artists stood out. Not only were they typically the sole woman in any given showband—if there were any women at all—but their very presence often signaled contemporary allure: chic hair styles, fashionable makeup, and glamorous stage outfits. One of the earliest women showband singers was Eileen Kelly, who joined the Nevada Showband in 1960. She was inspired by fashions she saw in magazines, particularly those worn by British and American celebrities: miniskirts, hot pants, long velvet dresses, and somewhat later, catsuits popularized by Elvis Presley (E. Kelly, interview, 2008). Kelly recalls her initial surprise when she realized how closely she and her fashion choices were followed, particularly by her women fans: "There were only a couple of girls in the business at the time. I didn't realize until years later and even now, people used to regard me as a sort of a fashion icon" (interview, 2008).

Many women showband artists report having been coached by the male bandleader about how to dress, but most note that after a short period of time, they were free to decide what to wear and how to appear. Vocalist Muriel Day of the Belfast-based Dave Glover Showband recalls having autonomy over her choice of clothes as well as the good fortune to be able to afford an excellent seamstress who made her individual dresses. Often changing her stage attire four times in the course of an evening, Muriel Day recalls that these outfits became part of the draw of the band, with her young women fans "standing in droves" just to see what she was wearing (interview, 2009).

So important was their stage appearance that, perhaps unsurprisingly, women showband artists are sometimes remembered less for their musical and performance skills and more for their appearance. And for some male fans, the often revealing and sexualized nature of the women performers' outfits, for better or worse, would become *the* memory. Eileen Kelly discovered this many years later in the early 2000s, when she encountered a former Nevada Showband fan: "He said, 'You used to wear these long hat-suits with the feathers. You wore these white boots with the miniskirts, you wore these hot pants and you wore the [jumpsuit].' . . . Yeah, I couldn't really remember half the outfits that he was taking about!" (interview, 2008).

Jukebox Saturday Night: Putting the "Show" in Showband

Apart from their new, eye-catching stage outfits, the members of the Clipper Carlton picked up on the importance of humor and improvisation in an evening's performance, recalls Art O'Hagan: "We were getting the crowds! And we were playing away and people were dancing around . . . [but] they weren't paying any attention to us. So we turned our backs away from the crowd. Turn around and forget about them, right, and play and let them dance away. And this would go on for two or three dances before they caught on . . . and they were all looking up on what freaks this band was!" (interview, 2007).

Building on this success, the Clippers next turned their attention to American and British popular musicians, bands, and entertainers for novel performance ideas. In particular, the Clippers were inspired by the Temperance Seven, a popular British traditional ("trad") jazz group whose members were known for their high level of musicianship as well as their quirky senses of humor. Early on, the Clipper Carlton developed a skit that essentially impersonated the members of the Temperance Seven, which they performed about halfway through the evening during the interval between dance sets. Their parody of the Temperance Seven was an immediate hit. Realizing the potential, the Clippers created parody skits of such well-known comedians as Laurel and Hardy and the Marx Brothers as well as singers Frankie Laine, Johnny Ray, Slim Whitman, and, somewhat later, Elvis Presley. The Clippers' ability to impersonate these international singing stars proved to be a huge draw: a 1960 *Irish Independent* article celebrated their success, noting their strength as "singers with real voices and built-in personalities. Bing Crosby, Frank Sinatra, people like that. Singers you *could* impersonate so that the listeners would know it" (*Irish Independent*, September 6, 1960, 6).

These skits became so popular that the Clipper Carlton eventually combined them into a fifteen- to twenty-minute segment that took place halfway through an evening performance. Called "Jukebox Saturday Night," the interval came to be known as "the show." Recalls Paddy Cole, "When you came back out after the interval, people knew that was the show, and they all moved up to the front and watched!" (interview, 2007). Clipper Carlton drummer Mickey O'Hanlon remembers: "We called it a wee show and it gave the people a wee rest that had been dancing all night and it gave them something to *look* at. . . . And they were looking forward to it. When I look back on it, it was a good night's entertainment for the people" (quoted in Maguire 2012, 65).

Apart from its entertainment value, there was also, at least initially, a pragmatic reason for including a show in their earliest performances, according to Fr. Brian D'Arcy. "They were young guys and they weren't good enough musicians to play all night, and they would readily admit that. . . . Because many bands had to play for five hours a night at that time. And to fill the time, they decided, 'Well, why don't we put on a little variety concert in the middle of our hall?' And so that's what they did" (D'Arcy, interview, 2007). A practical and innovative solution to their relative inexperience, the Clippers' show drew on the band members' accrued amateur dramatic experiences from local pantomimes and reflected the same stage strategies gleaned from the traveling fit-ups and other local theatrical productions. Ultimately, the show would come to form the basis of the name of a popular new music style that was about to sweep Ireland, recalls Mick O'Hanlon: "It started off as The Clipper Carlton—'Don't forget to see their show!' 'The band that does the *show!*' That's the way it started off and went from that to 'showband.' Then *every* band was called a showband but they weren't doing a show, they were just playing at a dance but they were known as showbands" (O'Hanlon, quoted in Maguire 2012, 65).

The Jolson Story: Cultural Ventriloquism

By far, the Clipper Carlton's best-remembered show was their staged reenactments of songs and impersonations of actors from the film *The Jolson Story*. Produced in 1946 at the height of Hollywood's wartime boom and starring Larry Parks in the title role, *The Jolson Story* garnered a majority of nominations at the 1946 Academy Awards and won one (Best Score and Sound). Until the 1960s, the film was one of Hollywood's most profitable releases.

By the early 1950s, Irish and Northern Irish audiences were well familiar with *The Jolson Story* (directed by Alfred E. Green) and its 1949 sequel, *Jolson Sings Again* (directed by Henry Levin). The original is a musical biopic about the renowned 1920s singer and actor, Asa Yoelson. The son of an orthodox Jewish cantor, Yoelson, against his parents' wishes, had ambitions to move beyond the confines of his traditional community and find success as an entertainer in Hollywood and the show business industry. Changing his name to Al Jolson, he did just that, eventually becoming a popular singer and actor known for his blackface performances. Jolson is best known for his role of Jakie, a would-be cantor turned jazz singer, in the first talking motion picture, *The Jazz Singer* (1927).

The Jolson Story is replete with memorable songs such as "Sewanee," "The Anniversary Song," and "By the Light of the Silvery Moon." Thanks, in part, to the strength of these long-enduring songs, *The Jolson Story* and its sequel were immediate hits with Irish and Northern Irish audiences, garnering near constant praise in newspaper reviews and advertisements: "A film you will long remember after all other films are forgotten. Voted the greatest film ever made"; "a warm, lively film, with [Jolson's] home and early vaudeville days providing a richly human background for the entertainer and the songs he made famous"; and this somewhat more nuanced assessment from one critic: "I liked this picture not because I admire Mr. Jolson's voice—which I don't—but because, in this particular instance, I admired Mr. Parks' superb handling of an exceedingly difficult characterization and Director [Henry] Levin's very skillful grasp of his subject."[4] What this anonymous film reviewer was referring to was the ability with which the actor, Larry Parks, portrayed Al Jolson, who, himself, impersonated an African American performer in *The Jazz Singer* by singing renditions of crooning ballads and songs in blackface.

The popularity of the films *The Jolson Story* and *Jolson Sings Again,* in combination with the Clipper Carlton's clever impersonation of its actors, made this their most requested show. Capitalizing on the theatricality of the film, the members of the Clippers added their own sonic and physical layers of performance. Impersonating Larry Parks, Mickey O'Hanlon lip-synched in blackface at the front of the stage. Behind O'Hanlon hung a sheer curtain. Behind that was Art O'Hagan, who sang the songs from the film using a microphone to project his voice. O'Hagan recalled,

> It was great *craic*! Mickey, the drummer, he done the actions [acting] at the front [of the stage]. And I was behind the curtain at the back, singing, you know? . . . The mics weren't good enough in those days to pick up the voice, you know. So you couldn't do the actions and sing at the same time, because you needed to have the microphone up close [to your mouth] to get the same Jolson [sound]. And I used to be at the back like, singing [he sings]: "Rock a bye, your baby, with a Dixie melody!" And Mickey here is doing all the actions.
>
> And it worked great. They went mad for it! Because Jolson's story was very popular that time. . . . That just went on for years; that was one of the successes from the start, you know? (Interview, 2007)

Rooted in American minstrelsy, blackface performance, argues Michael Rogin (1994, 11), "creates visual doubleness" inasmuch as it locates the racial "other" through the white actor. The Clipper Carlton's use of one band member to mime the gestures ("do the actions") while the other supplied the vocals not only paralleled the doubling effect of blackface performance but further complicated it by adding a second spatial layer through literally separating the voice from the actor.[5] Crucially, while the Clipper Carlton's presentation of Mickey O'Hanlon as Larry Parks in blackface visually depicted the racial "other," their Irish audiences heard the songs performed with a familiar Strabane accent—one that was an ocean apart from what audiences heard in the original Hollywood film. The Clippers' scenes thus embraced yet another type of doubling by juxtaposing the visual impersonation of the "other" (American blackface performance) with the familiar vocal cadences that reflected self, local community, and, in this case, Northern Ireland.[6]

The Clipper Carlton's iconic show also neatly underscores the argument of blackface performance as "a perfect metaphor for one's cultural ventriloquial self-expression through the art forms of someone else's" (Lott 1995, 92). The central themes of *The Jolson Story* easily translated to 1950s Irish audiences. With the realities of endemic unemployment, limited opportunities, and ensuing emigration, *The Jolson Story* offered audiences hopeful themes of personal transformation and the possibility of individual accomplishment despite everyday limitations. While the success of the Clipper Carlton's version of *The Jolson Story* certainly was in no small part a result of its enormous entertainment value, it also served, for audiences on both sides of the border, as a sort of cultural vent, one that reflected a fascination with modernity and popular culture from abroad as much as the familiarity of home and locality.

Early Showbands: The Melody Aces, Johnny Quigley and His Casino Aces, and the Maurice Lynch Band

While the Clipper Carlton is generally credited as the first showband with its revolutionary approach to Irish popular music, other bands were simultaneously experimenting with new ways of entertaining. Most of these early groups saw the benefit of touring, and taking their cue from the traveling fit-ups, they got on the road to tour regionally and nationally. In doing so, these early showbands began to carve out what would become a touring circuit.

Many of the earliest showbands, such as the renowned dance quartet, the Melody Aces from Omagh, County Tyrone, came from the border region between Northern Ireland and Ireland. In 1950, the Melody Aces were hired to perform at the popular Star Ballroom in Omagh. At the time, bandleaders and promoters were recognizing the financial potential of dances and, increasingly, sought out larger venues, such as the Star Ballroom, to accommodate larger audiences and maximize profits. These halls presented a very real acoustic challenge to bands, given that sound equipment at the time was largely inadequate to project across large spaces. The solution was to enlarge the band with more and louder instruments, particularly wind players, in order to be better heard by dancers across the sheer expanse of the dance floor. The Melody Aces added two additional musicians to become a six-piece band (piano/piano accordion, bass, drums, tenor sax, alto sax/clarinet, and trumpet). A few years later, the band recognized the need to further innovate. Recalls Melody Aces trumpeter, Gene Turbett, "It was a new era coming in, you know. Prior to that, we were sitting down. We decided to stand up all the time, playing. It was at the same time as the Clipper Carltons. . . . They did it, and we did it, we did it and they did it, either way you could talk" (interview, 2007).

Other bands followed suit. A *Connaught Tribune* (October 29, 1955, 12) advertisement placed by the New Savoy Ballroom in Castlerea promoted a performance of the Derry-based band, Johnny Quigley and His Casino Aces, noting that this band offered "Music in Clipper Carltons Manner." Johnny Quigley's band, in turn, influenced other musicians and bandleaders, such as clarinetist/saxophonist Paddy Cole, who, at the time, played in the County Monaghan–based Maurice Lynch Band: "The Johnny Quigley Band from Derry took the music stands away. But they went a step further: they were wearing very somber, dark suits, but then they would come out in orange and lime suits and all those sorts of things. And they had everything choreographed: all the steps, sidesteps, kicks with the feet, everything . . . swaying the instruments from side to side. Wonderful! It was fantastic" (Cole, interview, 2007).

The move from playing in a sit-down dance orchestra to playing in a showband was notable for many seasoned musicians who made the transition. After a storied career as a dance band vocalist and clarinetist/sax player, Sonny Knowles joined the Pacific Showband. The dynamic between the musicians and their dancing audiences ("punters") he recalls, was startlingly different as a member of the new showbands: "Punters, as we used to call them . . . wouldn't be looking at the [sit-down dance] band; they would be looking at the girls and you would hardly be noticed. They were chatting up the girls. . . . But it was not until the showbands started that people, dancing around, they used to look up at you, which was a big difference" (interview, 2009).

The transition from the older sit-down dance bands to the new showbands was felt also in the pacing of an evening's performance. Like the sit-down orchestras, a typical showband dance by the mid- to late 1950s began at 9:00 p.m. Halfway through the evening, there was an interval during which a trio or quartet played a short set of céilí dances and old-time waltzes. Not only did this mix of Irish traditional music and dance appeal to their audiences, but it also gave the other musicians a much-needed break. The difference between the old ways and the new became evident after the interval, when the full band returned. Instead of returning to their seats to play another set of dance numbers, the Maurice Lynch Band, according to Paddy Cole, kicked "into this 'show' for the rest of the night." He continues,

> We worked out [choreographies] ourselves . . . it was all down to what we called "presentation," to present the piece. The easy way out would have been to just rehearse the piece and then go out and play it, but we had to present it then as a show. Because in those days, the ballrooms were packed, but a lot of people just stood watching the band. So every song was presented, and choreographed.
>
> [This new style] was happening and none of us really realized it was coming along. . . . Suddenly it was expected from the bands to do this. (Interview, 2007)

In these ways, the members of these early showbands redefined their roles as musicians. While their work of creating dance music continued to be utilitarian, the new format and approach to stage performance now spelled out a musical identity that was increasingly common among popular musicians elsewhere—a status more akin to the stage personalities and celebrities.

Other early showbands included a "show" in an evening's entertainment in keeping with the precedent set by the Clipper Carlton. The Melody Aces, for example, introduced skits between dance music sets, some of which were humorous but others not. Trumpeter Gene Turbett recalls that his bandmate guitarist/vocalist Shay Hutchison became well known for his tearjerker monologues:

> Sad stories, you know. . . . There was one called the "Golden Guitar." It was very, very good. A person goes in and looks at a guitar hanging up in a bar, and it's got all these diamonds and all on it. . . . The father of the person who played the guitar was in the bar at the time and he explained that [the guitar] belonged to his son[who] was in a car crash. Usual performance, you know, he got killed, and his son now plays with a band of angels, and that's his golden guitar. (Interview, 2007)

Other bandleaders followed suit. In Derry, Gay McIntyre, for example, was a keen observer of how to best market his band and remain competitive. To this end, he integrated into his dance band's set list impersonations of American and British actors and singers. According to McIntyre, one of the musicians in his band, Vince Kelly, "could do all the Al Jolson stuff and different voices, so he was a great asset to the band. And other bands saw what was happening, so they started to do the same thing" (interview, 2008).

And then there were the occasional evenings when old habits simply died hard and where the innovation of the show itself was clearly irrelevant and fell on seemingly deaf ears. Mickey O'Hanlon recalls one particularly bizarre instance:

Figure 3.8 The Gay McIntyre Band, ca. 1955. *Left to right*: Roy Doherty, John Anderson, Jim McGonagle, Gordon Sweeney, Willie McIntyre, Gay McIntyre, and Joseph McIntyre. (Photo courtesy of Paul McIntyre.)

> Usually it was a big night out and they would come in, men looking for women. The people were always bright but an odd place you went to and the people in the area were dull in themselves.
>
> I remember one place and it was like everyone had had a row and fell out . . . nobody looking at anyone, no smiling and when they were dancing, they were like zombies. And I said to Hugo "I don't think the show will go here," but he said, "We'll do it anyway." Now to this day, I don't know if it was because they were so dumb or they were drugged or what it was, but I was out doing [the impersonation of] Groucho Marx with the cigar and all, and there were these boys . . . jiving away with these women and they were all dancing to me telling jokes! I was telling Hugo to cut it short. Fergie and Art were doing Laurel and Hardy and there wasn't one looked up at the stage, not *one*! They danced away through the whole show, jokes and all. (Interview, 2007)

Early Showband Repertoire: Variety and Hybridity

The emphasis on a diverse program was crucial as showbands selected their repertoire. Even those showbands known for a specific music style had to cater to their audiences' catholic tastes in music. The earliest showbands—the

Clipper Carlton, in particular—performed Dixieland jazz in addition to the popular dance music styles of the time: old-time waltzes, quicksteps, tangos, rumbas. They learned the popular Latin American hits of the day, such as "La Paloma" and "Tico-Tico," and songs heard on radio broadcasts by American pop idols Perry Como, Frank Sinatra, and Bing Crosby. Hugely popular also were cowboy songs by early country music stars such as Gene Autrey, Roy Rogers, and, according to Mickey O'Hanlon, "everybody played Hank Williams!" (interview, 2007).

The Melody Aces played a similar repertoire and excelled in their performance of country songs, sung by Shay Hutchinson, who quickly developed a reputation as an evocative country singer. The members of the Melody Aces took turns on lead vocals, with each singer specializing in a different genre. Similarly, much of the Melody Aces' versatility was also a result of their ability to double on instruments. (Shay Hutchinson played both guitar and tenor banjo; Edward McNamee played clarinet and alto saxophone, for example.) With this adaptability, the band could move seamlessly between styles, from the trad jazz music of the popular British clarinetist/bandleader Acker Bilk to American Dixieland and jazz classics and the Hank Williams country songs that were always in high demand.

The early showbands' ability to swap out the lead vocals and their mastery of a number of diverse musical styles meant they could offer their audiences new repertoires and dynamic performances but in a frame that referenced the familiar variety approach of the fit-ups. At the same time, it also established an important performative template that would ultimately come to define the showband industry. As the showband era blossomed into the 1960s, variety was an expected component of an evening's entertainment; most of the later showbands routinely swapped lead vocals and musical styles among band members. This strategy was crucial, in fact, to a band's success. Paddy Cole of the Capitol Showband recalls that while some performers naturally focused on a particular singing style, others had to be recruited to fill out a missing stylistic specialty. Once in place, band members spent hours polishing the repertoire: "We had [pianist] Eamonn Monaghan, who sang all the Jim Reeves type songs; [bassist] Des Kelly, who sang the country western songs; [drummer] Johnny Kelley[who] sang the Irish ballads and other tunes. Butch Moore was our lead singer; he was like a Pat Boone–type singer. So everybody sang and we worked out harmonies. . . . We spent a lot of time rehearsing" (Cole, interview, 2007).

In any given band, vocalists covered songs by such American and British rock 'n' roll stars as Elvis Presley, Carl Perkins, Bill Haley, Chuck Berry, Cliff Richard, and the Shadows, among many others. They catered to an array of country singing stars and pop singers such as Pat Boone and England's Dusty Springfield (whose real name was Mary O'Brien) and worked up contemporary R&B hits by such artists as the Temptations, Otis Redding, and Brook Benton. Some showband musicians served as local versions of international stars: most famously, Brendan Bowyer became known as "the Irish Elvis" while Dickie Rock emulated pop crooner Frank Sinatra. Dixies vocalist Brendan O'Brien recalls that channeling well known singers amply made up for the lack of original material: "Unless you recorded a song that the girl next door knew, you were a loser. Original stuff was not the thing to do, not the avenue to go. . . . [The Dixies] had a lot of original stuff. But nothing charted. You'd forget what you did! Because no stars came to Ireland then. So when I would sing a Buddy Holly number, I was Buddy Holly!" (interview, 2006).

For many musicians who grew up listening to a wide range of postwar popular music, the emphasis on variety reflected not only the range of available music genres but also their own restless musical imaginations as creative artists. For example, Van Morrison was raised hearing music from his father's eclectic record collection of 1940s/1950s African American gospel/spirituals, soul, R&B, and blues as well as American country music. Morrison recalls how he listened "with an open mind" without "restrictions of categories" (Morrison 1997/2012). This artistic process variety is evident in Van Morrison's continued embrace of varying musical styles—R&B, rock, and the occasional country-style song—in his own songwriting.

Perhaps more than anything, developing musical versatility made for a stronger musician in terms of developing playing technique, expanding musical vocabularies, and learning the craft of performance. When Van Morrison joined the Monarchs Showband in 1960, he had to quickly master a range of music styles. He recalls that this gave him, as a young musician, not only playing skills and improved technique but also access to music jobs: "Well, that's how one got work, you know, at that point. If you were a professional musician which I was at that point, then you had to work with somebody. So the showbands were probably the only entity in Ireland that were getting work" (interview in Heffernan 2001).

Cork-based blues/rock guitarist Rory Gallagher also learned a range of music styles from playing in showbands beginning at age fifteen, an experience he grimly accessed in a 1972 interview with *Rolling Stone*: "You've got to respect your audience. I played in Irish showbands years ago; you'd be playing for five hours at a time and never get a clap. It was all dancing . . . I only joined a showband 'cause there was no other place to go with an electric guitar. We'd have to play all the Top 20 stuff. You learn a lot of basic stuff.

Mostly you learn what sort of music you don't want to play" (quoted in M. Rock 1972). Viewed from a more positive perspective, Henry McCullough, who played in Joe Cocker's Grease Band and, from 1971 to 1973, as lead guitarist in Paul McCartney's band Wings, believed that playing in a showband challenged him to develop musical chops and ultimately prepared him for his future career as a rock musician: "I had all this experience in playing different types of music, you know. Everything from, you know, country to pop to old-time waltzes and all, everything, which was part of the showband dance band scene. You know, all standard fare. . . . And that's where my rock 'n' roll career came into being, that was the seed planted then because I knew I was on a different path" (interview, 2007).

While versatility certainly helped musicians develop skills as artists and performers, it also underscored the unabashed commercialism that permeated the showband industry. The best musicians were adept at reading and responding to their audiences and could pivot musically as needed. Albert Reynolds frequently observed this from his perch as a dancehall builder and showband promoter: "A good band would make their own judgment as to whether the customers were enjoying it or weren't enjoying it. They'd know if they were able to put them all on the floor dancing, that *that* tune must be popular around here. They would try and create a program that would attract people and bring them back the next night. That's what it was all about, trying to get them to return. Send them home happy" (interview, 2007).

With this enduring variety format, showbands, like the by-then defunct fit-ups, could offer something for everyone, an expectation that may have challenged individual musicians but ultimately pleased their audiences and accounted, in no small part, for their enduring popularity for over two decades from the mid 1950s to mid 1970s. Along with this, the showbands played covers of imported hits complete with dynamic stage shows, all framed in recognizable performance styles and accents. It was this combination of the novel with the familiar that not only built legions of showband fans but would also change the course of Irish popular music in the twentieth century and challenge notions of Irish identity among Irish youth.

Notes

1. Guitarists Billy McFadden and Barney Skillen were also members of the Clipper Carlton. Skillen was replaced by Jim Gunner by 1968.

2. Once common parlance, the term "g——y" is widely understood today as an ethnic slur for members of the Irish travellers community and Roma elsewhere in Europe.

3. Early showbands took their cue from the fit-ups and saw the financial potential of touring, initially moving out of the local to regional, national, and, for a handful, international stages.

4. Advertisement in *Western People*, March 1953, 4; review by "Our Film Critic," *Irish Independent*, January 23, 1950, 4; *Sunday Independent*, January 22, 1950, 4.

5. This type of ventriloquism was paralleled in the original film when Larry Parks's vocals were recorded by Al Jolson and then overdubbed. With the exception of one scene that features Al Jolson in a long shot, the audience sees the actor (Parks) but hears the singer (Jolson).

6. That the Clipper Carlton relied on blackface performance raises inevitable questions of race and racism. Of blackface performance in general, Eric Lott (1995, 3–5) writes that it is an "unstable and contradictory" form that borrows from "black performative practices as well as ridiculing them and which invest[s] desire and identification in simulated blackness as well as troping blackness as inherently comic and pathetic."

The Clipper Carlton's engagement with blackface was particularly complicated because there were relatively few people of color in Ireland at the time. John Brannigan (2009, 186) writes that despite this overall homogeneity, persistent narratives of a multiracial Ireland date back to 1925. Further, Brannigan (2024, 117) notes that in the years before and after Irish independence, "newspaper reviews [of blackface performances] show no sign of a critical or ironic understanding of blackface." The Clipper Carlton's use of blackface as a centerpiece of their show was similarly uncritical and unironic, perhaps because their intent was to imitate the performances of American entertainers. The Clipper Carlton and their audiences functioned as what Brannigan (2024, 117–18) describes as "passive consumers (or indeed active adopters) of the racial ideologies produced in Britain and the U.S." and, as such, serve as evidence of a "cultural complicity in the system of privilege that defines whiteness." Ultimately, the Clipper Carlton's engagement with blackface through their innovative show—with all its embedded racisms—unquestionably contributed to their success as a group, ultimately propelling both the band and the entire showband genre into the Irish mainstream.

4

"Traveling Jukeboxes"

Imitation, Translation, and Irishness

Oh, what a night that was. . . . The floor was a burning trampoline. The body was a pogo stick. I had never sweated so much in my life before. Oh, what delicious hell was this? . . . I saw now why dances had to be crowded; from a full heart I silently thanked the strangers all around me for creating for me, for everyone, this inspirational heat, this fabulous undulance in which we bobbed and dipped, bubbles forming, breaking, forming in richly seething stirabout.

George O'Brien, Dancehall Days

I loved the showband scene. I'd go to the dance and see the showbands. It was wonderful. And I loved the dancing and I loved to go into the dance and be the first one out on the floor. And 'twas smashing, 'twas great, 'twas great. I loved it!

Mildred Beirne, interview, 2007

By 1966, the showband era had firmly taken hold with a thriving circuit in place. An estimated eight hundred showbands of ambitious musicians, often guided by equally ambitious managers, crisscrossed Ireland and Northern Ireland in recently purchased vans to perform in large ballrooms, marquees, and parish dance halls. Most showband musicians worked day jobs in factories, agriculture, and the service industry. After a day's work, they met their bandmates and drove, sometimes for hours, to play a dance. Their audiences consisted largely of their peers: young men and women who held the same types of day jobs as did the musicians on stage. In this way, the showband world was largely a working-class phenomenon created and consumed essentially by neighbors and peers.

Showband fans themselves were starting to reap the benefits of a reviving Irish economy that afforded better employment opportunities and higher wages. With disposable income in their pockets, young Irish men and women had more choices for how to spend leisure time, and most chose dancing at their local ballroom. There they danced to the music of local and touring groups that personified the otherwise faceless rock 'n' roll and pop artists heard on the radio. This was especially significant in the early years of the showband era, recalls Fr. Brian D'Arcy:

> We weren't likely to get Elvis Presley here, but we could get Brendan Bowyer. . . . We weren't likely to get Jim Reeves, but we got Larry Cunningham and Shay Hutchinson and Gene Stuart and Brian Coll . . . all the other country singers at that time. . . . And we weren't likely to get somebody like Otis Redding, but we got Doc Carroll of the Royal Blues. So we had all of these fellows who were "traveling jukeboxes," that's really what they were. You know, they played the hits of the time live, and they brought excitement and they brought glamour. (Interview, 2007)

While showbands delighted their audiences with the sheer novelty of rock 'n' roll and stage choreographies that could and did turn working Irish musicians into local and regional pop stars, it was precisely this studied approach to performance that generated what would become the central critique of showbands for years to come. In 1994, music critic John Waters wrote, "Many of the early Irish attempts to create rock 'n' roll were crude and imitative, confused about whether to look to Britain or the US, unsure of what they were looking for, of what exactly this medium was supposed to be about" (49). This "blindly imitative" approach, according to Waters, was a result of a postcolonial mentality, a "constant war between the invading and the indigenous culture" and that the "strong connections between the bland, fixed smile of the Country and Irish showbands of the sixties and seventies . . . were a denial of real feeling . . . expressions of inferiority, fatalism, and self-hatred" (87–88).

Waters rightly points to postcolonial anxieties that often inform the politics of identity formation. And while Irish showbands were indeed imitative inasmuch as they mined repertoire from Britain and the United States, what does not follow are arguments that working-class Irish musicians—and, by extension, their audiences—struggled with feelings of self-hatred and inferiority.[1] A more generative perspective allows that showband musicians filled a need in the everyday lives of working-class audiences with entertainment and dance music that was, at the time, novel and refreshing and, for many, radical and even rebellious, all uniquely couched alongside familiar signifiers of Irish culture. Indeed, showband fans responded the same way that pop and rock fans have and do elsewhere—through the fun and pleasure of listening and dancing to live music. There were other factors: fans also recall the opportunity to socialize with old and new friends; the influence of the showbands on the newest fashions of the day (often underscoring the important role of the Irish diaspora); and the universal and always intriguing social dynamics of the dance hall. Mary Duffy and Eileen Lavin, for example, recall the anticipation of an evening of dancing to a showband as well as the dance itself:

RSM: Did you like going to the dances?

MARY DUFFY (MD): Oh, yes! Oh, yes! Just the music and the dancing, and that's what you did. That was your pastime, meeting up and—

EILEEN LAVIN (EL): Friends, and—

MD: —you'd be planning what you'd wear, and—

EL: That's right, yeah.

MD: Swap dresses, and just so excited when, you know, about going.

EL: And if you got a parcel from America, then you had a new dress. Yeah!

MD: Oh, yeah, you had the girls over one side [of the hall], the boys on the other, and the dance was announced, and *zoom*! [laughs]

EL: And you'd get up and dance! (Duffy and Lavin, interviews, 2009)

Arguments of cultural imperialism and musical imitation also tend to lose sight of the labor and often hard-won accomplishments of musicians who had to learn playing techniques that matched the variety of repertoire they performed. This was particularly true for inexperienced players, many of whom would ultimately go on to develop the skills needed to earn a living from music. Some, like Henry McCullough, grew into seasoned professionals. He recalls that this initial musical mastery was not only fun but also boosted his self-esteem and optimism: "I was seventeen when I joined the Skyrockets Showband. . . . Everybody in Ireland had a guitar, you know. And I think everybody had great fun. It was like the punk thing, you know: you could get on there with an acoustic guitar and if you rattled out 'Tom Dooley' or something like, you were doing great!" (interview, 2007).

There was also the kinetic and visceral pleasure of playing music, recalls Mildred Beirne, the drummer in the all-women Granada Girls Showband: "You know when you're a drummer, you're the heart of that band and without the drummer, you can give it up. The drummer gives it everything. . . . For me, it 'twas like magic to sit behind that set of drums and the girls playing. I got lost playing those drums. It was lovely, heaven!" (interview, 2007).

And as it is for many musicians of all stripes, there was the prestige of performance as well as the intoxicating attention generated from being on stage, recalls drummer Des Hopkins: "Every showband man was a kind of a star when he was up there, and you'd have all the girls around the band looking for autographs, and all. That was quite fun when you were twenty-one years of age [*laughs*]. Yeah, there was a certain amount of stardom attached to it, no matter what band you were with. When you were with a showband, you were kind of a peg up in society" (interview, 2007).

Also missing from Waters's analysis is a nuanced reading of the very notion of creativity. Indeed, there are many ways to be creative apart from composing original works and just as many understandings of the creative process itself. At one end of this argument is the perspective voiced by Miami Showband vocalist Dickie Rock: "Just because a thing is original doesn't mean it's good. And an awful lot of [original material] is quite the opposite: very bad" (interview, 2006). At the other extreme, some groups ignored the question altogether by doing whatever they wanted, notably the County Monaghan–based Big Tom and the Mainliners, one of the most popular Country and Irish bands. According to Paul Maguire, Big Tom and the Mainliners "demonstrated a studied indifference to the existing showband paradigm" of imitation given their lack of interest in creating a faithful reproduction of the original. In fact, Tom McBride ("Big Tom") introduced new material to his bandmates by learning the song himself and then playing his version of it for them. Recalls bassist Ginger Morgan, "The Mainliners' sound was based on *not* hearing the records" (Maguire 2012, 203).

The average showband fell between these two extremes. Much like the Clipper Carlton's reenactment of *The Jolson Story* in which American popular culture was translated to local audiences with Northern Irish accents, showbands combined familiar and uniquely Irish performance practices with the newest American and British popular songs and played them as closely as possible to the originals. The result was a style that emphasized variety, a distinctive stage presence, and a repertoire of the newest hits of the day with the occasional popular Irish song, old-time waltz, and sometimes, a céilí dance. What also emerged was a hybrid dance music rhythm that typified the showband sound and sent jive dancers whirling to the dance floor.

And finally, showband music can be characterized for what it was not, beginning with that distinctive dance rhythm. Unlike the title of the 1966 showband hit, "Ireland Swings," most showband music was played with a fairly straight pulse rather than slightly syncopated (or swing) feel. Additionally, showband covers of American blues songs often lost the critical "blue" notes, reflecting a strongly Irish rather than African American tonal aesthetic. Showbands borrowed non-Irish popular songs but, crucially, retained key elements of Irish popular music and, in doing so, did the creative work of translating the aesthetics and sounds of the modern world outside of Ireland into a recognizable Irish frame.

Wrapping the newest songs in this cloak of familiarity, showbands moved beyond being simply imitative. And while some showbands lacked

Figure 4.1 The Woodchoppers, Derry, ca. 1960. *Front, left to right*: George Hasson, Jack Malloy, Paddy Helferty, Jimmy Helferty, and Jim Tolland. *Back row, left to right*: Tommy Wright, Richard McManus, and Willie Bradley. (Photo courtesy of Willie Bradley.)

the musical virtuosity and polish heard on the slickly produced recordings, what they centrally provided was the excitement of live performance with its own palpable energy: new sounds, stage moves, occasional sexually suggestive lyrics, and sheer spectacle. How well they accomplished this would ultimately determine their status in the growing showband industry.

"Going Pro:" Showband Divisions

Showbands fell into an informal hierarchy, known as "divisions," starting with the professional bands (or "pros") that toured nationally (and occasionally internationally) and drew the largest crowds. Among the best known in this division were the Clipper Carlton, the Royal Showband, the Capitol Showband, the Dixies, the Miami Showband, the Freshmen, the Nevada Showband, the Plattermen, the Mighty Avons, Joe Dolan and the Drifters, the Dave Glover Band, Eileen Reid and the Cadets, Johnny Flynn Showband, and others. These top showbands were so in demand that their members were able to quit their day jobs and work full-time as musicians, performing six or even seven nights a week. The best-known professional bands garnered quite a lot of attention by the popular press, often to the neglect of the hundreds of other, less well-known showbands, observes drummer Des Hopkins: "It quite annoyed me from time to time over the years, obviously because any book or any article that has been written . . . always tends to just harp on the same five or six bands. You hear about the Capitol, the Royal, the Miami, the Clipper Carlton. But there was much, much more to it than that. Much, much more" (interview, 2007). Hopkins played in the Ohio Showband, a well-known professional band that he describes as belonging to the "B division" of the pro groups, which, he recalls, "were also very good professional bands earning very, very good money. Not quite as much as the bigger boys. . . . All these bands are fairly well known: the Kings, the Victors, the Ohio, the Graduates. I think every town had their band, you know? The Royal Blues, they were quite big. And then there was the Blues Aces and the Black Aces and I could go on and on" (interview, 2007).

Only a small number of showbands "went pro"; in fact, the largest percentage of showband musicians were the semiprofessionals ("semipros") who played regularly, mostly in local and regional venues. Most of the semipro showband musicians held on to their full- or part-time day jobs and performed largely on weekends, recalls Michael Coughlan, who played guitar in the Waterford-based (and aptly named) Intermediate Showband. As semipros, Coughlan recalls that their lives as part-time musicians with full-time day jobs were often grueling: "With us, it was always a case of [playing] just the weekend, and going off, we'll say, all day Sunday and coming back at maybe seven or eight o'clock on a Monday morning. And sometimes being dropped off directly outside your place of work. The van would go around dropping people off to work, having slept in the back of the van. . . . But we were young; it didn't seem crazy at the time" (interview, 2007).

The third tier of players were the so-called amateur showbands—musicians who played often, mostly locally, but, in contrast to the typical use of the term "amateur," sometimes received pay and other times not. Like the semipro musicians, amateur players also worked at daytime jobs and often opened for the visiting professional bands.

On the Road with the Showbands

Showband musicians selected the newest American and British hits from radio broadcasts via Radio Luxembourg, the American Armed Forces Network, and the BBC *Pick of the Pops*—the same broadcasts that youth throughout Ireland regularly listened to. On Sunday evenings, musicians gathered around their radios to hear and record some of the weekly Top 10 songs. If they had a job that night, they recruited a friend or family member to record the Top 10 for them and then listened repeatedly over the next twenty-four hours to one or two songs to learn the lyrics, melody, and chord progressions. Occasionally, a manager or bandleader might buy the newly released single of a particular song. In most cases, showband artists aimed to learn the new hits as closely to the originals as possible.

While some musicians came to showbands with formal musical training and experience, others had something of a do-it-yourself approach whereby anybody with musical inclination and basic mastery of an instrument could form or join a band and take to the stage. Some came to showband music with the advantage of having a background in Irish traditional music, a genre that, at its core, relies on learning music through listening and imitation rather than from written notation. Their skills were complemented in many instances by bandmates who possessed some level of music literacy and who could create lead sheets, recalls Barons Showband vocalist José (Joe) Fernandez: "As soon as a piece of music hit the Top 10, or the Top 20, or the Top 30 and one felt it was on its way up, the manager used to go out and buy the records. The manager's brother used to play the piano . . . [and he would] write out the chord structures and give it to the rest of the musicians. And I'd be then given the record to transcribe the words and to learn them" (interview, 2007).

By Monday afternoon, one or two band members would have created rough lead sheets containing chord progressions and sometimes melodies written out in music notation. The band members were pressured to quickly learn these new songs in preparation for their Tuesday through Sunday night performances, recalls Henry McCullough: "It [was] a bit of a scramble. You would shuffle through the Top 20 on the Monday afternoon and you would rehearse maybe two, three of these. The turnover was constant . . . you know, to try and keep up . . . and the more pop songs you knew that were close to the top of the charts, the better it was for everybody" (interview, 2007).

Armed with the most recent hits, many semipro and professional showbands performed six nights a week, from Tuesday through Sunday. They played year-round with the exception of the six weeks of Lent, when showbands were furloughed in Ireland in response to the Catholic Church's ban on public dancing. The Lenten season ban was challenging for professional showband musicians, who relied on the income generated by steady performances, recalls Nevada Showband saxophonist Tommy Hayden: "We literally went [to England] because we had a thing called Lenten period, which was a terrible period. . . . All the dance halls closed" (interview, 2008). While it was hard on the musicians, it was even harder on their wives and young families, recalls Tommy Hayden's wife, Anne: "For Lent every year, they

Figure 4.2 Tommy Hayden, ca. 1966. (Photo courtesy of Tommy Hayden.)

didn't have any work in Ireland. So they had to either go to Germany or America, England, and Scotland, you know, different countries to get work. In fact, when our second son was born, my husband was in Germany. Those weeks were the worst part, when they had to go abroad to get work" (interview, 2008). The limitations imposed around Lent also posed a quandary for fans because, despite the ban, a handful of ballrooms—mostly in Dublin and Belfast—remained open, according to Dixies drummer/comedian Joe McCarthy:

RSM: The parish priests looked down on dancing during Lent?

JOE MCCARTHY: Oh my God, yes.

RSM: But some people would still go out and dance?

JOE MCCARTHY: Yeah, but you'd be damned to hell! (Interview, 2007)

Aside from the Lenten ban on public dancing, showband players were challenged year-round by Ireland's rudimentary transportation infrastructure. Because motorways did not come to Ireland until 1983, showband players traveled in their crowded vans on notoriously narrow and poorly paved roads. Musicians routinely recall traveling four or more hours to get to a job. In a 2007 interview with RTÉ host, Eamon Dunphy, vocalist Adèle King recalled the rigors of driving for hours in a van with other musicians: "If I never saw the Nace Road again, let me tell you, what a pleasure that would be! . . . And then you were first on the scene of so many horrendous accidents on the road and you saw carnage on the roads firsthand. Just all sorts of ghastly nightmares that it brings back: sitting in that bloody van hour after hour (King 2007).

To cope with the tedium of travel, showband musicians recall the strategies they developed as well as the camaraderie that formed between bandmates:

> Adèle King: I started to learn Italian. . . . [Saxophonist] Paddy Cole, [trumpeter] Dave Coady, and myself became amateur lexicographers. We brought a dictionary and we studied a page a day and quizzed each other on each word. You had to do something if you had half a brain, to relieve the mind-numbing boredom of the whole thing. (King 2007)

> Des Hopkins: Yeah, it could be four, five, six hours in the back of a van, you know, and laughing and chatting. Sleeping, mostly. (Interview, 2007)

> Maxi McCoubrey (vocalist): [The musicians] also had crazy interests like cowboy books. And they'd talk about—a lot of them came from Artane, the school where the kids were abused . . . the brass players, wind instruments. So the conversations would be absolutely riveting. For me, that was an upside. (Interview, 2009)

Their destination was one of the many dance halls, marquees, parish halls, and newly built ballrooms that dotted Ireland and Northern Ireland. Bass-player Billy Robinson recalls some of the dance venues near his home in County Donegal:

> Around here, there would have been a hall, the Mountain Wood, every Saturday night. The Kilmacrenan every Tuesday night. There was a huge dance hall, the Fiesta in Letterkenny every Friday, the Butt Hall in Ballybofey near here every Thursday. These dance halls would hold maybe 1,500 people, and then the smaller ones maybe 400 to 500. Every night of the week, within maybe twenty-five miles, there were at least two dances, all with bands. And there were so many local bands that played all over the northwest that came from Letterkenny and this area. (Interview, 2009)

The showband typically arrived at the venue in the late afternoon. Some of the professional bands had help from hired roadies, but for the most part, the work of unloading and setting up instruments and sound equipment fell to the musicians themselves. Mildred Beirne recalls the challenge:

> We might be four, five hours on the road. And we'd arrive and we'd have all to unpack. Get out of the van, everybody to carry in their stuff, set up the stuff. Rehearse for maybe another two hours on stage. And then there'd always be a meal waiting for you. And we'd go to the hotel or the house, a private house or something. And if it was a priest that booked you for a carnival or something, you'd go to the priest's house and you'd get your meal there. And we'd be back on stage again and we'd start playing at nine o'clock at night. And we would have to play 'til two in the morning. That's a long time playing. (Interview, 2007)

Getting ready for the evening's performance posed its own challenges, given that the dance halls and even newer ballrooms were not set up with the needs of the musicians in mind, according to vocalist Eileen Kelly: "The ballroom mightn't even have a dressing room. Or it might have something at the side of the stage where everybody would have to go in and change. When you've got a gang of guys around, they would leave . . . and I learned very quickly how to undress and dress again. . . . Those days were primitive. The roads were primitive. Everything was primitive so you kind of just got on with it" (interview, 2008).

By 9:00 p.m., the band was set up and ready to go and audience streamed into the dance hall. The band's manager, dance hall owner, or, if it was a parish-sponsored dance, a local priest used a handheld clicker counter at the door to keep count of ticket buyers—particularly important because the band typically split the proceeds with the venue owner. In the early years of the showband scene, bands charged venue owners a set fee, but as their popularity increased and as they became better versed in business practice, bands (and their managers) increasingly required a split of the proceeds with the venue. A typical showband might demand a forty-sixty split and, as they became better known, fifty-fifty. For the really well-known groups, the split was closer to sixty-forty.

Some dances in the larger halls often featured a warm-up band—in many instances, a local amateur group—after which the featured band played. Semiprofessional bands mostly played the entire evening, from 9:00 p.m. to 2:00 a.m. or later. Like the sit-down dance bands before them, showbands played in sets of three: three fast jive dances, followed by three old-time waltzes, and then three foxtrots, for example.[2] Halfway through the evening was the interval when dancing audiences could have a cup of tea,

Figure 4.3 The Comets Showbands, 1961. (Photo courtesy of Bob Kearney.)

a sandwich and snacks, and a cold beverage at the mineral bar; there was no alcohol served at the venues.

By the 1960s, showbands had largely dispensed with the formal "show" during the interval, although occasional elements of the show lived on in some groups. (The Cork-based Dixies Showband, for example, routinely peppered their performances with short dramatic and comedic skits, not to mention their well-known outbursts of off-color humor.) Some groups offered nonstop music by breaking into trios and taking turns providing music during the interval, eventually giving all members a short break. If there was demand, one of these trios might play traditional Irish dance music to accompany a ceílí dance or two. For those musicians who were taking a well-deserved break, their respite was scant, recalls Comets Showband member Bob Kearney: "You might get a cup of tea or something in that, if you were lucky" (interview, 2007). Dancing resumed until as late as 2:00 or 3:00 a.m. At the end of the evening, the musicians in professional bands might stay over in a hotel; most semipro and amateur showband artists broke down the gear, packed it up, and began their drive home, sometimes traveling for hours and arriving home just in time to return to their day jobs.[3]

Figure 4.4 Earl Gill Showband. Publicity postcard. (Collection of Jimmy Higgins.)

Naming the Bands

Showbands sported a wide range of names, from those that simply named the bandleader (Earl Gill Showband, Jack Ruane Showband, among many others) to the aspirational (Millionaires Showband, Cadillac Showband, Fab Five Showband) and the playful (Mad Lads Showband). Other bands likened themselves to forces of nature (Dambusters Showband, two Hurricanes Showbands—one in Ballymena and the other in Dundalk); while still others opted for the sinister (the Assassins) or the dancingly descriptive (Jivenaires Showband).

Given the outsized influence of the United States on the showbands, many unsurprisingly adopted names that specifically located American signs, symbols, and locations. Some embraced contemporary American bands and music styles (Bluegrass Country Bandshow, Dixies Showband, Beach Boys Showband) while others seized on American locations (Miami Showband, Nevada Showband, Idaho Showband, Ohio Showband, Boston Showband, Denver Showband, Florida Showband, Niagara Showband, Detroit Showband, and, most unambiguously, the U.S.A. Showband). A spate of showbands targeted the American south (Hoot'nannys, the Virginians, the Hillbillies, Memphis Showband, Confederates Showband, Texan

Figure 4.5 The Millionaires Showband meets Chicago's Mayor Richard J. Daly, ca. 1967. *Left to right*: Jimmy Higgins, Terry Cash, Michael O'Brien, Mayor Richard J. Daly, Gene Bannon, Joe Doherty, Billy Doyle, and Michael Conn. (Collection of Jimmy Higgins.)

Showband, Creole Showband). Still other bands embraced symbols of the American West, Canada, and Mexico, including the Cowboys Showband, the Mounties, Yukon Showband, and the Mexicans.

Some showbands appropriated the names and imagery of various African and Native American cultures and capitalized on the racist gimmick of performing in regalia and face paint, echoing the earlier blackface performances by the Clipper Carltons. Indeed, gimmick showbands of all stripes were a micro-phenomenon unto themselves. Beginning in the early- and mid-1970s, gimmick showbands aimed to carve a marketing niche in what was an increasingly crowded and competitive circuit. Among these groups were the Zulus, the Apaches, and one of the longest running showbands in Irish history, the Indians.

Formerly known as the Casino Showband, the Indians performed for some forty years and enjoyed great commercial success, thanks in part to their "gimmick," that is, their unabashed appropriation of Native American costuming. The Indians performed a range of material—from Steve Earle's "Galway Girl" to objectively offensive songs like "Wig Wam Wiggle" and

Figure 4.6 Dickie Rock and the Miami. Publicity postcard. (Collection of Jimmy Higgins.)

Figure 4.7 Detroit Showband. Publicity photo. (Collection of Jimmy Higgins.)

Figure 4.8 The Mounties Showband. Publicity photo. (Collection of Jimmy Higgins.)

"Your Chief's on the Warpath Tonight." While the politics of identity and cultural representation have changed since the band's inception, their choice of costuming and performance practice did not and has generated strident criticism by Native American activists. A 2011 article in *The Irish Independent*, entitled "Indians Told to Disband by PC Posse," reports that an unnamed "US campaign group" called out the Indians on their offensive appropriation of Native American symbols and called for boycotts of the band by Irish concert promoters. Bandleader Eamon Keane was unapologetic in his response: "All we ever get are positive comments about our show. This is PC gone mad. I don't want to give this added publicity but it's madness."[4]

The approximation and representation of Native American culture as other was further conflated, amplified, and misunderstood. Guitarist/vocalist Roly Daniels, who was born in Jabalpur, India, and raised in Dublin, recalls being routinely perceived also as other (that is, not Irish) but often incorrectly so: "When they're told I'm from India, some punters seem surprised I don't go around with feathers in my hair, scalping people. They get confused with the Red Indian bit" (quoted in "Popeye View," *Top Ten Weekly*, February 17, 1967).

Figure 4.9 The Zulus, ca. 1972. Publicity photo. (Collection of Jimmy Higgins.)

The American Influence: Covering Country Music

Apart from band names, the influence of popular American music on showbands was profound and contributed to arguments that showbands simply reflected the worst kind of cultural imperialism. In writing about these anxieties in the context of modern Ireland, Fintan O'Toole (1997, 21) argues that this issue can "miss the point that American mass culture may well contain buried elements of other cultures," a concept aptly demonstrated by the longtime popularity of American country music throughout Ireland in the twentieth century. So popular was this genre that, by the showband era, the inclusion of country songs in most showbands was a given and nearly mandatory.

Tracing the genesis of country music to Ireland underscores the earliest moments of cultural exchange between the United States and Ireland. Beginning in the late seventeenth century, Scots-Irish immigrants settled primarily in the southeastern United States and particularly in the southern Appalachians. With these immigrants came fiddle-heavy instrumental dance music as well as folk songs and ballads, and unaccompanied singing styles. Over the years, these musics combined with elements of African American music and dance, eventually developing into old-time string

Figure 4.10 Hoot'nanny's. Publicity photo. (Collection of Jimmy Higgins.)

band music ("hillbilly" music). In addition to forming the basis of bluegrass music in the years surrounding World War II, old-time music also was critical to the development of country music. A textbook example of musical syncretism—the largely organic process of cultural exchange that occurs when two or more disparate genres interact over time—country music shares elements of structure, tonality, and often lyrical narratives with Irish folk traditions. Because of this—and despite centuries of major and subtle change—country music has long retained a sonic familiarity for Irish audiences as well as an enduring popularity.

For decades, country music was widely heard on both sides of the border, in part due to broadcasts by Radio Luxembourg and, beginning in 1942, the American Armed Forces Network for American troops abroad (see Miller 1996). These iconic sounds were, in turn, embraced and re-created by Irish musicians and bands and, by the late 1950s, had become a staple part of many showbands' repertoires. Women showband artists covered the hits of Patsy Cline, Jean Shepard, Skeeter Davis, Kitty Wells, and Dolly Parton, while their male colleagues focused on songs by such country stars as Hank Williams, Johnny Cash, George Jones, and others. By the mid-1960s, the demand for country music was so great that some showbands shed their horn section altogether and revamped their repertoire to better emulate the "new Nashville" style of country with its own use of pop styling and instrumentation. Some groups, such as Ray Lynam and the Hillbillies, Hoot'nanny's, Cotton Mill Boys, and Brian Coll and the Buckaroos, added a Nashville-style fiddle and pedal steel to solidify their sound as centrally country. By 1966, the demand for country western music was so notable that it spawned the showband subgenre Country and Irish, with some showbands moving entirely to this repertoire.[5]

The American Influence: African American Blues and R&B

The sounds of African American blues and R&B were powerful sources of inspiration for many young players who were then motivated to learn instruments and join showbands. Jazz saxophonist Jim McDermott played with the Derry-based Esquires Showband before joining the Witnesses. He recalls the moment in the mid-1950s when, as a teenager, he first heard a musical and tonal language that was leagues away from his native Derry: "I remember practicing one day in my room. I'd heard this stuff on radio, and I'd actually found the basis of the twelve-bar blues. The Black American blues. . . . For a young guy of my age at that time, [it was] like an unbelievable revelation which totally, totally changed my direction in music (interview, 2008).

Van Morrison's early showband career coincided with his introduction to Leadbelly and other African American blues players and gospel artists. His visceral response upon first hearing African American music would lead to a decades-long engagement, as he describes in a June 4, 2015, interview in *The Guardian*:

> It was some sort of a spiritual experience. I just absorbed it. I reacted later, but I was absorbing it when I was first hearing it . . . there was some sort of energy. . . . The whole thing. The voice, the 12-string guitar, the amazing sound. I was hearing Sonny Terry and Brownie McGhee at the same time. I was hearing Josh White, Louis Armstrong recordings and stuff like this, and Muddy Waters and gospel. It wasn't just an isolated thing; it was part of a whole framework of this type of music—blues and gospel . . . and also John Lee Hooker, which I absorbed more than anybody . . . all that stuff over a long period of time from the 50s to the 60s. (Interview, Denselow, *The Guardian*, June 4, 2015)

By the 1960s, a spate of showbands embraced the sounds and repertoire of blues and R&B and signaled this through band names such as the Blue Aces (Waterford), the Royal Blues Showband (Claremorris), D.J. Curtin and the Kerry Blues (Tralee), Blue Beats Showband (Dublin), the Bluebeats

Showband (Belfast), two Blue Notes Showbands (one that was Derry-based, the other from Arklow), and others. While some of these bands certainly incorporated elements of blues and R&B into their repertoire choices and playing styles, others did so more in theory than in actual musical practice, retaining a pop music sensibility, despite monikers that located blues.

The American Influence: Rock 'n' Roll Showbands

With its raw, unbridled energy, rock 'n' roll arrived in Ireland full force by the early 1960s. The influence of rock 'n' roll cannot be overestimated: along with the music came the new concept of adolescence as a discrete demographic and a distinctive teen culture that had already taken shape in the United States and in England. In Ireland, rock 'n' roll and teen culture went head to head with the conservative mores firmly in place at the time, recalls Eamon Carr, drummer with the early Irish fusion group, Horslips.

> People frowning at kids sort of; it happened I suppose in England as well. I mean, there was an explosion in England in the 50s, when adolescents suddenly—well, in America too—adolescents "appeared." And in Ireland, it was slightly later. So it wasn't 'til the '60s. And you know, we were assuredly hidebound by convention and by religious convention. . . . [B]ut we all had rock 'n' roll radio beamed in [on TV] and so we were picking up on all that stuff and . . . there was a sort of a cultural swing. (Interview, 2009)

This cultural swing was also felt in Northern Ireland, which by the mid-1950s, was emerging from the deprivations of World War II. With material goods now readily accessible, the early 1960s ushered in an era of relative security. According to Jim McDermott, "people were becoming more happy-go-lucky. . . . Parents let [their children] out to meet [at dance halls] because they were safe: there was no alcohol, there was no drugs, you know, even cigarette smoking was frowned upon. It was a tremendous time, really opening up of the whole personality of the country and the people in it. . . . I still find that very mesmeric, that sort of amazing transition. You know? Things were dark and all of a sudden, things were bright!" (interview, 2008).

The images and sounds of African American popular music were an important source of inspiration for the members of the newly formed Royal Showband. After seeing films of the Platters and the Coasters and hearing recordings of Motown artists such as the Temptations, Royal Showband member Brendan Bowyer recalls incorporating similar light choreographies into the Royals' onstage performances—routines that became known as the "showband step": "We would have seen the Platters' 'Rock Around the Clock.' . . . And they were visually good in those old movies. It was nothing

Figure 4.11 Brendan Bowyer, The Royal Showband, ca. 1964. (Photo courtesy of T. J. Byrne.)

extraordinary, but some showbands took it to a level where they were side-stepping and crossing and everything. But I think it was important at that time, you know, if we were doing a fast, up-tempo number, that we were together, back and forward" (interview, 2006).

In 1960, the Royal Showband from Waterford emerged as arguably Ireland's premiere showband, setting a new standard for other bands in terms of overall musicianship and performance skills. While their stage performances were clearly influenced by the Clipper Carlton, the members of the Royal Showband drew more explicitly on American rock 'n' roll. The Royal Showband also established what would eventually become standard showband instrumentation: a strong rhythm section that included electric guitar and bass, drums, and piano, and a frontline horn section (trombone, trumpet, and saxophone/clarinet).[6] With Brendan Bowyer as lead singer, the Royal Showband also built on the practice of earlier showbands of distributing lead vocals to others in the group, thereby capitalizing on the skills and preferences of individual band members.

The Royal Showband was almost entirely a covers band, rarely composing their own songs, and instead, translating the new sounds of rock 'n' roll for showband instrumentation. Their approach and stage charisma proved to be spot on: by 1962, the Royal Showband received a Carl Alan Award (the British equivalent of the Grammys). They were just completing a triumphant tour of Britain when they were booked to play the Liverpool Empire

Figure 4.12 The Royal Showband. Publicity postcard, ca. 1966. (Collection of Jimmy Higgins.)

Theatre. Opening for the Royals that night was an early version of the Beatles (John Lennon, Paul McCartney, George Harrison, and Pete Best) when that band was just on the cusp of international stardom. The group was so atypical of the popular bands in those years that Bowyer remembers this iteration of the Beatles as "being good, but with only four of them and no brass instruments, would they make it?" (interview, 1992).

> I do remember McCartney. I can remember his baby face eating a bag of chips. And he was looking at the Royal Showbands' big Mercedes bus outside and all our trappings of success. And I actually said, "I thought you guys were great! If you stick together, you should do very well." But what really struck me, during the course of the evening was even though they would do other people's music, which we were doing all the time, they would intersperse one, like "Here's one we wrote ourselves." And I thought, for a group that was starving, you know, this was really something. The lesson we should have learned from the Beatles was that we should have gotten away and started to do our own stuff. (Interview, 1992)

Despite being a cover band, the Royal Showband enjoyed a string of firsts in the showband industry: they were the first to "go pro" and the first to make a record (*Come Down the Mountain Katy Daly*, 1962). They were also the first to have a number-one hit on the Irish charts ("Kiss Me Quick," 1963). But it was the Royal Showband's 1964 cover of the 1949 American R&B hit, "The Hucklebuck," that was arguably their most memorable contribution to showband history.[7] Having performed "The Hucklebuck" as a dance number for two years, the group recorded it as something of an afterthought for the B side of the single "I Ran All The Way Home":

Figure 4.13 Brendan Bowyer, ca. 1964. (Photo courtesy of T. J. Byrne.)

> We rattled off one take [of "The Hucklebuck"]. And [Royal Showband producer Walter J. Ridley] said, "That's great, that's great! Spontaneity in that now." "Now," he said "Brendan, you double track and we'll have the blend . . . on the back beat and shout 'hey.'" So the band clapped on the backbeat and shouted "hey," and I double tracked my voice, sang direct, exactly the same thing I sang before. So there was two takes and that was the Hucklebuck in thirty minutes. It's become the biggest party song ever in Ireland. (Bowyer, interview, 2006)

As the unofficial anthem of the showband era, "The Hucklebuck" was the first single showband record to sell upwards of 50,000 copies in Ireland, ultimately going Platinum in the 1980s. Part of the song's success was that it was not only very danceable but also came with its own particular dance choreography. Also appealing to 1960s Irish audiences were the song's lyrics that contain thinly veiled sexual innuendo—risqué and thrilling at the time. As such, writes Gerry Smyth, "The Hucklebuck" was "a hymn to the dance floor . . . and a paradoxical *recording* success" (G. Smyth 2005, 15). The Royal Showband's cover of the song was successful for other reasons as well, including its arrangement, which, John Waters writes in a revised assessment of showbands, is "a blistering three minutes as good as anything since" (Waters 1994, 96 as cited in G. Smyth 2005, 14).

Showband Rhythms: From Old-Time Waltzes to "Chop" and Jive

Emphatically upbeat and played in a bright duple meter, the Royal Showband's version of "The Hucklebuck" retains the song's standard twelve-bar blues progression and straightforward three-chord progression. But like many renditions of R&B and rock songs in the hands of showbands, the Royal Showband's "Hucklebuck" jettisons the "blue" notes so distinctive in the original. And unlike the original R&B and subsequent jazz versions that swing the beat (e.g., played with a slightly syncopated rhythm or groove), the Royal Showband's version features a more precise, squared rhythmic feel with virtually no swing. Theirs is a perfect example of the uniquely Irish "showband beat," one characterized by bassist Barry Scully of Gene and the Gents, as "a quickstep, dance-y beat with a drummer playing the leg of a chair offbeat. Bash away there! Very agricultural, but it was dance-y!" (interview, 2006). Drummer/guitarist Gerry Anderson (2008, 20) describes this as the "show-band chop" or a "peculiar pulsing but clipped offbeat, known to the aficionado as the 'Galway Wallop . . . the beat that activates the natural jiver." With the Royal Showband's squared-up dance rhythm and recognizable tonality, "The Hucklebuck" felt accessible; as Brendan Bowyer observed, "a sound doesn't have to be difficult to be great" (interview, 2007).

A smaller but still significant percentage of showband numbers are in waltz (three-four) time. A mainstay of European social dancing since the sixteenth century, waltzes were, by the mid-twentieth century, still immensely popular in Ireland and were a staple of evenings of céilí and ballroom dancing both. Because of their association with the past, this portion of a showband's repertoire was typically referred to as "old-time" waltzes, and their inclusion at a dance was an expected part of an evening's entertainment.

As performed by showbands, a significant percentage of waltz-time songs contained lyrics that make explicit reference to Ireland and, in doing so, further linked this dance rhythm to an Irish sensibility. Some showband waltz songs portray a specific Irish person, such as Brian Coll's version of "Give an Irish Girl to Me" and Dermot O'Brien and the Clubmen's recording, "Turfman from Ardee." Others nostalgically locate a place in Ireland, such as Frankie McBride's recording of "A Cottage in Old Donegal," and Pat Hanrahan and the Nomads' "Lough Sheelin." Still other showband favorites include Republican ballads such as Brendan Bowyer and the Royal Showband's hit cover of the Clancy Brothers' "The Croppy Boy" and Sean Dunphy and the Hoedowner's recording, "Black and Tan Gun." In this way, showband musicians layered explicit references to Ireland with a familiar,

Figure 4.14 Gene and the Gents, ca. 1964. *Left to right*: Dermot Doherty, Pete Watson, Paddy McDermot, Pete Creswell, Tony Gallagher, Gene Chetty, and Barry Scully. (Collection of Jimmy Higgins.)

old-time waltz rhythm—lyrical and sonic references that were both well understood and culturally significant to their audiences.

Showband audiences—jiving and waltzing couples both—responded to other musical cues. Most showband music is in major keys, a tonal strategy common to rock 'n' roll and pop in general and one that emphasizes the music's overall upbeat feel. In Western musical cultures, major keys largely signify optimistic and happy feelings in contrast to minor keys, which tend to suggest sorrow or difficulty. So prevalent are major key songs in the showband repertoire that a distinctive and somewhat peculiar subcategory of songs exists that juxtaposes these relentlessly perky keys with abjectly depressing and sometimes horrifying lyrics. Some of these songs depict alcoholism, child abuse, and neglect ("The Drunkard's Son" as performed by the Jimmie Johnston Showband); fatal airplane accidents (Brendan O'Brien and the Dixies' and Frankie McBride and the Polka Dots Showband's respective covers of the Everly Brothers' hit "Ebony Eyes"); and songs that recount revenge killings ("I Did What I Did For Maria," as performed by Brendan Bowyer and the Royal Showband, among others).

To add dramatic tension and musical interest, many showband songs begin in one key and, as the song nears its lyrical climactic moment, modulate up a step or more to a higher and brighter key. An admittedly unscientific survey of 135 song hits recorded by a number of showbands between 1960 and 1975 demonstrates that nearly 20 percent modulate up. The sonic effect is an unexpected and refreshing tonal shift that also forces the singer into a higher end of his or her range, thus heightening the emotional intensity and impact before bringing the song to its end.

The British Influence: Trad Jazz and Skiffle

Equally influential to the showbands and their audiences were the enduring fashions, sounds, and popular culture of Britain thanks to its proximity to Ireland as well as centuries of colonial and postcolonial domination. This cultural dynamic continued through the twentieth century, first with the repertoire as played by Irish sit-down dance orchestras and, second, by 1952, the ever-influential English hit parade.

One of the formative influences on the early showbands were the "trad jazz" (traditional jazz) bands that played a combination of Dixieland and ragtime music. Originating in the United States in the 1920s, trad jazz took shape in Britain around 1943 with pianist/bandleader George Webb and the band, the Dixielanders. A revival of British trad jazz coincided with the showband era: artists such as Humphrey Lyttelton, Chris Barber, Sid Phillips, and the famed jazz clarinetist/vocalist Acker Bilk and His Paramount Jazz Band were known for their virtuosic playing and their hit records which arrived in Ireland from the 1950s into the 1960s. By the mid- to late 1960s, however, showbands had largely turned their attention away from trad jazz. Showband saxophonist/agent Tommy Hayden recalls that the soloistic format of trad jazz, which included improvisation, was not appreciated by Irish audiences, who, he asserted, saw this type of playing as "egotistical": "The people, I suppose they'd just look at you and say, 'Full of his own importance.' And you were just playing over their heads. . . . And so, you didn't go down that road really. You kept on the popular fast lane" (interview, 2008).

The short-lived skiffle music phenomenon was also influential. Originating in the United States in the 1920s and then revived in the mid-1950s in Britain, skiffle musicians played both folk and "found" instruments (guitar and banjo as well as basses made from tea chests, washboards that were scraped and tapped with thimbles, and others). In addition to novelty songs, skiffle bands combined elements of jazz, blues, and folk music from England and the United States. Despite their short window of popularity, skiffle bands laid some of the foundation for British rock and popular music, proving attractive to future members of well-known rock bands such as Deep Purple, the Hollies, Led Zeppelin, the Shadows, and the Beatles. Many of these musicians were influenced by British skiffle singer/songwriter, Lonnie Donegan, a guitarist and plectrum banjo player who came to personify this upbeat musical style. Hugely successful on Britain's hit parade, Donegan's best-known song was the 1954 cover of American blues artist Leadbelly's "Rock Island Line." While Donegan had little knowledge of blues guitar (and, indeed, his guitar playing on some recordings of "Rock Island Line" is rudimentary), his vocals emulated a distinctive African American singing style so compelling that one reviewer noted that Donegan "really captured the spirit of the Negro singing" (M. O'D., "Record Reviews," *Limerick Leader*, February 6, 1957). Donegan's popularity in Ireland was helped along by the fact that he was born in Glasgow to Irish parents, a fact readily seized on by Irish media: a 1956 article in the *Irish Press* complicates genre, origin, and ethnicity by describing Donegan, who, "in the U.S. . . . is known as the 'Irish Hill Billy'" (Desmond Fisher, "Britain To-day," *Irish Press*, April 12, 1956, 7).

Skiffle emerged on both sides of the border around the same time as showbands when musical change and variety were in the air. One of the early songs in the Clipper Carlton's repertoire was reportedly their cover of Donegan's "Rock Island Line." In 1957, Van Morrison's first band, the Sputniks, played skiffle; showband-turned-rock guitarist Henry McCullough and vocalist Muriel Day also began their careers in skiffle bands. In keeping up with the constantly changing styles, some of the leading sit-down Irish dance orchestras in the mid- to late-1950s felt obliged to include a handful of skiffle numbers in an evening's performance. Paddy Cole played in the Maurice Lynch Band at the time and remembers some of the band's older musicians who, already irritated with the popularity of the emerging showbands, found the skiffle fad insufferable:

> When the skiffle craze came, it was really big here, and four or five of us would go out . . . and we'd do all the skiffle tunes. And this would drive those musicians bananas altogether because you were playing things like an old tea chest [with] the handle of a brush and that was known as a bass. And you were trying to get a musical sound out of it. And maybe you couldn't get a musical sound out of it, but it was visual. It was all visual (interview, 2007).

"Ireland Swings Like Nowhere Else Can"

By 1966, the showband era was at its apex. It was also the year that the Omagh-based Brian Coll and The Plattermen came out with their hit song, "Ireland

Swings," an adaptation of Roger Miller's 1965 British hit, "England Swings." Like many showband songs, "Ireland Swings" is upbeat, cheerful, and highly danceable and features a refrain that points to a modern and united Ireland, thanks, in no small part, to the ubiquity of the showbands:

> Ireland swings like nowhere else can,
> Swings to the sound of the big showband.
> Dublin and Belfast and village and town,
> Everywhere swings to the big, big sound!

At the same time, the song references an Ireland familiar to Irish audiences with lyrics that underscore the significance of locality and place, both rural and urban (villages, towns, Dublin, Belfast, Cork, and Limerick). The song also speaks directly to its young, male, working-class audiences:

> If your work is done and you want to have some fun,
> Maybe even meet someone you met and have a night you won't forget!
> Plan it right before you leave tonight, let me tell you where to go,
> Go, go a-dancin' no?

Young women showband fans are also the focus of attention here. If she's lucky, she could go to a dance and perhaps meet a nice boy and, potentially, the wonderful musicians themselves:

> There's no just sitting, not if things get warm,
> Trying to get an autograph written on your arm.
> Asking that a tune be played specially for you,
> Sitting talking to the boys, when the dance is through.

"Ireland Swings" ends with a plug for the Plattermen themselves, turning it into a musical marketing tool very much in keeping with the tenor of the showband industry and the times:

> Ireland swings like nowhere else can,
> Swings to the sound of the big showband.
> Big Season, Freshmen, The Capitol too
> Maybe the Plattermen's the band for you!

Ironically, "Ireland Swings," like most showband music, is played with a straight, almost march-like rhythm, with virtually no swing rhythm whatsoever. This detail is perhaps incidental in light of the song's larger message of Irish emergent modernity and the cultural moment that produced the showbands in the first place. Merging the new sounds of pop and rock from outside of Ireland with familiar elements of Irish performance culture, showbands translated, in a fashion, the popular hits from beyond Ireland to their local audiences, offering young Irish fans a taste of the world outside of their own. For the showband musicians, playing on a stage in front of audiences of hundreds, if not thousands, opened up the doors of possibility and of their own potential. The result was a music scene that quickly ignited into an industry, one that was market driven and unapologetically commercial.

Notes

1. Stuart Hall's now classic essay, "Notes on Deconstructing 'The Popular'" (1981), argues that members of the working class are not "cultural dopes"; they are not easily manipulated or entirely passive. This argument extends to the thousands of Irish youth——both showband musicians and their fans——who were fully aware of the origins of the music, actively chose to participate as musicians and as dancers, and, most significantly, found pleasure and meaning in the form as it pertained to their lives.

2. Derived from the popular American jitterbug from the 1930s, jive dancing is a partner dance with a defined leader and a follower. Jive dancers are in constant motion with lots of turning of one partner by the other. Jiving requires keeping one's feet entirely on or quite close to the floor and is at its best as a fast-paced dance. Like the Twist and other popular dances at the time, jiving brought to the dance floor a new sensibility of modernity from beyond the nation's borders.

3. After finishing a dance, packing up their gear, and starting their drive home around the same time at night, showbands often encountered each other on the road. Band manager/sound engineer Pat Maguire remembers these scenes vividly: "All bands have got the name of the band . . . on the back of their vehicle. You could be driving and if . . . a band [was] coming from behind and they see the name of your band, they probably roll down the windows. And they have got loads of eggs and they just slashed them, smashed them, off the windscreen. And the one rule was that you never put your wipers on. Because eggs [get] smeary and [then] you can't really see" (interview, 2009).

4. *The Irish Independent*, July 1, 2011. https://www.independent.ie/irish-news/indians-told-to-disband-by-pc-posse-26747510.html, accessed August 16, 2024.

5. A younger cousin to showbands, Country and Irish bands specialized by combining elements of country music with Irish song. The term originated from a 1969 album entitled *A Little Bit of Country—and Irish* by one of the most popular singers of the genre, Big Tom and the Mainliners (Maguire 2013b).

6. In response to the changing aesthetic of popular music that foregrounded a new electric sound, the Royal Showband and their contemporaries also made use of emerging instrument technology: electric guitar and bass replaced the acoustic guitar and upright bass and electric organ replaced piano.

7. With lyrics written by Roy Alfred, the music for "The Hucklebuck" was adapted by Andy Gibson, who, in turn, was inspired by legendary American jazz saxophonist Charlie Parker's 1945 tune, "Now's the Time." "The Hucklebuck" in the United States also set off a dance craze at the time of its release.

5

"Blarney Sounds"

Making and Marketing the Showband Industry

In 1962, Des Hopkins, a young jazz and pop drummer living in England, placed an advertisement in the *Irish Independent*'s dance band column: "Irish-born drummer. At present with English Dixieland. Requires position with Irish showband." Shortly thereafter, offers started rolling in:

> I got a reply from the Clefonaires Showband in Sligo, who offered me eleven pounds a week. I got a reply from Jack Browery's showband in Cork, who offered me eleven pounds, ten shillings a week. There was four or five replies. Anyway, I took up the offer from Dave Dixon's Dixonaire Showband in Clones, County Monaghan, who offered me a whopping thirteen pounds a week, and that was too good to refuse in those days. . . . So, my parents put me on the train with a bag and it was quite a reverse really, 'cause everyone at the time was saying goodbye from Ireland [and] going to England to emigrate. (Hopkins, interview, 2007)

Like many young Irish at the time, Des Hopkins was on the move—though as he notes, in reverse. With high unemployment throughout Ireland at the time, thousands of young Irish were seeking work in England and, to a lesser extent, the United States. But Hopkins saw a specific opportunity in Ireland: a booming showband scene in which a young but skilled drummer could make a generous living.

Des Hopkins' good fortune in joining Ireland's rapidly growing showband industry reflected the many social and economic changes afoot in

Ireland at the time—shifts that facilitated the emergence of showbands as an industry. In turn, the rapidly growing commercial showband scene itself generated new and much-needed work opportunities in Ireland. By contributing infusions of capital and jobs back into impoverished rural communities, the showband industry became part of Ireland's domestic economic growth at a time when the nation was turning away from decades of its formerly inward-looking, protectionist, and, ultimately, strangling economic policy.

Beginning in the mid-1950s, various initiatives and developments—domestic and foreign—were instrumental in growing Ireland's economy. One of the most personal and best remembered domestic developments was the rapid expansion of Ireland's hire purchase (buying on credit) industry, which for better or worse, encouraged consumerism among the working and middle classes. Around the same time, Irish political leaders looked abroad with a number of foreign investment schemes and trade agreements aimed at trade liberalization and facilitating industrial growth. There was also a concerted effort to expand Ireland's economy into a broader engagement with Europe, including efforts to join the European Economic Community, and to attract foreign direct investment into the nation. To this end, Irish industry leaders at the time aimed to rebrand Ireland as modern and forward-looking. The new showband scene offered just that: an ideal image of the nation as fresh, youthful, and charismatic. By the early 1960s, showbands and showband stars were, on occasion, pressed into representing Ireland's embrace of modernity, a vision that neatly characterized a nation that was reinventing itself after years of isolationism.

The showband industry itself stimulated the Irish economy through directly contributing to Ireland's brightening employment picture. In generating a bevy of jobs—conventional positions as well as those in response to the needs of a new industry—the showband scene strengthened local economies and put increasing numbers of Irish youth to work. In this way, the growing industry helped staunch the flow of near constant emigration of young Irish to the United Kingdom and the United States. The nascent showband industry also spurred the birth and genesis of Ireland's pop music recording industry, further contributing to job and economic growth at the time and laying the groundwork for future pop and rock artists.

Setting the Economic Stage

Historian Diarmaid Ferriter notes the prevalence of terms like "doom," "drift," "stagnation," "crisis," and "malaise" to describe Ireland in the 1950s.

Indeed, the exceptionally high unemployment and immigration statistics from this decade were indicative of a sluggish economy that Ferriter (2004, 462) writes "was eating away at Irish confidence like a cancer." Various historical factors contributed to this economic landscape. Beginning in 1922, partition split off the single heavily industrialized region that was centered in Belfast, leaving the Republic with very little industry (Bowen 1983, 90). Coupled with that were decades of overreliance on the United Kingdom for trade: in 1926, for example, 99 percent of all Irish exports were headed to the UK; by 1950, this figure narrowed slightly to 93 percent (J. Bradley 2004, 109). Nearly 35 percent of Ireland's top 115 companies were externally controlled, resulting in a full-blown balance-of-payment crisis as well as steady tax increases. In 1938, the Anglo-Irish Trade Agreement ushered in inward-looking, protectionist economic policies that restricted trade between Ireland and countries other than Great Britain. These policies established tariff structures that adversely affected industrial efficiency and curtailed Irish exports.

By 1952, there was very little industrial development, and after several years of stagnant national income overall, Ireland had the slowest economic growth than anywhere else in Western Europe (Ferriter 2004, 467). The discourse surrounding the economy was telling: in political scientist Tom Garvin's (2004, 171) view, "opinion rather than knowledge seems to have dominated much of the discussion; Irish elites, inexperienced in managing an economy, were unsure how best to go forward." Indeed, a 1960 editorial in a New Year's Day issue of the *Waterford Star* opines about the absence of generative policymaking by the Irish government:

> No nation can afford to come to a standstill in its efforts towards progress and perhaps the fault all around lies in too much talk and too little action. There is so much to be done, from housing the people in a decent manner to virtually attacking our economic problems, that in all phases of our national life the great need is for incisive and effective methods in tackling what obstacles may stand in our way. (*Waterford News and Star*, January 1, 1960, 6)

Along with this bleak economic landscape, Ireland had been submerged in decades of cultural isolationism largely put into place by the administration of then Taoiseach Éamon de Valera. In a now legendary 1949 radio broadcast, de Valera's vision of a provincial Ireland presented the country as a "parochial, rural, neo-Gaelic, and above all, Catholic arcadia" (Garvin 2004, 37). This was compounded by what Garvin argues was a result of a generation's worth of "massive, popular and satisfied, if not fatalistic, conservatism," experienced and enforced by leaders from the independence generation. Trade unions, businesses, parts of the bureaucracy, and the Catholic Church all largely defended and held in place the status quo and with it, a pervasive institutional conservatism that stymied new directions in domestic policy and reinforced antimodernist and anti-intellectual tendencies (ibid.).

The chronically floundering, underdeveloped economy and infrastructure, coupled with endemic unemployment, was challenging to populations throughout Ireland, and particularly to rural residents from the west and north. County Mayo drummer Mildred Beirne vividly recalls these years: "There was no jobs. You just simply left and took the boat and went to England and got a job there. There was very little education. There wouldn't have been money to send us to school. Once you left national school, that was it. . . . There was a lot of people that didn't have money for food. They didn't. That's why the boats were full going to England and going to America" (interview, 2007). Compounding the problem of high unemployment were the traditional inheritance customs specific to rural Irish communities, whereby the eldest son inherited the farm, leaving his brothers and sisters to either emigrate or look for scarce work. Saxophonist and showband leader Mick Wood had little choice in this regard: "Well, there wasn't any jobs to get. It was only people that were born on land stayed on land, some of them. And I didn't do anything on land whatsoever. . . . I was married to music all the time" (interview, 2007).

The psychological effect of what was often pervasive poverty was profound, remembers Cork showband musician Bob Kearney. "People's standard of living would've been very low. But it was also their expectations, so from that point of view it didn't bother them too much because everybody else was in the same boat" (interview, 2007). Kearney's narrative points to a population that was more or less resigned to its impoverished status. Indeed, historian Dermot Keogh (2004, 25) recalls these years in similarly personal terms and, specifically, the overwhelming sensibility of people "grimly accepting the status quo":

> Even in the fiercest years of my late adolescence, it never occurred to me that I could change anything. True, I knew I could change my personal circumstances, by getting out of Wexford certainly, and, if possible, out of Ireland as well, and I intended to do so at the first opportunity and did. But the society in which I grew up, and out of which I was striving to grow, seemed to me monolithic, impregnable, eternal. The structures of it appeared not man-made but the result of natural and inevitable forces before which the individual must bend or break. This feeling of impotence was endemic, I think. It must have been, for otherwise, surely, change could have come.

The perception of Ireland as economically and culturally stagnant was palpable, particularly to visitors in Ireland. In a 1958 essay in *The Capuchin Annual*, Katherine Edelman (1958, 54–55) records her observations of the Ireland she encountered during a return visit, after having immigrated to the United States some years before:

> Up to this time, we have said nothing about the shadow lying across the face of Ireland. Yet everywhere we went, its dark reflection was in evidence. It lay in town and village, and across the green countryside. The youth of Ireland were leaving their homeland by the hundreds; and so far, there seemed to be no known or sure way to stay their flight.
>
> We thought of things that could be done. American and English capital? A few of the Irish who had become great tycoons of industry in America coming over and starting the wheels of ingenuity to turn? Something like these might give the answer. The drive and dynamic energy of the Western world sparking and energizing the now listless Island; sweeping before it the lethargy, the "what's-the-use" attitude that seemed to prevail! If only this could be done, we thought, and without taking away the undefinable charm and sense of tranquility that was such a special and treasured part of the country!

Economist Liam Kennedy argues that despite the narratives that describe this discouraging climate, these years were also generative of economic solutions. He observes that it was "during the 1950s that the foundations for a decisive break with a mediocre past were laid. Investment in infrastructure and, even more importantly, a variety of institutional innovations, helped lay the basis for future development" (quoted in Ferriter 2004, 464). Many of the ideas for economic reform arrived in 1955 with the appointment of T. K. Whitaker to the post of secretary to the Department of Finance. Heralding an optimistic new era of economic expansion and planning, Whitaker's multifaceted vision was initially articulated in the 1958 white paper *Economic Development*, which served as the basis for Ireland's *First Programme for Economic Expansion* (1958–1963). Implemented by Whitaker and then-Minister for Industry and Education Séan Lemass (who, one year later, was elected as Ireland's taoiseach), the *First Programme for Economic Expansion* signaled a decisive shift from protectionist policies toward those that espoused free trade and underscored the nation's changing trade relationship with the rest of Europe. In addition to the explicit encouragement of foreign investment in Ireland, Whitaker outlined a policy of retrenchment with regard to existing practices as well as an emphasis on planning—an agenda that historian J. J. Lee calls "revolutionary in the context of Irish governance" (1979, 170–71; see also Lee 1989, 344).

Buying on the "Never-Never"

In line with T. K. Whitaker's initiative of economic development through planning was the government's increased regulation of Ireland's hire purchase industry. An integral part of Irish consumer culture, hire purchase enjoyed meteoric growth from the mid-1940s on—an expansion that took place against the backdrop of a lean Irish economy. Both a product of and driven by widespread poverty, the hire purchase industry promoted consumerism by providing the means to acquire goods generally, and, in some instances, the materials needed to earn a living in an era of little or no disposable income. For would-be musicians hoping to join the emerging showband scene, hire purchase often offered the only means for cash-poor young people to purchase instruments and basic sound equipment and potentially, a path toward upward mobility.

In one form or another, hire purchase had been well in place in both Britain and Ireland since the latter half of the nineteenth century (Ó Gráda 2006, 58–59). As a financial device designed to generally make possible sales in an underheated market, hire purchase customers paid an initial deposit for an item and followed up with weekly payment installments for a set period of time, along with significant interest charges. This arrangement was known colloquially as "payment on the never, never system," because it was often the case that it would take so long to pay for the item that the purchaser would never own it outright or that consumers who defaulted on their payments would never be out of debt. Showband singer John Kelly of Knock, County Mayo, recalls that, buying on the "never-never" often ended with consumers seeing the goods repossessed by the store owner—again, never ultimately owning the product: "[If] you never paid, probably [the store owner] came and lifted it" (interview, 2007).

Hire purchase plans were so integral to Irish consumer culture that people relied on them for purchases large and small. The industry itself generated local financial ecosystems, including a bevy of jobs associated with sales, delivery, and collection. Guitarist/singer Daíthí Sproule's father worked as a driver for a store in Derry. Sproule recalls that his father "was involved with bringing blankets and irons and stuff like that to people and then collecting the weekly money. . . . You know everybody lived on hire purchase which was paying by the week. Because nobody had any money" (interview, 2009). Given the nature of this industry, those who made a living by selling hire purchase agreements (and by doing so, indebting their colleagues and neighbors) were sometimes ambivalent about their work. T. J. Byrne, the longtime manager of the renowned Royal Showband, for example, worked as a hire purchase agent before he moved into the showband world: "It was a kind of an embarrassment to say that you were doing that kind of business" (interview, 2007).

By the mid-twentieth century, the number of hire purchase agreements had increased nationally so enormously that the Dáil and Seanad Éireann periodically debated bills to regulate this industry, beginning with the Hire Purchase Act of 1946. Aimed primarily at consumer protection, the Hire Purchase Act was further amended in 1956 and again in 1957, when the members of the Oireachtas addressed the nation's unemployment crisis and a concurrent credit squeeze experienced by Irish consumers.[1] Relaxing the credit squeeze, it was hoped, would expand spending and investment, create jobs, and stem the flow of emigrants. One of the ways to accomplish this was to address specific conditions that governed consumer credit in the form of hire purchase agreements. The result, by 1958, was a fourfold increase in the number of agreements overall, from a total of 64,000 transactions in 1938 to 242,000 in 1958.[2] The 1960 Second Stage Amendment of the Hire Purchase Act gave the government further regulatory control over the volume of transacted hire purchase business in an attempt to address and control the nation's balance of payments. This amendment also strengthened consumer rights, such as price transparency, more favorable terms of payment, and consumer protections in the event of nonpayment.

By no means was hire purchase a magic bullet for Ireland's economic woes and no credit industry is without its flaws and ethical issues. Among many concerns was that a significant number of hire purchase companies were British-owned and headquartered not in Ireland but in the UK, thereby creating difficulties in terms of legal oversight. More crucially, the considerable profits generated by the hire purchase industry essentially left Ireland for the UK, a concern articulated in the May 18, 1960, Seanad Éireann debates by Senator John B. O'Quigley:

> Quite an amount of the interest earned in hire purchase transactions flows out of this country to Great Britain where, to my own knowledge, some of the hire purchase credit companies—I do not know how many—have their headquarters . . . and for that reason, if for no other, the rate of interest should be controlled by legislation and as it appears to be possible to do so only by regulation under this Bill [Hire purchase Amendment Bill, 1957—Second Stage]. (O'Quigley, Seanad Éireann Debate, May 18, 1960)

In response to Senator O'Quigley's concern and underscoring the growing domestic financial interest in the industry, Minister for Industry and Commerce Jack Lynch (1960) responded that, in fact, Irish banks and companies were also jumping on the hire purchase bandwagon:

> Too much of this capital was leaving the country. The fact now that Irish banks and Irish hire purchase companies, as such, have been going into this business

> is, I think, an answer to such a complaint and the only effective answer. I think nobody will complain if Irish companies go into this business, and, if there is a profit to be made out of it, make a reasonable profit and retain as much of the profits at home for use in this country as is possible.

Senator O'Quigley (1960) also noted that the enormous profitability of hire purchase on a local level skewed the dynamic between shopkeepers and customers: "If a person goes into a shop with the intention of buying for cash certain commodities, the last thing certain shopkeepers want the person to do is to pay for the goods in cash. That person will always be advised to use the cash to pay deposits on a variety of goods, some of which he or she does not want."

Far from deterring individuals from acquiring goods, the full effect of the 1960 Amendment to the Hire Purchase Act quickly became evident throughout Ireland. José ("Joe") Fernandez, lead singer in the Dublin-based Barons Showband, emigrated from Goa, India, to attend medical school at University College, Dublin. Dr. Fernandez recalls the profound changes he saw in Dublin's urban landscape between 1958 and 1963:

> I used to live in University Hall on Hatch Street. And at that time, there used to be a nursing home and the only cars that one saw were the Rolls Royces or very large Jaguars belonging to the consultants who came to deliver children at that nursing home on Hatch Street. Apart from those three cars, there was nothing on that street. It started off as a very barren place, but after the advent of [amended] hire purchase, gradually the street started filling up with motor cars. And clearly, people had not all bought them with ready cash. (Interview, 2007)

Hire purchase agreements also paved the way for people to more easily consume popular culture. Working- and middle-class Irish used hire purchase to acquire radios, phonographs, and recordings. This was a boon for the emerging showbands: more frequent and wider distribution of music via recordings and radio broadcasts built audiences and spurred Ireland's nascent recording industry. By late 1961, hire purchase plans also helped Irish families acquire the newest form of media—televisions. With the inaugural broadcast of Telefís Éireann (the television arm of RTÉ), television brought the world into people's living rooms, arguably upending how the Irish saw themselves. In José Fernandez' view, access to this knowledge altered their expectations: "It made them aspire towards those material things that were either never looked for or taken for granted that one had to live without them. I have a feeling that that change in expectancy is what caused people to look for the better things in life, and it certainly served as a catalyst at that time, or a stimulus, shall we say . . . for people to try and improve their lot" (interview, 2007).

Television, in combination with the ubiquitous hire purchase plans that allowed easy access to material goods, contributed to a new and unfamiliar consumerism in Ireland. Viewed by some as selfish individualism, this emerging mentality evoked a degree of anxiety that, by 1965, warranted mention by then Taoiseach Seán Lemass. During a public celebration in Dublin of the Golden Jubilee of the 1916 Rising, Lemass opined that one result of the national emphasis on economic achievement was a growing materialism, an attitude that he believed the leaders of 1916 would not have understood (see Holohan 2014, 177–78).[3]

For aspiring showband musicians, however, hire purchase agreements often served as the only means of acquiring a musical instrument and essential sound equipment to begin or further their lives as performers. Music store owners seized on this: a 1956 advertisement for Pigott's in Dublin, for example, lists available stock (brass, woodwinds, percussion, and string instruments) and notes that "Friendly Hire Purchase Terms are available" (*Irish Press*, March 30/31, 1956, 10). Hire purchase agreements enabled the members of the newly formed Royal Showband to not only purchase their first instruments, but by chance, it also introduced them to their future manager, T. J. Byrne. Byrne had been hired in 1960 as a salesman for the hire purchase company Cotts of Kilcock in Kildare to cover the five counties of Carlow, Kilkenny, Wexford, Tipperary, and Waterford. Recalls Byrne,

> When [the Royal Showband] was starting, one of the lads wrote in for a guitar to this company. I got this inquiry from Jim Conlon for the guitar and I went to Waterford and was told he was rehearsing in a ballroom down there, the whole band was rehearsing. . . . They were young kids and they had a fabulous sound. When I sold [them] the guitar, I got another inquiry for a set of drums. And I went and I sold the drums and I happened to just say to them, "You're fantastic. You need to get yourselves a manager." And they said, "What's a manager, what's a manager do?" "He'll get you dates and publicity and get on the road." So I said, "Look, I wouldn't mind being your manager." (Interview, 2007)

Joe McCarthy ("Joe Mac") similarly relied on hire purchase to get his start in building what would eventually be a hugely successful career as a professional musician in the popular Cork-based showband, the Dixies. In 1954, when he was eighteen years old, Joe Mac recalls asking his father for help in buying a drum kit: "I wanted to get a kit of drums and my father said, 'Of course we'll have to buy them on the hire purchase,' you see. My father said he would co-guarantor or sign for them" (interview, 2007). The investment paid off almost immediately for Joe Mac, who owned his drum kit for all of one week when opportunity literally knocked:

> I started to drive the neighbors mad practicing in the front room of my home. And about a week after I got the drums, a fellow knocked at the front door and said, "Do you play drums?" I said, "Yes." He said, "Have you drums?" I said, "Yes, I have." He said, "Will you play with us next Sunday night?" He gave me the venue and he said, "We're playing from 8 o'clock until 11. And you'll get paid one pound." . . . I had to get the bus with the drums strapped onto my back and arrived and played!

Joe Mac's first gig as a professional musician underscores some of the realities of Irish life and culture in the mid-1950s. Like most working-class families at the time, the McCarthys did not own a car, and Joe Mac faced the Herculean task of getting onto a bus with a full drum kit. That accomplished, his pay of one pound for his first music job was quite good, given that a day laborer in Ireland at the time earned five to six pounds weekly. His initial investment through a hire purchase agreement eventually paid off handsomely and allowed him to get a start in what would eventually become a very successful musical career.

Hire purchase agreements also made it possible for emerging showband musicians to invest in sound equipment that was necessary in order to be heard in the new, larger ballrooms. But the initial investment was never enough: bands needed to continually upgrade their sound system to keep up with the constantly changing technology and remain competitive as a band. To do so, they often took out subsequent hire purchase agreements. Recalls guitarist Michael Coughlan:

> The equipment was starting to get a bit more sophisticated. You'd get away with what you had as long as you could, but then the band down the road got this new, better kit, like. And you were looking at it and saying, "Well, you know, we're starting to sound a bit dead compared to the way they're starting to sound." So you had to compete, in other words. So you went and you got your hire purchase . . . and got somebody to sign on a line for you and you know, your next six months' gigs were all [about] paying back. (Interview, 2007)

These investments, however frequent, generally paid off. Showbands of all stripes—professional, semiprofessional, and amateur—could see immediate or eventual returns on their hire purchase goods as there was plenty of work and as demand for music in the dance halls and ballrooms grew.

"This Phenomenal Showband Business": Showbands and the Brightening Economy

The success of the showband industry was tied not only to generative domestic economic policies but also to various international initiatives, notably Secretary T. K. Whitaker's program aimed at opening up trade agreements with countries other than Britain. In a letter to the Central Bank of Ireland in 1959, Whitaker took aim at Ireland's longtime protectionist policies, noting the "inadequacy of a policy of protection as a remedy for the problems of unemployment and emigration."[4] Shortly thereafter, the Department of Industry and Commerce was charged with examining the potential effects on Irish industry if Ireland were to join the European Free Trade Association. By 1961, the end of the era of protectionism was signaled with Ireland's first application for membership in the European Economic Community. While the application lapsed as a consequence of France's then-President Charles de Gaulle's veto in 1963, it did eventually lead to the 1965 Anglo-Irish Free Trade Agreement that allowed Irish industry tariff-free access to the British market. Historian Joe Lee (1989, 353) notes this Agreement was "less an end in itself than a further step in the direction of fostering Irish competitiveness for the beckoning opportunities."

What followed was Ireland's slow but steady economic turnaround: between 1960 and 1967, the economy started to grow at a previously unheard of rate of 4 percent per annum (Garvin 2004, 115). At the same time, Irish planners placed new urgency on expanding Ireland's tourism market and on attracting export-oriented industries. Indeed, between 1960 and 1969 alone, Ireland attracted more than 350 new foreign-owned companies (Walsh 1979, 32). A second bid to join the EEC in 1967 was again rebuffed by de Gaulle, but by 1969, his successor, Georges Pompidou, expressed his support. In 1973, Ireland gained membership in the European Economic Community, resulting in the opening of trade and markets throughout Europe as well as an increase in foreign investment in Ireland, among other benefits.

The growth of private enterprise was a driving force in stimulating Ireland's economy, a fact underscored by the April 1958 launch of the trade journal *Development, Agriculture and Industry: The Journal of Ireland's Economic Recovery*. An article in the *Irish Examiner* heralded this new publication, describing it as "lively and provocative, and sometime controversial" and quoting its publishers in their assertion that the journal had "no political or other connections or affiliations of any sort. It is independent of any organization" (*Irish Examiner*, April 24, 1958, 4). (That said, the *Irish Examiner* article also notes that the chairman of *Development* was, in fact, the president of the Irish Exporters' Association; one vice-chairman was "the worthy president" of the National Farmers' Association, and the other was the president of *Macra na Feirme*.)[5] The first issue of the journal was devoted to Ireland's cross-channel trade via "shipping position" in addition to "boosting, angling, our embryonic film industry, marketing agricultural produce, and steel production" (ibid.). Subsequent issues highlight Limerick as an industrial center and Cork's industrial development and economic prospects.

Figure 5.1 The Millionaires Showband, publicity flyer, ca. 1964. *Back row, left to right*: Joe Doherty, Penny Trent, and Gene Bannon; *front row, left to right*: Billy Doyle, (unidentified), Michael O'Brien, and Michael Conn.

By 1965, Ireland's brightening economy was reflected in the renaming of the journal to *Development: The Journal of Ireland's Economic Progress*.[6] The new title underscored the ongoing aim to attract foreign investment into Ireland and served as a positive public relations spin of forward movement: no longer was Ireland in "recovery," rather, the nation was enjoying "economic progress." This shift in perspective was neatly reflected in an advertisement in a 1965 issue of *Development* placed by the Industrial Development Authority (IDA).[7] Aimed at investors and young industries in England, Europe, and North America, the ad is explicit and direct: "Ireland wants new industry. Not the transferral of static industries—but the establishment of new or expanding industry from overcrowded areas such as South East England" (*Development*, no. 72 [June 1965]). Extoling Ireland as an ideal location for industrial development, the advertisement notes that the country is well placed geographically to serve both European and North American markets, boasts an extensive infrastructure and surplus of manpower, and has a reputation for excellent workers, high educational standards, and citizens with forward-thinking attitudes on social and economic problems. There are further incentives: new industries that act immediately are promised an exemption from income tax and corporation profits tax for ten years as well as nonrepayable cash grants.

If this invitation to lure foreign investment to Ireland was not convincing, then all the reader need do is turn the page to an article in the journal on how Ireland is competitive with other European nations, specifically West Germany. Entitled "this developing world—West Germany: excruciations of affluence," the article pokes fun at West German industry and changing consumerism as the nation emerged into a period of postwar growth and affluence (*Development*, no. 72 [June 1965], 14–15).[8] Accompanied by three cartoon drawings of a stereotyped jolly, corpulent German man, the article speaks to various successful (and failed) business strategies aimed to stimulate consumerism in the West German food, drink, and fashion sectors. The larger message here is that despite its fits and starts, consumer consumption drives economies and therefore materialism is to be encouraged, a value in place in West Germany and, ideally now, in Ireland.

"The Blarney Sound"

The rest of this issue of *Development* is devoted to Ireland's showband industry. While at first blush this may seem like an editorial non sequitur, it is, in fact, entirely logical: for Ireland, the showband scene was not only unique but also a vital new industry. And it was presented throughout the pages of this journal as exactly that—youthful, engaging, charismatic—in short, representative of a modern Ireland. The implication here is that this success would also be enjoyed by the new, international companies that the IDA was aiming to lure to Ireland.

By 1965, the showband industry was nearing its peak in terms of sheer numbers of participants and profitability and was hard to ignore. These successes contributed to the growth of associated allied industries, not least of which was a spate of new popular media, including the preeimnent showband magazine at the time, *New Spotlight: Ireland's Teenage Pop Magazine*. In the 1965 issue of *Development*, an advertisement for *New Spotlight* promoted its own advertising space and celebrated its reach and popularity: "Ireland has its own Big Beat Scene! Its own Pop Scene! The Showband scene. 75,000 Irish teenagers read the Irish Showband and Music full colour Magazine, *New Spotlight*, each month. This is an important market" (*Development*, no. 72 [June 1965], 28).

Singing the praises of the showbands and their versatility and sheer profitability is an article in this issue of *Development* by Barbara Byrne entitled "this phenomenal showband business." Here, Byrne quotes the manager of the Bandits Showband, who optimistically suggests that the well-known British "Mersey Beat" could one day be replaced by the "Blarney Sound." Detailing the showband industry's overall contributions—both real and potential—to Ireland's growing economy, Byrne describes the widespread media attention enjoyed by the top showbands and the sizeable profits earned by these bands and their managers/agents. Her article ends on an upbeat note regarding the potential of showbands that tour outside of Ireland and their ability to contribute to the national economy. Byrne (1965, 26) draws on historic and gendered symbolism to underscore the rebranding of Ireland as the nation moved into modernity: "The Showbands . . . are the modern Wild Geese. But with this difference. They are not fighting other people's battles this time. They *are* fighting to build up a modern, virile image of Tir na n-Og.[9] And they are not doing it at the public expense. In fact they are adding to the national income while they work, or should I say, play."

In a similar vein is John Coughlan's article, "there's profit in the world of 'pop.'" Coughlan was the editor of the renamed *New Spotlight Magazine*.[10] Like Byrne, Coughlan emphasizes that showbands are "the most important [part] of the Irish entertainment industry" but that the term "showband" is, itself, outdated, considering that few, if any, of the bands at the time of writing included the fabled "show" in an evening's entertainment. He also describes their audiences—"thousands of young people get 'turned on' to the sounds. . . . Girls scream and even faint in the accepted world-wide fashion and the men watch and listen, nonchalantly but admiringly" (Coughlan 1965, 27, 29)—and points to a streak of conservatism among showband musicians, particularly in contrast to the popular British Beat and rock 'n' roll bands at the time: "Showbands are probably the least maligned people in the 'pop' world. With their 'short back and sides,' respectable middle-class backgrounds and down-to-earth approach about the whole business being really just a way of earning an exceptionally good living, they have been 'accepted' as respected members of every community. They are the least offensive and at the same time probably the most entertaining type of 'pop' groups to be found anywhere in this world to-day" (ibid., 29). Coughlan is oddly more critical (perhaps realistic) and guarded in his estimation of the potential of Irish showbands. Indeed, accompanying his article is a photograph of the Beatles that bears the caption: "The fabulous Beatles (M.B.E.) are not exactly in the same category as most Irish showbands." Writing that the "rewards of success here in Ireland" far outweigh the possibilities for showbands that tour abroad, Coughlan concludes that while the showband craze may never "cross the Irish Sea or the Atlantic . . . it's keeping a lot of people happy in Ireland" (ibid., 27).

Figure 5.2 Joe Dolan and The Drifters Showband. Publicity postcard.

The rest of the showband coverage in this issue of *Development* consists of eight sidebar profiles, each celebrating a different professional showband—their domestic and international accomplishments, strengths, successes, and future plans.[11] Each is accompanied by a headshot of the band's lead singer, underscoring a subtle shift from what had once been the cooperative model of showband membership to a more hierarchical designation of the lead singer as bandleader (e.g., the Drifters Showband vs. Joe Dolan and the Drifters Showband).[12] Each showband has a half-page advertisement near their profile that includes a photograph of the entire band as well as promotional material and contact information for the bands' manager. The overall effect here is one of visibility and perhaps reciprocity: featured showbands benefited from the publicity and promotion in return for being part of Ireland's rebranding, at least in this journal, as a modern, business-friendly culture.

Working in the Showband Industry

Just as the improving Irish economy helped the showband industry gain momentum, the industry itself contributed to Ireland's continuing economic growth. It was a two-way street: for the first time in decades, an uptick in job opportunities offered young Irish options apart from emigration.[13] With disposable incomes in their pockets, this swelling demographic flocked to the newly constructed ballrooms throughout Ireland—venues that could accommodate as many as 2,000 or 2,500 dancers at a time. The size and popularity of these events meant unheard of profits for the musicians, promoters, managers, agents, and dance hall owners. It also meant regular infusions of cash revenues into impoverished parishes on both sides of the border.

Crucially, the showband industry generated thousands of new jobs in both rural and urban communities; its financial impact was felt in all sectors of the service industry, beginning with the musicians themselves. During the peak years of the showband era, an estimated eight hundred showbands of all levels of professionalism performed throughout the Republic. Each band consisted of seven to ten musicians—therefore, a minimum of 6,000 musicians.[14] According to the 1971 Irish census, Ireland's population between the ages of 15 and 64 totaled 1,717,248.[15] Thus, nearly 0.4 percent of the overall population—or nearly 1 out of 250 people in this cohort—made their living or part of their living by performing in a showband. In addition, many showbands had a manager or agent to help with bookings and logistics and, while it is impossible to know exactly how many managers there were, it is safe to assume that at least half of the professional and semipro groups had someone other than a band member booking jobs.[16] Add to this one or more office and clerical staff for many of the managers and promoters.

And then there were thousands of jobs generated by the estimated 1,252 venues in Ireland and Northern Ireland—ballrooms, dance halls, hotels, and marquees.[17] Owners and/or proprietors maintained the venues; they were supported by a small number of staff—often family members—who set up and ran the dances, prepared sandwiches, and sold soft drinks. Venue owners also promoted the dances and sometimes hired publicists. Dances were regularly promoted by paid advertising in local newspapers, oftentimes large banner-type ads, thus contributing to the financial health of local publications.

The showband industry spun off work and generated financial resources in other areas. Showband musicians wished to look dapper and professional. To this end, they ordered custom-made matching mohair suits, putting local tailors to work. Some of the top professional groups went several steps further, sparing no expense to cement their image as modern entertainers. The Dublin-based Capitol Showband, for example, hired Dougie Millings, a London-based specialty tailor who catered to show business stars, including the Beatles. In contrast to the suits worn by other showbands, Millings's were subdued in terms of color but extremely well-tailored. According to Capitol Showband bassist Des Kelly, each suit cost ten times the normal price but "it was worth it; it was all part of the image" (interview, 2006).[18] This emphasis was typical: Gene Turbett, trumpeter in the Melody Aces, recalls that their

Figure 5.3 The Capitol Showband with Butch Moore. Publicity postcard, ca. 1964. (Photo courtesy of Paddy Cole.)

agent, Jim Aiken, sent them to another expensive Belfast tailor while encouraging the band members with the thought that "if you look the part, you'll make it" (Turbett, as cited in Maguire 2012, 77).

The financial impact of the growing showband industry was felt in other sectors. Showband musicians needed musical instruments, supplies, and occasional repairs done to their instruments—all of which brought business to local music store owners and their workers. (Along these lines, Barbara Byrne [1965, 25] in *Development* estimated that "the cost of equipping a seven-piece group with instruments alone is between £700 and £1,500. Amplification will cost another £1,000.") Inspired by the showband musicians they saw on stage, others caught the showband music bug and, according to Byrne, "the number of fans investing in instruments for themselves has led to a big jump in instrument sales." Musicians also needed vans ("showband wagons") that cost upward of £1,000 each to transport them to gigs and petrol to fuel those vans. All showbands needed publicity materials: photographs,

Figure 5.4 Dave Glover All Stars. Publicity postcard, ca. 1965. (Photo courtesy of Muriel Day.)

postcard-sized business cards, and flyers that advertised individual performances, requiring the work of photographers, designers, and printers. Given the sheer number of bands and the frequency of their performances, it stands to reason that the showband industry generated an enormous amount of work in many allied businesses.

Pop Cheirníní Gael Linn: Irish Language Showband Songs

Perhaps one of the most significant contributions of the showband era was the creation of Ireland's popular music recording industry, which up until that point, simply had not existed. Indeed, the few record labels in Ireland at that time were devoted largely, if not exclusively, to Irish traditional music and song. Most prominent among these was the pioneering traditional Irish music label, Gael Linn Records, which released its first albums in December 1957. Established some four years earlier in 1953, Gael Linn's aim from the start was to "restore and renew the Irish language . . . in a society devastated by poverty, emigration and a kind of generalised cultural hopelessness, in which the Irish language had lamentably fallen into general disuse and, moreover, become associated more with want than with wealth."[19] Garnering national interest, Gael Linn steadily expanded its projects, notably the production and sponsorship of Ireland's first Irish language radio program on Radió Éireann. Gael Linn subsequently established Irish-language institutions and projects, including Irish-language schools, Irish-language theater and drama festivals as well as traditional music *seisiúns* and concerts, and produced the first ever Irish-language feature film, *Mise Éire,* with a music score by the renowned composer, Seán Ó Riada.

By the early 1960s, interest in Irish showband music was so widespread that even the staunchly traditionalist Gael Linn briefly seized on the genre. For one year, beginning in December 1961, Gael Linn released a five-part series of 45 rpm recordings—*Pop Cheirníní Gael Linn*—popular songs sung in Irish by such showband stars as Sonny Knowles and Seán Fagan (both of the Pacific Showband), Roy Donnelly (Johnny Flynn Showband), and others. Máire Harris of Gael Linn Records noted that the label's embrace of showband songs sung in Irish served both as a marketing strategy to expand Gael Linn's audiences and "to make the [Irish] language more accessible and attractive to young people."[20] This latter objective was helped along by the inclusion of Irish lyrics to each pop song printed on the back of the record sleeve. Because 45 rpm releases in general rarely provided song lyrics, their inclusion on these Gael Linn recordings made a clear statement of the label's larger mission of teaching and generating interest in the Irish language.

A December 25, 1961, article by Ken Stewart in the *Dublin Evening Mail* documents a Dublin press conference on the occasion of Gael Linn's release of the first recording in the *Pop Cheirníní Gael Linn* series T—a 45 rpm featuring Sonny Knowles singing "*Mí iomlán*" and, on the flip side, Johnny Christopher's rendition of "*Síúiuín.*" Writes Stewart, "The broad approach Gael Linn has adopted toward reviving the national language was indicated by the release of the first pop disk in Irish. Speaking at the Shelbourne Hotel, Dublin, the chairman of the company said: 'Believing as we do that Irish must find its place in all the recreational and other activities, we have issued more records of traditional music and songs than has ever been done before, and we propose extending the range considerably more. Now we want to cater for those interested mainly in modern international light music.'"[21] While Gael Linn's foray into showband music began and ended with these 45 rpms, the company's passing interest in the genre underscored not only the widespread popularity of showband music at the time but also its utilization in the promotion of other cultural projects, in this case, Gael Linn's Irish-language recordings.

The Birth and Growth of Ireland's Pop Recording Industry

Apart from the few Irish record labels dedicated to traditional music, virtually all of the earliest pop and showband recording prior to 1963 were made in England by Columbia (an American label) as well as the British labels—Decca, HMV, and Pye Records. By 1963, the executives of Pye Records recognized the financial potential of the Irish showband industry and set up shop in Dublin, diligently signing and recording mostly 45 rpm singles of many of the professional showbands. The following year, Belfast- and Dublin-based Emerald Records, owned by Mervyn Solomon, became the first major Irish record label to record showbands as well as the early recordings of Irish rock legends Rory Gallagher and Van Morrison. The Irish popular record industry steadily expanded through the 1960s and into the 1970s to include, among others, Major Minor (founded by Philip Solomon, Mervyn Solomon's brother), Release Records (Mick Clerkin, Jimmy Magee, and Dermot Hegarty), and other smaller companies devoted primarily to showband music, such as the Dublin-based Hawk Records.[22]

For many reasons, record sales yielded little by way of income for band members. In a 1965 *Spotlight Magazine* article, John Coughlan points out that while a handful of records had sold very well for the top three showbands, sales in Ireland rarely exceed a thousand copies.[23] Showbands were valued primarily for the excitement generated during live performances as they kept their audiences entertained and dancing; studio recordings minimized this lived experience and energy. Moreover, because the bulk of showband repertoire consisted of covers of existing hits, fans were more interested in purchasing the originals than the covers made by the showbands.

There were other reasons. "Many first records from the small bands have flopped badly," writes Coughlan. "Showband records have yet to be taken seriously by people outside of Ireland, as the material, on the whole, has been very weak." Nor was the quality of the recordings particularly good—Pye Records' products, according to Coughlan, were not "A-1." A pity, he notes, because making hit records could be the showbands' ticket to international success. That said, he concedes that Ireland's pop recording industry was still very much in its infancy, with the first showband records having been made only two years earlier and only half a dozen showbands having released more than one recording (Coughlan 1965, 28).

While the financial rewards of making a record varied from band to band, there were other reasons to record, not least of which was the possibility of the record selling enough copies to make the charts. For any pop band, a record that charts is a prestigious badge of success and generates excellent publicity. Because many of the showband recordings sold poorly, there are countless stories about how showband musicians and/or their managers would purchase hundreds of copies of their own, newly released recordings in an effort to artificially bump up their sales numbers so as to make it to the charts. After the bands made sure that the two sponsored programs on Radio Éireann—*The Hospital Requests Program* and the *Chart Show*—received copies, the question of what to do with the rest of these copies loomed large. Clipper Carlton bassist Art O'Hagan was the manager of the College Boys Showband in the late 1960s. He recalls that hundreds of the band's leftover albums often wound up at the bottom of the River Liffey: "Aye the charts! . . . Sent people 'round the shops, buying records. And you went to the Liffey and you see the whole frigging lot [thrown] into the Liffey! (Laughs). Until we found out that you could sell them back to the record company for so much. Then they'd get them back again (laughs)! It was the biggest racket I ever, ever imagined! [The] charts were meaningless! Jeepers" (interview, 2007).

The benefit of the practice of buying and then dumping records to inflate sales figures was short-lived, however, as it raised the number of sales for the charts only briefly. Dave Pennyfeather played drums in the Greenbeats and, by 1968, in the Real McCoy. In 1970, he worked for the Dublin-based record label, Hawk Records. He remembers that showband recordings were best used for record plugging. Pennyfeather recalls going to radio stations "with a bag of records in your hand and talk to the guys and pray that they would do you favors. . . . I've had a few thrown in the bin!" (interview, 2009).

The "Biscuit-Tin" Economy

In the end, the precise amounts of money earned and the overall financial contribution of the showbands to the Irish economy must contain a measure of conjecture. The showband industry was almost entirely a cash industry, and there are few if any detailed financial records left behind. Drummer Eamon Carr characterizes the showband world as a "black economy" owing to its wholesale rejection of receipts and nonpayment of taxes. He recalls how money was collected at the door of parish hall dances: "Inside is the priest with a collar on, and he's just taking, folding money, right? Like loads of it. And beside him, he's got a biscuit tin. It's probably only like a pound or ten shilling note or something, and it's all just going into this biscuit tin. The biscuit tin economy! And then that gets whisked away, you know? It's not like Ticketmaster we're dealing with here (interview, 2009).

Along these lines, promoters, managers, agents, workers, dance hall owners, and many musicians uniformly recall the showband industry as a huge moneymaker.[24] Even the younger showband musicians could earn generous

Figure 5.5 The Tropical Showband, ca. 1963. (Photo courtesy of Leo O'Kelly.)

pay. In 1963, fourteen-year-old Leo O'Kelly joined the Carlow-based Tropical Showband on guitar. Playing up to three nights a week from 9:00 p.m. to 2:00 a.m., O'Kelly reckons that he "must have been the youngest [player] in showbands at the time." Despite his youth, O'Kelly earned in those three nights what his widowed mother earned in a full week (approximately five pounds per week) (O'Kelly, interview, 2007). A portion of his earnings went toward his school expenses and toward supporting his family.

Better-known semiprofessional musicians worked similar hours but could earn more. Pat Lynch, vocalist in the Airchords Showband and in the second iteration of the Clipper Carlton, recalls that a semiprofessional musician could earn between eight and thirty pounds a week at a time when a welder, for example, would have earned around eleven pounds a week (interview, 2007). Professional showband musicians earned in the range of fifty pounds a week, and some could earn a great deal more. Eamon Carr recalls an occasion when his friend, the late Fran O'Toole, who was playing in a Beat band, got a lucrative job offer with the renowned Miami Showband:

> Well, Fran said, "The money is phenomenal." . . . It might've been something like eighty pounds a week at a time when we were probably earning, you know, ten pounds a week. But anyway, we were saying, "You're not going to do that are

Figure 5.6 The Raindrops Showband, ca. 1965. (Photo courtesy of Jimmy Higgins.)

> you? You're selling out!" And he said, "Oh, but the money is incredible. And I'll be more or less leading the band."
>
> And anyway, he took the job. And the headline on the paper, the press story that broke was "Young Musician Earns More Money than President de Valera." (Interview, 2009)

For some semipro bands, playing the showband circuit meant a huge investment of their time as well as capital expenditures on sound systems, vehicles, publicity, and the like. But unlike the top professional bands, they did not necessarily enjoy similar earnings. Brendan Mulhaire of the Raindrops Showband in Galway, for example, recalls that despite his band playing five to six nights a week (and seven nights a week in the summer), the band members "never made good money," in contrast to the promoters and the "top of the pile [that] would do well" (pers. comm., 2006). Moreover, among those musicians who earned legendary amounts of money, many failed to invest wisely or think toward the future. Paddy Cole notes that some former showband stars squandered their savings or suffered financial loss in the hands of ill-informed advisors:

> A lot of the showband musicians got ripped off because they really weren't great businesspeople. All they wanted to do was play music, they traveled a lot, all over Ireland and abroad as well. And they always assumed that somebody else was looking after their affairs. . . . But you'll always get wily people that will see that and move in and take advantage of it, you know. . . . But we thought the rainy day was never going to come. We thought this was there forever. And we never saw that coming and a lot of guys weren't prepared for it, and hadn't invested properly and hadn't looked after their finances. (Interview, 2018)

Looking Forward

Beyond the limited opportunities and vague horizons generated by decades of a stagnant Irish economy and high unemployment, the sounds and performance culture of showbands offered the young Irish a renewed sense of opportunity, ambition, and expectation. Domestic policies and trends paved the way for Ireland's growing showband music and recording industries. The showbands themselves focused the attention of their young audiences outward, away from Ireland and toward American and British popular culture, much in the same way that Ireland's political and industry leaders simultaneously looked toward new financial and trade partnerships beyond the UK and toward the rest of Europe. And for the musicians, the showband world meant not only the possibility of earning a living—and for many, an excellent living—but also the possibility of moving physically and psychologically beyond the boundaries of Ireland. Mildred Beirne recalls the excitement of her band touring and performing in England as well as simply crossing the border into Northern Ireland: "All we wanted was [to] go and play and be in Northern Ireland. And we loved it. It was different! I suppose it was so far away from home. It was an adventure. You were taken from nothing to the most wonderful things that could happen to you!" (interview, 2007). What emerged from this era in Ireland, recalls former Taoiseach Albert Reynolds, was a much-needed and renewed sense of hope and optimism: "We were very parochial. . . . But [the showbands] opened up the world for us, you know. It definitely changed the whole of Ireland, there's no question about it" (interview, 2006). Together with Ireland's changing economic landscape, the showbands, driven in no small part by a new generation of entrepreneurs, demonstrated that not only did the rest of the world beckon, but so did opportunities and new ways of thinking about one's role in it.

Notes

1. A credit squeeze is an economic policy that controls and typically reduces the general availability of loans and credit.

2. Jack Lynch, Minister for Industry and Commerce, *Díospóireachtaí Parlaiminte / Parliamentary Debates, Seanad Éireann* 52 (May 18, 1960).

3. National Archives of Ireland, Department of the Taoiseach, Taoiseach papers 97/6/159, October 9, 1965, as cited in Holohan 2014, 177–78.

4. T. K. Whitaker papers, letter dated December 14, 1959, University College Dublin Archives, Catalogue Number P175/50.

5. Founded in 1944 by Stephen Cullinan, the aim of *Macra na Feirme* (Stalwarts of the Land) was to provide young Irish farmers and other rural youth with training as well as social opportunities.

6. Like the subtitle of the journal—*the journal of Ireland's economic progress*—the use of lower case type in 1965 was a shift from its earlier typeface. Using lower case type was radical in its time and signified a progressive design aesthetic that was clearly in step with a modern Ireland.

7. Founded in 1949, the IDA was charged to research new industries and expand those in existence. By 1958, the scope of the IDA widened in the interest of creating new ways of thinking outside of existing infrastructures, as reflected in this ad.

8. "this developing world—West Germany: excruciations of affluence" focuses specifically on the ups and downs of the West German clothing, food, and drink industries. There are also articles on a campaign from the German Cravat Institute urging German men to buy more ties; businesses that are described as dangerous "novelties" and quickly go bankrupt; a checklist for West German bosses of all the no-win situations that they must deal with as authority figures; and a section that offers "a box seat to watch the transformation of German eating habits, and it's quite a show!" (*Development*, no. 72 [June 1965], 3'6).

9. "Wild Geese" refers to the Irish soldiers from the sixteenth through the eighteenth centuries who left Ireland to serve in Continental European armies.

That Byrne describes Ireland in terms of virility stands out in stark contrast to the historical construct of Ireland as female, which dates to the eighteenth century (Ingman 2007, 7). Byrne's regendering of Ireland here can be read as a post–World War II rethinking of the nation in terms of economic vitality, independence, and strength.

10. The showband industry also gave rise to Ireland's early popular music print media with *Spotlight Magazine* being the most significant magazine in this emerging industry. Billing itself as "Ireland's No. 1 Young Entertainment Weekly," *Spotlight* started out as a monthly publication in April 1963, moved to a weekly format in May 1967, and, over the years, was renamed *New Spotlight* and then *Starlight*. By 1973, *Spotlight* reported weekly sales of over forty-seven thousand copies (Irish-Showbands.com, accessed May 10, 2016, http://www.irish-showbands.com/spotlightcovers.htm).

11. The featured showbands include Roly Daniels/the Memphis Showband, the Drifters Showband, the Kamels, Butch Moore and the Capitol Showband, Miami Showband, the Cadets, Derek and the Freshmen, and the Airchords Showband.

12. Paul Maguire argues that this change from the cooperative model was a consequence of showband managers and agents who believed that it was easier to sell a band based on the lead singer's charisma. At that point, managers and agents had "wrested a large degree of control from the musicians who had created the industry" (Maguire 2012, 80).

13. The timing of the reversal of unemployment rates in Ireland was fortuitous for other reasons, not least of which were the concomitant changes in both British and American immigration laws that no longer favored western European migrants (see Miller 1996; Delaney 2007).

14. These calculations are conservative. The estimate of eight hundred showbands is based on an average suggested by many of the musicians, managers, and dance hall owners I have interviewed. Other sources bear this out. For example, Barbara Byrne's article "This Phenomenal Showband Business," in *Development*, estimates that, by 1965, Ireland had "over six hundred showbands, comprising about five thousand musicians" (25). In the same publication, John Coughlan provides a similar count: six hundred showbands comprising five thousand to six thousand musicians. Given that the showband era continued another ten years after this article was published, an additional two hundred showbands is, if anything, a conservative estimate, and there were likely more.

This estimate is also borne out by the fan-based website Irish-Showbands.com, which identifies 991 Irish showbands that were active in Ireland and Northern Ireland. The website lists each showband by name; a tally of these names brings this number closer to 1,600. Webmaster Gerry Gallagher notes that this latter figure may include some duplications and explains his criteria for inclusion: "We consider any band playing before 1970 a 'showband,' however, many of the showbands continued well into the 1980's sometimes as a pop or country band and we have listed them in those categories as well" (Irish-Showbands.com, http://www.irish-showbands.com/).

Some showband musicians, however, assert that these figures are exaggerated, particularly the number of professional showbands that performed full time. Paul Maguire (2012, 55–56) notes that these assessments are more qualitative than quantitative, that is, they take into account, rather subjectively, which ensembles were truly "musical"—an imprecise determinant at best—rather than the mere fact of the existence of bands that performed, whether frequently or infrequently, musically or otherwise.

15. The total population in Ireland in 1971 was 2,978,248. Of these, 931,200 were fourteen or younger and 329,800 were sixty-five or older. The total Irish population, then, between ages fifteen and sixty-four was 1,717,248 (Central Statistics Office, comp., *Census of Population of Ireland, 1971*, vol. 2, *Ages and Conjugal Conditions* [Dublin: Stationery Office, 1973]), 7, http://www.cso.ie/en/media/csoie/census/census1971results/volume2/A_C_1_1971_V2.pdf.

16. Gallagher's compiled list on the fan website Irish-Showbands.com indicates 414 showband managers/promoters.

17. Irish-Showbands.com home page, https://www.irish-showbands.com/ballrooms.htm.

18. Fastidious attention to appearance was the norm. Niagara Showband vocalist John Kelly recalls that the band had suits made for them with false pockets so that they "couldn't bring anything on the stage or put [the pockets] out of shape" (interview, 2007).

19. Gael Linn, "About Us: History," accessed May 13, 2021, https://www.gael-linn.ie/en/about-us/history.

20. Máire Harris, e-mail communication with author, July 7, 2014. The five Gael Linn recordings are "Mí iomlán" / "Síúiuín," performed, respectively, by Sonny Knowles and Johnny Christopher; "An bhfuil an fonn sin ort?" / "Bí Liom," performed by Sonny Knowles; "Olagón"/ "Fill," performed by Joe Lynch with piano accompaniment by Ian Henry; "Palabra d'Amor" / "Neilí Mhící Óig," performed, respectively, by Roy Donnelly and Seán Fagan; and "An Tiún Agus Tú" / "Féirín Nollag," performed by Seán Fagan.

21. Ken Stewart, *Dublin Evening Mail*, December 25, 1961. The press conference also marked the release of another album on the Gael Linn label featuring renowned uilleann piper

Seamus Ennis that, according to Stewart, had the distinction of being "the first album the company has issued by an individual artist."

22. Gerry Gallagher, moderator of Irish-showbands.com, has compiled an astounding collection of images of many of the small record labels. He notes that "unfortunately, most of the labels that issued the bulk of the Irish Showband era singles and albums . . . have gone out of business, or been absorbed by other companies and many of their back catalogs never made the transition to CD and are, for all intents and purposes, lost forever." See Irish-Showbands.com, "Record Labels (Archive to 1990), www.irish-showbands.com/recordlabels.htm, accessed April 1, 2016.

23. Coughlan (1965, 28) writes that the highest-selling showband record in Ireland by 1965 was the Royal Showband's "The Hucklebuck," which "held the No. 1 position in the Irish 'Top 10' for several weeks, and sold a phenomenal total of 30,000 copies."

24. Virtually everybody I spoke with noted the significant money made by promoters and agents in particular; when I interviewed some of these agents, they acknowledged making good money but were not forthcoming with precise figures.

6

Builders, Promoters, Managers, and Priests

Profiles of Showband Entrepreneurs

> These guys had to break into [and] create a form of market. They had to spend money building halls, had to run them. They were geniuses! I don't think anybody has ever given them credit for dragging Ireland out of the dark ages [so that] guys that would have been shoveling drains in England became stars. . . . I learned everything that I've learned about communicating from those guys, because their phrase was "the punter is always right."
>
> *Fr. Brian D'Arcy, interview, 2007*

"For a Dubliner, it was a matter of standing still," recalls showband aficionado John Doyle, "The bands came to the capitol. However, I did travel to dances in the New Arcadia Ballroom in Bray, County Wicklow" (pers. comm., 2006). Along with hundreds of other showband fans, Doyle was happy to go a distance to hear the best-known touring showbands. His trip was made easier by an entrepreneurial Dublin-based bus company that ably capitalized on the need for late night bus service:

> There was a good bus service to Dublin from the Arcadia. They were double-deck buses from what is now Dublin Bus. . . . The bus to town after a dance *cost twice the normal fare,* between Dublin and Bray.
>
> On entering the ballroom, one went to a booth for bus tickets. The closing time for this booth was 11:00 p.m. That was the time the numbers of buses were ordered, determined by the ticket sales. The Arcadia had a legal attendance figure of 3,500. At the end of a dance, on a night of high attendance, the ballroom was encircled by double-deck buses and more buses queuing to get into the circle. The circles of buses around the Arcadia always gave me the

impression of covered wagons, in western films. (Doyle, pers. comm., 2006, emphasis added)

High-priced bus service was but one example of the many projects put into motion by entrepreneurs who were quick to recognize the market potential of the showband phenomenon. With the rapid growth of this industry, there were ample opportunities for entrepreneurs of all stripes, the largest demographic of whom were young Irish men. Less visible and certainly not as well-known but equally significant were the Irish women entrepreneurs whose labors often went unrecorded and uncelebrated but who worked both behind the scenes and out front alongside their husbands and other family members. As a group, these individuals chose not to emigrate and instead, remained in Ireland, shouldering the risk of establishing new businesses outside of existing models.[1]

The best-known entrepreneurs recognized early a growing public demand for large social spaces to accommodate dancing. They designed and built ballrooms (sometimes entire chains), obtained essential licensing, and learned the art of promotion and publicity as they booked bands and planned events. The growing showband industry additionally saw the emergence of a new class of entertainment professionals: the agents, managers, and promoters who worked directly with the professional showbands, both locally and on tour. These include, most famously, the Clipper Carlton's Vic Craig, the Royal Showband's T. J. Byrne, Tom Costello, Tony Loughman, Jim Aiken, George O'Reilly, Tommy Hayden, and others who could earn substantial livings by promoting showbands and individual performers. Their efforts ultimately contributed to creating a star system among popular Irish musicians and promoters both, one that arguably has endured in Ireland into the present.

The entrepreneurial nature of the showband industry also extended to Catholic clergy, specifically parish priests. Their involvement in community music and dance was nothing new; indeed, it expanded on a practice that dated back decades to parish-sponsored dances that variously featured céilí bands and popular dance bands. Like the generation before, local priests recognized the potential of community-based showband dances to create social opportunities for young Irish in an effort to encourage them to remain in Ireland rather than emigrate. Yet there was also the undeniable fact that parochial hall dances, particularly those in impoverished rural areas, served as great fundraisers. Chronically underfunded parishes thus looked toward the frankly commercial nature of the showband industry and the regular cash infusions generated from dances to pay for basic costs of parish buildings, maintenance, programming, and other expenses. In embracing these benefits of sponsoring dances, many parish priests simply ignored the ongoing condemnations regarding popular music and dance regularly issued by Archbishop John Charles McQuaid and others in the Church hierarchy at the time. As a result, many parish dance halls became regular stops along the showband touring circuit. And while some parish priests certainly saw the sponsorship of showband dances as a way to maintain some level of control over morality and behavior in general—particularly in contrast to those held in public dance halls where parish priests held little sway—still others, most famously Monsignor James Horan of Knock, County Mayo, themselves reportedly enjoyed the music and the very social nature of the showband scene.

As a group, the earliest showband entrepreneurs, lay and otherwise, were forced to generate innovative solutions to the numerous novel—and inevitable—challenges that came with creating a new business model. At the same time, many followed the practice of prior generations of Irish business owners who drew on informal relationships with the immediate and extended community: indeed, many agreements in the showband industry were cemented with a handshake. What emerged was a new business model that carved out and solidified a touring circuit, ensured the financial success of dance hall owners and promoters, and kept showband musicians employed. Some of this was facilitated by the timing of domestic economic initiatives beginning in the late 1940s and gaining steam through the 1950s. Aimed at developing entrepreneurship in Ireland, these programs, at the very least, established a national tone that signaled to young entrepreneurs the possibilities of innovation that come with stepping outside of conventional Irish business practice.

Setting the Stage for Irish Entrepreneurship

The showband era coincided with the emergence of Ireland from decades of conservative leadership and cultural isolationism, an era where any impulse toward entrepreneurial creativity was all but stymied, argues Tom Garvin: "State enterprise looked patriotic, private enterprise looked selfish and greedy; an ideological mind-set that justified the crowding-out of potential entrepreneurs existed in the minds of many power-holders in Fianna Fáil in particular" (Garvin 2004, 170). This outlook began to change in the aftermath of World War II which coincided with soaring Irish unemployment and renewed emigration. One influential semi-state[2] initiative was the Industrial Development Authority (IDA), established in 1949 to foster domestic Irish industrial development and to advise the Irish government accordingly. In

1958, the scope of the IDA was expanded by then Tánaiste and Minister of Industry and Commerce Seán Lemass to include conducting research "with an explicit emphasis on entrepreneurship in the interest of creating new ways of thinking outside of existing infrastructures" (Garvin 2004, 173–74). By the early 1960s, the IDA's goals were further strengthened through Fianna Fail's developmentalist platform aimed at entrepreneurs, which was intended "to build up among younger people a culture of work discipline, hands-on capacity, entrepreneurship and management . . . [including] on-the-job training, experience, and education of a kind that, up to the fairly recent past, had not been given to large numbers of young men and (latterly) women, typically of Catholic and modest backgrounds" (Garvin 2004, 178). With an emphasis on kick-starting the economy, these initiatives contributed to a growing climate of inventiveness and openness that, in turn, stimulated young adults to think beyond the status quo. Young Irish entrepreneurs, particularly those in the nascent showband industry, thus combined a new model of doing business with older approaches that drew on community, particularly when it came to acquiring start-up capital, obtaining licensing and permits, and greasing the wheels of cooperation with local church leaders.

While a precise count of the total number of dance halls and ballrooms is nearly impossible, some estimates catalog a total of 1,200 or more in Ireland and Northern Ireland between 1955 and 1985. These include ballrooms, dance halls, marquees, lounge bars, parish halls, and hotels with ballrooms.[3] So robust was this growing ballroom industry by the 1960s that some promoters and owners of the new and largest ballroom chains became as well-known as the showbands that they hired. These included, among others, Albert and Jim Reynolds, the Lucey brothers in Cork, Dee O'Kane and Jimmy Hamilton's Adelphi Ballrooms in Dundalk, and mining magnate Con Hynes's Associated Ballrooms chain. With their near celebrity status, some of these entrepreneurs moved into positions of national political leadership, most notably Albert Reynolds, who served as Ireland's eighth taoiseach from 1992 to 1994.[4]

While the builders and owners of the large chains of ballrooms may have been the best known nationally, it was arguably the hundreds of other dance hall owners—those who built or managed a single, often smaller, venue—who played key roles in growing the burgeoning showband industry. A March 1956 article in the *Irish Press* summarizes, in the most celebratory terms, the vision and strategies of this growing group of entrepreneurs:

> The ballroom owners and managers are a level-headed lot. They watched the new trends; they saw the old dances—in particular, and to the regret of most of them, the lovely waltz—go out of vogue, they witnessed the rocket-like rise of popularity of the new styles. . . . They built new halls . . . and they took their time

> over them, for they expected them to last a long time. . . . They hand-picked the men and women who staff the halls. They chose people who like their work and do their best to make things pleasant for the dancers.
>
> Then the bands have to be chosen; and here no mistakes can be made. Not only are the Irish natural dancers, they are natural musicians, for the enormous demand of recent years for dance-band musicians has met with an ample response.

The most successful of these smaller-scale venues were strategically located so as not to compete with the larger chains of ballrooms. Those that thrived were conveniently located midway between two larger ballrooms; touring bands were therefore able to pick up another night en route from one larger venue to the next. As such, many of the smaller dance halls, particularly those in rural areas, served as critical nodes in the broader showband circuit. These dance halls also functioned as local community centers and their owners often assumed positions of prominence as civic leaders. For these proprietors, running a dance hall was often an extended-family affair, with their spouses and teenage children preparing sandwiches and selling soft drinks during evening dances.

One such dance hall owner was Seamus Gallagher, who built and ran the Ray River Inn in Falcarragh, County Donegal. His life story and contributions as a proprietor and, eventually, a community leader, parallels, in many respects, those of the better-known team of Albert and Jim Reynolds, who built and owned a famous chain of ballrooms throughout Ireland. Despite the differences of scale between Seamus Gallagher's and the Reynolds brothers' respective enterprises, their profiles as entrepreneurs in Ireland's popular music circuit are strikingly similar in terms of their staunch work ethic, leadership skills, entrepreneurial confidence, and sheer ambition.

Building the –Lands: Albert and Jim Reynolds

In 1954, Albert Reynolds had just finished his secondary school examinations. He was living with his parents near Roosky, County Longford, and working as a clerical officer at CIE, Ireland's national railway company. On the side, he volunteered for his local parish council as the organizer of two weeks of fundraising dances held under a marquee. Reynolds became quite good at organizing these dances. But by the end of the second year, the local priest told him that the parish no longer needed these fundraisers but, if he wished, Reynolds was free to take over the marquee dances and run them not for the Church but on his own.[5] Reynolds seized the opportunity: he had the skills, connections, and most importantly, could envision the commercial potential:

> Up to that, the only places where dances or céilís were being run belonged to the parish. . . . The [dance] marquees pointed to an opportunity that was there if you wanted to decide to go and try and develop it. So that's what we did. We set out to make it commercial. You know, it is a question of trying to make it successfully and make money. There was a margin to be made. (A. Reynolds, interview, 2006)

In 1957, Reynolds's older brother, Jim Reynolds, returned from Australia and New Zealand, where he had immigrated five years earlier to work in construction. Together, the Reynolds brothers set to building and branding their string of ballrooms, ultimately a total of fourteen, throughout Ireland. They had the combined skills to do this work as independent contractors: Jim Reynolds was a seasoned builder, and Albert Reynolds's prior experience running and promoting local dances, along with his growing list of contacts throughout the Irish business world, contributed to a successful business model.

The Reynolds brothers also drew on their family's background in the hospitality business. Their earliest model came from their father, John Patrick Reynolds, who, in the 1940s and 1950s, ran weekly Sunday night dances from his woodworking shop in Kilglass, near Roosky. These dances were modest, attracting audiences of one hundred and featuring four-piece popular dance bands. It was very much a family enterprise: John Patrick's wife, Catherine, served tea and sandwiches at the interval and their children, including Albert and Jim, were all put to work. Jim Reynolds recalls that it was always his father's ambition to build a larger venue but was stymied by the finances: "I'd have to be honest, I set out to do what he wanted to do but wasn't able to" (interview, 2008).

The Reynolds brothers began building a string of large, lucrative ballrooms across Ireland, all of which ended in the suffix *-land*.[6] Their first, Cloudland, opened in 1957 in Roosky. In contrast to the parochial halls typically found in the center of towns, the Reynolds brothers intentionally located theirs between two or three towns, thereby drawing dancing audiences from throughout the region—as far as twenty and forty miles away. In an era when mobility was comparatively limited—few people owned cars and young people typically traveled by bike—this strategy was enormously important, and the Reynolds brothers saw a handsome expansion of their profit margin. Part of this was due to the fact that young people from different parishes were delighted to mix, socialize, and expand their social networks well beyond the eyes of their elders and their local priests. Attending a dance some distance from home therefore came with a new sense of freedom from what many recall as the often stifling social restrictions of their small towns. Albert Reynolds remembers that this strategy alone amounted

Figure 6.1 Jim Reynolds, July 12, 2008, Longford, County Longford. (Photo by author.)

to "a social revolution in Ireland because it was a question of people moving out and meeting . . . you know, boy meets girl. And you could go down the marriages that came out of the ballroom business. I mean, it was there!" (interview, 2006).

The Reynolds brothers' ballrooms stood out in other ways. First, theirs were much larger than the typical parish or commercial dance hall at the time and could accommodate thousands rather than hundreds of dancers. Secondly, rural dance halls tended to be roughly constructed from inexpensive materials and are remembered by showband musicians and fans alike as "primitive." Summer dances, held in outdoor marquees and often in tandem with parish carnivals, were set up in fields that, during rainstorms, became legendary pools of mud. Albert and Jim Reynolds aimed to address both issues through modernizing and brightening their ballrooms and keeping creature comforts in mind. While some dancers and musicians remember the Reynolds brothers' ballrooms as a cut above the average dance hall in general because of their safer electrical wiring, nicer interiors, and better amenities, others, like Capitol Showband saxophonist Paddy Cole, recalls the new venues in more nuanced terms: "It wouldn't have been hard to be much nicer" (interview, 2007).

Albert Reynolds knew the value of publicity and the opening of their newest ballroom typically garnered nothing short of major, celebratory coverage. A 1963 newspaper feature on the opening of Jetland in Limerick, offers descriptions of a "floating dance floor of unique design," the "artistic use of colours in side walls, end wall, ceilings, rails, stage, entrance porch, pillars, etc.," the excellent acoustics ("no sound fading or distortion, no annoying echo or dead spots"), two snack/mineral bars, and a dancing area "framed in a raised sitting-out surround and is floodlit from concealed lighting at floor level." The article celebrates the Reynolds brothers' commitment to excellence: "In keeping with the Reynolds policy only top bands will be employed. Like all the 'Land' ballrooms the construction of 'Jetland' is substantial . . . nothing shoddy or gimerack . . . good solid masonry and joinery, first-class plaster and paintwork and the most up-to-date fittings" (*Limerick Leader*, July 27, 1963, 4).

Aside from their attention to ballroom construction, much of the Reynolds brothers' success stemmed from sheer persistence: "You had to take them chances, you know. That was it. Push ahead!" (J. Reynolds, interview, 2008). This is precisely what they did, despite a rocky start. Albert Reynolds recalls that the Longford-based Munster and Leinster Bank (now AIB) matched the small amount of money that the Reynolds brothers had to build Cloudland (Power 1990, 106). It was still not enough financing, and they faced serious cash deficits. Jim Reynolds recalls that this reluctance by Irish banks to fully finance the project forced him to rely on personal relationships:[7]

> A chap called Joe Quinn had Quinn Brothers Building Providers. And I had priced all the materials with him. I met Joe a couple weeks afterwards and he says, "Jim, are you going on with that job?" And I says "I can't, Joe." Up and told him about the bank, wouldn't give me no money. . . . And he turned around—and I'll never forget—he said, "Jim," he said, "You go on with the job," he says, "and when you get your money, I get my money." And I built whatever it was—thirteen or fourteen or fifteen ballrooms throughout Ireland and I bought all my material from him down the years. (Interview, 2008)

The Reynoldses used the cash flow from each newly operating dance hall to finance the next project. At the start of building a new ballroom, they introduced themselves to the local Garda and the parish priests. While this process generally went smoothly, there were moments of conflict, particularly with priests who had been running their own parish dances and who were understandably concerned about competing with the Reynolds brothers' newly built ballrooms. Recalls Jim Reynolds, they "didn't like that it was taking the revenue from them. 'Twas a bit thorny on them. [I] just said, 'Sorry,' but kept going, you know. That's the nature of the beast" (interview, 2008). The Reynolds brothers also negotiated with priests from adjacent parishes, as was the case with the 1959 construction of Roseland in Moate, County Westmeath:

> Moate was my first clash. We were digging the foundations. The priest arrived, [and] he said nobody was going to build a hall in his parish or in his town. So I says, "Fair enough. Father, I'll leave your parish altogether and go down to the other end of the town." . . . There was different priests down there, and they were Carmelites, and they were a lot more open-minded. And eventually he said, "No," he said, "You stay where you are, build your hall," that's it. Couldn't have been a better friend to me afterwards. (J. Reynolds, interview, 2008)

Building Jetland in Limerick brought its own set of challenges. Both the Church of Ireland and the Catholic Church opposed its construction and went to court to contest the granting of the required dance license:

> [The judge] granted the license to me. And when the court was over, I went up to the two ministers and shook hands with them. I said, "I'm sorry that this is the way you feel about things. But," I said, "if you ever want [to use] the premises, you're very welcome to it, anytime." It wasn't six months after, when we used to have to clean it out on a Saturday for a Sunday mass! (J. Reynolds, interview, 2008)

Once a new ballroom was completed, Albert Reynolds went into promoter mode—hiring bands and negotiating with local politicians, business people, and the clergy. He publicized the dances in ads in local newspapers, and, in 1965, in yet another stroke of entrepreneurial ingenuity, through his own national publication, the *Dancing News*. Edited by Jimmy Molloy, the *Dancing News* promoted ballrooms, showbands, and dancing in Ireland. One of the main writers was then twenty-year-old Brian D'Arcy, who recalls a chance meeting with Molloy, Reynolds, and "another great character in the band business, a [solicitor/song writer] called Eddie Masterson" (interview, 2007).

> *The Dancing News*, which was started by Albert Reynolds who, at that time, had 17 ballrooms and no notion of politics at all. He stopped me in the street in Dublin when I was still a student at UC-D and said: "You know all the bands, so write for me—I won't be able to pay you." I said "I'm not even allowed to read the paper [as a clerical novice] never mind write for it." But it was suggested that I write under the pen name of Hughie.[8] And I did that for five years. (D'Arcy, quoted in Sweeney 2017)

Weekly parish hall dances tended to begin and end early (by midnight) and were limited largely to local audiences. A priest often patrolled these dances, oversaw ticket sales and kept an eye on the behavior of young people. Indeed, there are many anecdotes about priests who roamed the dance floor, using a ruler to enforce a required distance between dancing bodies. At the newer commercial ballrooms, such as those owned and run by Albert and Jim Reynolds, not only could young people go out dancing more often—five or six nights a week—but, significantly, they could avoid the watchful eyes of the parish priest and presumably dance as close together as they wished. Clergy from the affected neighboring parishes were at the least unimpressed, probably irritated, and often challenged by the Reynolds brothers' dance halls:

> We extended the hours of dancing. It was opposed by some of the priests at the time, some of the parish churches, that the dancing shouldn't go beyond twelve o'clock. So we said, "No, not when people are traveling that far and everything. Ours was different." . . . So we looked for a certain amount of nights [that ended] at 2:00 [a.m.] and a certain amount of nights at 1:30. Certainly we weren't that popular [with local clergy], I'd say at the start, no. (A. Reynolds, interview, 2006)

Both Jim and Albert Reynolds remembered that their ballrooms were only as strong as the relationships they built with the community, their dancing audiences, and the members of each band. From the perspective of showband musicians, a job at one of their ballrooms was highly prized as the Reynolds brothers were well known for their fairness, decent pay, and hospitality, recalls bassist Barry Scully: "You'd get something to eat before you go on. And I remember, Albert, like, going around with the teapot. You know, very, 'Are ye alright for tea, lads?'" (interview, 2006). From the perspective of an entrepreneur and a business man, Jim Reynolds recalls additional benefits of kind treatment: "I feel that [the musicians] perform better, you know, if they're in a homey atmosphere. And we always tried that to keep them happy" (interview, 2008).

Building the Ray River Inn and Ballroom: Seamus ("the Wee Gent") Gallagher

On an entirely different scale, local entrepreneurs also seized the showband era moment as they built and ran a single dance hall, devised strategies to solve problems, and worked with community members to accomplish their goals. Seamus Gallagher's life story is typical of this type of entrepreneur. Born in 1926 in Falcarragh, County Donegal, Gallagher was six months old when his father left Ireland in search of work to support his family. The elder Gallagher immigrated to Philadelphia, found work as a boiler man in a hospital, and regularly sent his wages back to his wife in Falcarragh. Seamus wouldn't see his father again until he was nine years old.

Like his father, Seamus Gallagher was no stranger to hard work: his first job, when he was fifteen, was cutting peat in Muckish, County Donegal. A year later, he joined thousands of other laborers and immigrated to Scotland to find employment. His first job was in Dumfries, where he signed on to work on a farm, digging potatoes ("tattie hoking"). He and the other workers were housed in a bothy (a small hut outside the main farm), sleeping three to a bed—"two up and one down"—with Gallagher, because he was small, always in the middle (Gallagher, interview, 2008). Gallagher subsequently worked for seven years at various jobs throughout Scotland and in London as a builder and bartender before securing work as a merchant seaman with the P&O Company, where he worked his way up to head barman on a cruising ship. In 1963, Gallagher married and became a father to his oldest son, Martin, who, like Seamus, wouldn't know his father until the elder Gallagher returned to County Donegal for good in 1965.

When he did return home, Seamus Gallagher found that in his absence, his wife, Chrissy Gallagher, had leased a pub and a bed-and-breakfast in Falcarragh and was running both. Of her entrepreneurial initiative (and his initial resistance), Gallagher recalls that her determination ultimately paved the way for his own: "[She] was a great businesswoman. She worked hard: she went into this bar business and she did it all up, the whole pub. I came back, and I said, 'I'm not staying here in a bar.' She said, 'Try it out,' so we tried it out for three or four months and that was the start of it" (interview, 2008).

By the mid-1960s, Ireland's showband industry was in full swing. Singing lounges—dance halls that sold alcohol—were just coming into vogue. At the time, the only dance hall in Falcarragh was Cloughaneely Hall, a parochial hall that did not serve alcohol. Gallagher seized the opportunity: he purchased three acres of land in 1968, hired a contractor, and built the Ray River Inn: "I saw an opening, at that time, for a good lounge. [There was] nothing here! People thought I was mad. They thought I was mad! So did the family! It would have been the first singing lounge I suppose, in Donegal" (Gallagher, interview, 2008).

As part of his calculations as to what would draw audiences, Gallagher invested in the required two liquor licenses. He also saw an advantage to creating a more hospitable social space than the standard cavernous ballrooms that engendered the awkward dynamic of men and women who gathered on opposite sides of the dance floor, with men crossing the hall to ask women

Figure 6.2 Seamus Gallagher, Falcarragh, County Donegal, ca. 1960. (Photo courtesy of Martin Gallagher.)

to dance. Instead, the Ray River Inn was set up with individual tables and comfortable chairs circling a spacious dance floor. People could sit between dances and be served drinks by the floor staff. Apart from these spatial innovations, the Ray River Inn was centrally conceived as a dance hall, one that featured a formal stage and a large dance space. Recalls Gallagher, "I knew what I wanted: I knew I wanted to get artists in. I knew it would draw a crowd" (interview, 2008).

On opening night in October 1969, Gallagher was lucky to hire the internationally renowned singer Bridie Gallagher, who, conveniently, had grown up in nearby Creeslough, County Donegal. Gambling on the power of local pride as well as Bridie Gallagher's immense and widespread appeal as a popular singer, Seamus Gallagher took yet another entrepreneurial risk:

> I knew I would get the Creeslough crowd to come to see her. And I put a cover charge on. I was the first lounge in Donegal to put a cover charge on. People

> had a lot of controversy about it, they said they wouldn't pay coming in. And I thought, "Well, it's sink or swim," that's the way it was. I put on three shillings at the door, that would be fifteen pence. That was my first cover charge. (Interview, 2008)

Opening night was unpredictable and Gallagher had to quickly pivot in response to the unfolding situation. To counter the challenges that often accompany innovation, Gallagher embraced the time-honored approach of reaching out to members of his community:

> At nine o'clock, I had nobody on the premises. At half past nine, a few cars came in and sat there. This fellow came up to the door, and he says, "You're charging money to get in here, Seamus?" I says, "Yeah," and he says, "It's hard to be paying money to come in and get a drink." And I says, "I tell you what, you come in for nothing and take your friends in with you." All I wanted to get was a couple of cars sitting in front of the building. That was at half past nine. At quarter to ten, I had Bridie Gallagher paid for! She cost me thirty pounds. And I didn't look back after that. (Interview, 2008)

Working as a ticket seller as well as the bouncer, Gallagher ran hugely successful dances every Sunday night and, during the summer, up to seven nights a week. With a capacity of 350–400 patrons, the Ray River Inn often was forced to curtail admissions to a dance as early as 8:00 p.m. in response to the crush of dancers at the door. But for every hurdle, Seamus Gallagher found a strategy. For example, local laws required that dances end by 11:00 p.m., unless the establishment served a meal; in that case, the venue could remain open an extra hour. Gallagher received permission to extend his hours by (mostly) serving meals of chicken in a basket. "It was an excuse really because they didn't know whether I'd served a meal, or whether I hadn't served a meal. So with the basket, some people had them and some people didn't have them, but it gave me that extra [hour]" (Gallagher, interview, 2008).

With its kitchen and dining area, the Ray River Inn grew into more than a dance hall and like many similar venues, served the community well beyond sponsoring dances. Friday nights, for example, were reserved for use by football clubs, civic groups, and other local organizations for meetings, benefits, and fundraising events. Other evenings were devoted to wedding receptions and social and life cycle events. As proprietor, Gallagher increasingly took on a variety of leadership roles in his community, from working as an auctioneer to undertaking:

> I might get the call at four o'clock in the morning: somebody was dead, and you'd have to get up and go. But then I was doing [funeral] meals: soup, chicken

and ham, potatoes with veg, tea or coffee and biscuits. There were maybe a hundred there for the dinner, all their neighbors would be asked, that was the pattern. Well, then they sat, when the meal was over, they drank all day, at the bar. And they were all people I knew. So I'd look after them and they looked after me. (Interview, 2008)

By 1976, Gallagher saw that business was declining. The showband era was giving way to the new discos that were becoming the rage of the younger generation. Feeling the exhaustion of working eighteen-hour days, Gallagher sold the Ray River Inn to concert promoter Tony Loughman, ultimately ending his work as an entrepreneur who took a chance on building a dance hall, providing entertainment, and, in doing so, created a social center for his community. The Ray River Inn was destroyed in a fire in the early 1980s.

Parish Fundraisers and Dancing Priests

Much like the commercial builders and promoters, parish priests played an important role in creating the showband circuit because parochial halls were often used as dance venues. As such, parish priests, despite the formal ongoing condemnation by the Church hierarchy, were often as entrepreneurial as the commercial dance hall developers. Their involvement was affirmed and strengthened by the timing of the showband era, which roughly coincided with the Second Ecumenical Vatican Council, beginning in 1962. In addressing ways to reformulate Church doctrine in contemporary terms, Vatican II aimed for better integration of Catholicism into the modern world. In response, argues Diarmaid Ferriter, the once outsized control of people's daily lives and beliefs by Ireland's Catholic Church gave way in the face of increasingly vocal opposition to long-held Church doctrine. A growing liberalism emerged in response to restrictions imposed by the Catholic Right, notably, a "growing awareness and acceptance of materialism that was outweighing attachment to tradition" (Ferriter 2004, 463–64, 607).

Indeed, one of the best-known religious figures in the showband world was Fr. Brian D'Arcy, who seamlessly combined his world of the priesthood with that of showbands. His fascination with the music began when he was a teenager; by time he joined the priesthood, he had befriended many of the showband musicians: "I was going to hear the music, and I was also the chaplain. And certainly at dance halls in Dublin, any of the guys will tell you, every night, they'd look down and I'd be somewhere in the hall. Some of them would come down and chat with me. I heard more confessions in dance halls than I ever heard in the church for those fifteen years!" (interview, 2007).

For local priests, particularly those in rural parishes, showband dances served as a means to generate much-needed funds. Revenues from dances went a long way toward supporting essential basic parish expenses such as general maintenance of buildings and schools, renovation projects, assisting local schools, and underwriting the cost of youth clubs, among other initiatives, recalls Fr. Cathal Stanley, who was a young priest in Kiltullagh, County Galway in the late 1960s. At the time, Fr. Stanley organized an annual carnival festival that featured, among others, the Athenry-based Swingtime Aces Showband. The revenues from this festival, combined with those from the regular dances that he also produced, supported his parish's expenses as well as nonessential but very welcome initiatives, such as maintaining a swimming pool for the children of the parish. Apart from this, Fr. Stanley recalls the social importance of these dances: "I think they were really more instrumental as a social thing for young people and [for] people to meet and get out, really. Because there wasn't a lot of outlets. You didn't have a lot of cars and transport and people couldn't go too far at the time and so on. So they were a good outlet for young people, you know" (interview, 2013).

The pleasure of dancing to showbands was by no means limited to lay audiences. Mildred Beirne of the Granada Girls Showband vividly recalls the nuns in a County Mayo convent delight in taking to the dance floor: "There would be about three hundred nuns in the convent. So every Christmas, we would play for free for the nuns. We used to love playing for the nuns! . . . They loved it then when we'd play the Irish [music] for them. And we'd play rock 'n' roll and we'd play waltzes and jives and we'd bring the nuns out and jive and they absolutely loved it!" (interview, 2007). Similarly, Fr. Stanley recognized that dances often provided a social outlet for clergy as well as an opportunity for them to meet and socialize with their parishioners. His superior, a ninety-one-year old parish priest agreed, as Stanley recalls:

> I said to him, "We want to run the dance" And he said, "If I was able to get up myself and dance, I'd be down [there] with you!" So he gave his approval. I could do some of the modern dancing, you know. Wouldn't have been great at it. Generally if you were there, you might go for a dance at some stage or some woman might come over and take pity on you and say, "Come on out," and bring you out kind of thing. And the good thing about it was a bit of exercise as well. You get out on the floor, and it kept you fit, anyway! (Interview, 2013)

While the rumors shared among the Church hierarchy and parish priests often centered around the possibility of rampant sin occurring at showband dances, Fr. Stanley's recollection of these years is somewhat more nuanced and realistic:

> There was an odd tumble in the hay, as they said, I'm sure. But generally, the dance hall days were a glorious era really, in the sense that people were very innocent and free, and great times and people really enjoyed them, you know.

Figure 6.3 Father Cathal Stanley, June 5, 2013, Portumna, Galway. (Photo by author.)

> There was these wakes and dances and stuff, and unfortunately, a lot of them at times finished up with a bit of drinking and a bit of carrying on and that kind of thing. But stories were told and so on and parish priests listened to these stories. Generally [the dances] were pretty harmless. (Interview, 2013)

Facing the Devil: Monsignor James Horan and the Toreen Dance Hall

A common trope regarding the evils of dance and the dangers of the dance hall involved an individual—typically somebody from outside the parish—who shows up at dances with the aim of seducing or otherwise luring a young woman over to the dark side. This image also served as a warning: if you attend dances, you do so at your own risk of encountering wickedness and a fall from grace. By 1954, this narrative shifted from the level of personal failing to the frightening possibility of a dangerous encounter with evil incarnate. In 1954, a widely distributed pamphlet published by a Limerick-based Redemptorist priest entitled "The Devil at Dances" reported that the devil was now frequenting dance halls. The pamphlet tells of a young woman who was asked to dance by a nattily dressed young man, who, upon closer inspection, possessed cloven feet. Once the young woman realized who she was dancing with, the stranger "vanished in the midst of a cloud of Sulphur smoke. The smell of Sulphur permeated the air in the hall" (Horan 1992, 102). The "devil at the dance hall," as it became known, took on a life of its own in communities throughout Ireland and even further afield in Britain.

On the evening of December 23, 1954, the devil was reported to have made his way to a recently constructed dance hall in Tooreen, a small village near Ballyhaunis in County Mayo. Tooreen Hall, as it was known, was built and run by the renowned priest and entrepreneur Monsignor James Horan. Well remembered for his skillful fundraising, Monsignor Horan's vision and dogged work ultimately turned Knock into a major Catholic pilgrimage site beginning in 1967 with the development of Our Lady, Queen of Ireland, at Knock Shrine. Monsignor Horan's efforts also extended to his very successful lobbying of the Irish government for a new regional airport, an initiative that ultimately resulted in the opening of Knock Airport in 1985.

Monsignor Horan's combination of business acumen and confidence served him well, particularly when it came to the potentially damaging rumor of the devil appearing at Tooreen Hall. Tom Neary was the chief steward at Knock Shrine and one of Monsignor Horan's longtime associates from 1963 until Monsignor Horan's death in 1986. Neary suspects that the rumor was the result of local friction between owners of the nearby dance halls:

> It was a nasty kind of story that was put out, and I maintain it came from the neighboring hall. Because [Monsignor Horan] was getting the crowds and they weren't and they tried to damage him that way.
>
> [Monsignor Horan] never dismissed [the story] but he knew exactly why the thing was put out, that they wanted to damage the hall and close it down, you see? Of course, the media got hold of it and they made a big, big story out of it. But there was absolutely nothing, no truth in it at all... he wouldn't subscribe to that kind of nonsense and he never did and didn't close the hall. In fact, it did twice as well after. (Interview, 2008)

In other accounts, Monsignor Horan accused Albert Reynolds of starting the rumor of the devil frequenting his dance hall. Indeed, there was often friction between Monsignor Horan and the Reynolds brothers regarding a nearby dance hall in Ballyhaunis that they leased and ran dances out of—one that directly competed with Monsignor Horan's Tooreen Hall. Recalled Albert Reynolds, "It used to drive [Monsignor Horan] mad. And next thing the story came out and he always blamed me" (quoted in Reilly 2006, 9). Ultimately, none of this prevented Monsignor Horan and the Reynolds brothers from conducting business together, recalls Jim Reynolds:

> I wanted the Clipper Carlton for a particular dance in [Cloudland], Roosky. I really wanted them. And Monsignor Horne had the date. So I approached him one night and I offered him two dates with the Clipper Carlton if he gave me that particular date, but he wouldn't budge. He was like pure iron: he was

Figure 6.4 Monsignor James Horan at the official opening of Knock Airport, May, 1986 (© Knock Shrine Archives.)

> fighting his corner, and fair play to him. We just belted away. Let the best horse jump the ditch. And he won and we won some, you know. But I have great admiration for the man, you know. He was a fantastic man, give him his due. (Interview, 2007)

Early on, Monsignor Horan set his entrepreneurial sights on the construction of a major ballroom and community center near Ballyhaunis, in County Mayo. In his memoir, Monsignor Horan writes that such an institution could address the problems of near constant emigration through providing entertainment, alleviating boredom, and improving the social lives of young people in his parish. The hall was initially planned for the town of Aghamore; ultimately, Fr. Horan's superiors moved the project to nearby Tooreen, where Fr. Horan worked as the parish priest. Also, there were no pubs in Tooreen at the time and, as Monsignor Horan (1992, 100–101) writes, "[The Church hierarchy] wanted the new social centre to be a distance from pubs." To build this dance hall, Monsignor Horan traveled to the United States in 1949 and, for nine months, fundraised in many of the Irish-American communities. He ultimately raised £8,000, a small fortune at the time. He returned and built the dance hall that opened in 1951. Recalls Tom Neary,

> [Monsignor Horan] would say that, you know, there has to be a little bit of a gambler in you if you want to achieve or if you want to do anything worthwhile. He would say, have a go. Take a chance. Most things work out. If something doesn't, forget about it and move on. He would not accept no for an answer. And he'd go always to what we called the horse's mouth, meaning going to the top and get your business dealt with. (Interview, 2008)

Monsignor Horan also understood the potential of popular culture generally and dances specifically to cement community bonds. And, unlike some of his peers in the Church hierarchy, Monsignor Horan saw no harm in popular music and dance:

> He knew the world and nothing ruffled him. He didn't mind: music for him was music. It made sense to have music because this was a social thing that people enjoyed, and he didn't go into the nitty gritty behind that at all. . . . He wasn't afraid of anybody. And if he believed in something, he would go through fire and water to achieve it. And he'd say, "You know, it's a good thing, there's nothing wrong with it. And if you don't agree with it, that's your business." (Neary, interview, 2008)

By all accounts, Tooreen Hall saw quick success and generated significant profits, most of which were reinvested in the community infrastructure, including bringing electricity to the parish in 1953.[9] Moreover, Tooreen Hall brought some level of prosperity to the surrounding community by generating much needed jobs. Recalls parishioner Mary Duffy:

> When Monsignor Horan was in Tooreen, there was no work in the area, absolutely no work. And his whole idea about building the hall in Tooreen was to give work to the people, which is what he did. There were women who worked in the cloakroom, there were women who made tea, and there were men who cleaned up the hall, men who stood at the door. And it just meant a little income for people in the area. And in every parish where he worked, he did the same thing . . . wherever he worked, wherever he was stationed, he saw the needs of the people, and he worked towards that. (Interview, 2009)

By all accounts, Tooreen Hall set a very high standard for dance halls and quickly became the stuff of legend. Monsignor Horan himself organized and was the compère for most concerts and dances, which, in his memoir, he writes, "gave [people] a different image of the priest from the one they saw on the pulpit . . . somebody very human who enjoys life, a joke, or a song" (Horan 1992, 103). Tooreen Hall quickly became a popular stop for sit-down dance bands and céilí bands, and by the late 1950s, it became a favorite stop for showbands as well, recalls Fr. Brian D'Arcy. "The bands always liked Monsignor Horan. You know, some of the people who ran the Clipper Carlton were not Catholics but [the manager] always maintained that no matter where he was in the West of Ireland, as long as Monsignor Horan was there, he went in to have a glass of whiskey with him" (D'Arcy, interview, 2007).

In addition to his entrepreneurial skills, Monsignor Horan's success as a community leader had its roots, in part, in his ability to combine conservative morality with socially progressive opportunity, a fact not lost on visiting showband musicians such as Dixies drummer Joe McCarthy: "Fr. Horan would keep an eye out at the dances and he'd make sure there'd be no close dancing—all night I think—and watch people going off home, that they weren't sneaking off in the back of cars. So he was kind of a go-ahead priest with some old-fashioned qualities" (interview, 2007).

Managers, Agents, and Drivers: Vic Craig, T. J. Byrne, and Tommy and Anne Hayden

The showband era introduced increasingly professionalized and entrepreneurial approaches to Ireland's nascent entertainment industry, including new layers of management between hall owners and musicians. Until that point, the duties of booking and management had largely been the purview of the bandleader. As the showband industry took shape, these responsibilities shifted to an emerging cadre of middlemen—band managers and booking agents—who, for either a regular salary or percentage of revenue from gigs, assisted bands with marketing, publicity, and the logistics of physically getting from one job to the next. As the profits from the showband industry expanded, bands often hired other workers, such as van drivers and roadies to facilitate hauling, setting up, running, and, at the end of the evening, tearing down sound systems, among other duties.

One of the earliest showband managers was Victor ("Vic") Craig, the assistant postmaster in Strabane, County Tyrone. Craig had long been friendly with the members of the Clipper Carlton who, beginning in 1952, hired him as their agent. Given that there was little precedent, no job description, and no expectations for band agents at the time, he enjoyed a wide-open field with which to make bold demands. Craig's tenure as band manager began with the question of pay scales and haggling with venue owners over the standard payment of ten shillings per musician, which Craig saw as wholly inadequate:

> [Double-bass player] Art O'Hagan stated that it was very acceptable, since he had to work a full week in his day-job to earn ten shillings. Arguing that "this was different," Craig offered to look after the engagements for the band. He announced to the organiser of the first of those engagements, that the fee . . . would be fifteen pounds rather than the prevailing rate of four or five pounds, in

> the knowledge that it was unlikely that an alternative band could be arranged at such a late date. The organiser agreed to pay the greatly increased fee with considerable reluctance but was heard to complain afterwards that "the band nearly robbed us." (Maguire 2012, 85)

Vic Craig essentially transformed the dynamic of risk and profit between dance promoter and band members. Instead of a flat fee paid to the band, as had been common with sit-down dance bands and céilí bands, Craig negotiated a percentage system whereby the band was paid 40 percent of ticket revenues, which soon became the model for other showbands. His entrepreneurial instincts were so successful, that, in combination with the band's sound and novel approach to entertainment, the Clippers quickly moved well beyond Strabane, touring in their custom-built bus throughout Ireland and Britain, and in September 1958, across the Atlantic for their first United States tour.

Given Vic Craig's success as their agent, the members of the Clipper Carlton recognized their need for additional support and so hired a manager, Maxie Muldoon. From 1954 to 1963, Muldoon traveled with the band, shouldering myriad responsibilities such as tracking ticket sales at the venue, calculating the percentages owed to the dance hall owner and to the band at the end of the evening, booking the hotels, paying the bills, and driving the band from job to job. Recalls Muldoon:

> The fellas used to sit in the front with me, smoking. You'd just have to open the window in the wintertime to see if Mickey [O'Hanlon] was still in the back!
>
> Money! Money! Money! Used to do percentages and all that all the time, you know, and somebody had to be there. So I used to carry the money, do the hotels, do the whole lot. . . . [At the door], I used to do 1,500 an hour at any price, just handing out tickets, bang bang bang! (Interview, 2009)

Similarly, the Royal Showband benefited from the efforts of one of the earliest band managers, T. J. Byrne. Like Vic Craig, Byrne was able to spot an opportunity and nimbly respond with strategies that drew on longtime relationships as well as his training in sales. Byrne initially faced formidable challenges: not only was the concept of a band manager new to Irish cultural and community groups, but both he and the Royal Showband were entirely unknown to dance hall owners at the time. Moreover, Byrne was marketing a novel and largely untested popular music that was only just starting to sweep Ireland. Undaunted, Byrne started with the associations that he knew best: the farmers.

> Just imagine now. I took on seven unknown boys, never heard of. I had to sell them, so the only way to sell them was to get 'em into venues that are already guaranteed a thousand or eight hundred or two thousand people. And by going after the farmers who were very huge—big dancers in every county and the agricultural

students in Dublin from all over Ireland, north, south, east and west—and there were maybe two or three thousand every night at the dance. And they went home and spread the word for me about the band. (Byrne, interview, 2007)

T. J. Byrne relied on his intuition, sales skills, and a healthy dose of self-confidence. He also had a good eye for entertainment and showmanship:

> "And you know what," I said, "I'm going to get four girls or five girls to do this onstage with you." And the boys [in the band], they didn't want to know about girls. . . . They just were seven lads and they were a success and they didn't feel like they wanted the girls, you see. I talked them into it anyway, and I got the girls.
>
> I got the girls together and I said, "Look, I want you to wear short, nice, not you know, but nice and short [skirts], and white boots and that." And when they came out on the stage the first night . . . it clicked! The girls actually helped build up the crowds even higher, because they wanted to go and see the girls onstage, you know. And I called them the "Hucklebuck Girls."
>
> It's just something that just comes to me: that'll be a hit, or that could be a hit. And I could be wrong but I've never been wrong. And so far things have worked out very right for me, you know. (Byrne, interview, 2007)

The Royal Showband's success spelled T. J. Byrne's personal success: "I could see that I was probably going to have a quite, what do you call it, nice living for myself and my family and that was one of the main things" (ibid.).

There were varying levels of business and financial integrity among showband managers and agents and more than one had questionable ways of supplementing their income. It was often the case that new managers were recruited to clean up the mess left by their more unscrupulous colleagues. A case in point involved the highly accomplished Omagh-based showband, the Plattermen. Initially managed by bandleader Pat Chesters, the Plattermen opted in 1965 to hire a professional manager—or, as trumpeter/arranger Ray Moore puts it, "that was the start of our many crooks who managed the band." He continues,

> [One] got us the bookings OK, but he was taking backhanders to get, because the band was so popular. The way he would do it was if some firm wanted the Plattermen for a dinner dance or something, slap down twenty-five quid, and he'll get you the band. On top of the fee. And then he got his cut off the band as well. [We had] no idea we were being skimmed [until band agent] Jim [Aiken] saw things were starting to go bad for us at one stage [and] he took us under his wing. (Interview, 2007)

"It Was Never a Burden": Women Entrepreneurs

There is scant record of the work of women entrepreneurs during the showband era despite the fact that many, like Chrissy Gallagher, were centrally

Figure 6.5 T. J. Byrne, Carlow, 2006. (Photo courtesy of T. J. Byrne.)

involved. Indeed, it was very common for Irish women to work in dance halls, as secretaries to agents and parish priests who produced dances, and as drivers, among other diverse roles. It goes without saying that women encountered similar challenges and concerns and, with just as much entrepreneurial spirit, devised innovative strategies to resolve the inevitable problems associated with small business ownership. Anne Hayden, for example, was the wife of musician and band manager Tommy Hayden of Greystones, County Wicklow. A working mother with young children, she was instrumental to the success of her husband's bands and his management agency.

Tommy Hayden played sax and clarinet in the semipro Artones/Jets Showband and, later, in the professional Nevada Showband. Like other semiprofessional musicians who were just starting out, Hayden worked full time as a motor mechanic, a skill that came in handy given the band's wagon near-constant need for repair. Hayden's full-time work, in addition to steady evening music jobs, took a toll on their family life, recalls Anne Hayden:

> It was a lonely kind of a life because, at that time in Ireland, we didn't have the road system we have now. So it took so long to get to the venues. Plus the fact that most of the guys had day jobs. Between them being at work all day and then come home in the evenings, if it wasn't rehearsals midweek, it was playing at a venue. So they literally were from bed to work type of thing, you know? The hours were very long so for the wives. It was pretty lonely. (Interview, 2008)

In 1967, Hayden took over the management of the Nevada Showband and, some years later, opened his own Dublin-based entertainment management company called T.H.E. (Tommy Hayden Enterprises). Anne Hayden was

Figure 6.6 Anne and Tommy Hayden, July 11, 2008, Greystones, County Wicklow. (Photo by author.)

central to many aspects of band booking and management, especially in the early 1960s before telephone service in Ireland was widespread:

> When he first took over the management, we couldn't get a phone installed in the house. It was like that at that time. You had to order a phone and you might not get it for six months or maybe even a year. But we lived on the main street in Greystones and there was a public telephone just across the street. That was our telephone for the business! We gave people that number and people would call us. The people in the news agents, who were right beside the public phone, would answer the phone sometimes, or just somebody passing. And they would just come and knock on the door and tell us there was a call for us. And that's how the management started. And I was busy because it was I who was there with the two children, naturally, and trying to take the phone calls and the messages and all that goes with having a band on the road with five people in it. (A. Hayden, interview, 2008)

Before the band turned professional, Anne Hayden was frequently called on to be the band's driver. Leaving their young children in the care of her mother-in-law, Hayden drove with her husband to the venues, both those nearby and those as far afield as County Donegal. She was frequently among the last to return home the next morning:

> [Tommy] would drive home in the car because he had a day job and get a couple of hours rest and then go to work again. . . . And sometimes he would arrive home at seven in the morning and literally, you know, have a change of clothes and bath, and his breakfast. And go straight to work. So, I would drive the wagon with the gear, the instruments, and maybe a couple members of the band who weren't working during the day.
>
> [Or] if they had a breakdown on the way home, which might happen at four in the morning, and it might be two hours away from Greystones, I would get a phone call and be asked to drive to where the breakdown was. And give the guys who had to work the car to come home. And I would have to stay with the wagon and have it repaired and then drive home. . . . When you'd have a breakdown in the middle of winter—and we had bad winters—you'd have to sleep then in the wagons. And you'd wake up at nine in the morning, maybe, and the frost was so thick on the windows of the car, the windscreen, that you couldn't even see out. (A. Hayden, interview, 2008)

Like many entrepreneurs, Anne Hayden recalls that despite the "hard work and long hours," she, her husband, and the rest of the band were inspired by the knowledge that they were involved with something that was new and different and had great potential. Moreover, for Anne Hayden, working with the showbands meant moving well beyond the routine life of her home and community:

> To me, it was very enjoyable. . . . I like driving anyway! And it meant, too, that you did a lot of things that your friends never got to do, like, even to travel to Killarney, say, or to Tralee. And I'd be just going down, literally, to drive this wagon home. For them, it was like somewhere exciting that they couldn't get to. I was just literally going there and sitting for maybe five hours, six hours sometimes, and driving a wagon home. But they thought I had the best lifestyle! (Interview, 2008)

As an industry, the growing showband scene not only ushered in a new era of popular culture but also new ways of doing business for both men and women. For the ballroom owners, promoters, band managers, agents, and others affiliated with the burgeoning industry, being part of it enlarged their perspective, whether it was learning the ropes of representing, negotiating, and booking a band tour; seeing other parts of Ireland; or going on tour to the United States or England and, in the process, envisioning one's own potential beyond the parochial. Their collective vision changed the way that popular music and dance was produced and consumed and, arguably, laid the foundation for Ireland's contemporary popular music industry.

Notes

1. The term "entrepreneur" was first coined and the concept advanced in a 1755 publication by the French economist and entrepreneur Richard Cantillon, who was himself born and raised in County Kerry in the 1680s. While there are some differences, subtle and otherwise, as to how entrepreneurship has come to be understood in the twenty-first century, it generally refers to an individual who organizes and manages any enterprise usually with considerable initiative and risk (Nelson 2012).

2. Specific to Ireland, semi-state enterprises are technically owned by the state but largely privately managed.

3. Irish-Showbands.com, accessed August 23, 2024, https://www.irish-showbands.com/ballrooms.htm.

4. Daniel ("Donie") Cassidy, a businessman from Westmeath, started out in 1963 as a saxophonist in the showband Jim Tobin and the Firehouse and then moved into entertainment management. He eventually became a *Teachta Dála* ("TD," or member of Dáil Éireann, the lower house of the Oireachtas, the Irish Parliament) and then, in 2007, a member of the Seanad (Senate) of the Oireachtas.

5. Fr. Brian D'Arcy observes that "[in] Albert's case, that must have been the first priest in history [who] said, 'We have raised enough money from in the church, so cancel that carnival. We don't need the money!'" (interview, 2007).

6. Albert Reynolds and Jim Reynolds' chain of dance halls included, among others, Barrowland (New Ross, County Wexford), Borderland (Muff, County Donegal), Borderland (Clones, County Monaghan), Cloudland (Roosky, County Roscommon), Danceland (Portlaoise, County Laois), Dreamland (Athy, County Kildare), Fairyland (Roscommon, County Roscommon), Hi-Land (Newmarket, County Cork), Jetland (Limerick, County Limerick), Lakeland (Mullingar, County Westmeath), Moyland (Ballina, County Mayo), Rockland (Borris-in-Ossory, County Laois), Roseland (Moate, County Westmeath), and Wonderland (Bawnboy, County Cavan). They also enlarged their stock of ballrooms through leasing venues elsewhere in Ireland.

7. Another strategy, such as "the brown envelope," or payment under the table, was useful to grease the palm of those who issued permits and licenses or who could otherwise resolve a sticking point in business negotiations and transactions. When I asked Royal Showband manager T. J. Byrne about "the brown envelope," he just laughed. Later, when I asked Jim Reynolds if these types of transactions involved actual brown envelopes, he explained, "That's right. This happened in political circles, you know. But I wouldn't be surprised at anything" (interview, 2008).

8. The pseudonym "Hughie" was borrowed from Fr. D'Arcy's father, Hugh D'Arcy, a well-known GAA athlete.

9. Electricity Supply Board, "1927–1978 Connecting All Homes to the National Grid," Google Maps, https://www.google.com/maps/d/u/0/viewer?mid=1R6t46z_YjERI_4pn-fFzVhWuCsU&hl=en&ll=53.32579648490526%2C-8.247642765890305&z=7. Accessed August 25, 2024.

7

"Aching the Notes" and Challenging the Industry

Negotiating Gender on the Showband Stage

In 1962, Mildred Beirne of County Mayo went out on her first music job with the Granada Girls Showband, one of the rare, if not the only, all-women showbands in Ireland. She and four other young women, ranging in age from sixteen to eighteen, drove with their band manager, Leo Beirne, to Killybegs, County Donegal. After a stop to buy sweets, they arrived at the dance hall and set up their equipment, had their tea, and then played until 3:00 a.m. Mildred Beirne sang and played the drums and then went out on the dance floor and danced the steps to the hit "The Hucklebuck."

Before the show, the Granada Girls received permission from their band manager to watch the fishing boats come in to the docks in Killybegs. There, the fishermen gave each young woman a bag of fish to take home with them: "Can you imagine the smell in the van coming home? But, for me, I had a bag of fish. . . . And when I landed home, Leo Beirne gave me a pound note. Like, that to me was heaven. I had money and I had food. And you know, from that day to this, I was never short of either money or food" (Beirne, interview, 2007).

Mildred Beirne's account speaks to a number of economic and social conditions in Ireland in the late 1950s and early 1960s. She lived at home with her mother, who, like Beirne, was also largely unemployed.[1] They survived on money sent home by Beirne's father and siblings, who, like thousands of Irish, had immigrated to London throughout the 1940s and 1950s to find work: "In the fifties and early sixties, there was no jobs. There really wasn't a job. You just simply left and took the boat and went to England and got a job there. There was very little education. I know, my older sister, she got educated. . . . She was the only one of eight of us that were sent to school" (ibid.). The opportunity to play in a commercial showband offered Mildred Beirne an unusual measure of security and financial stability for herself and her mother. Given Ireland's soaring unemployment rates, particularly in rural areas, Beirne, like many young people, had limited opportunities and impaired visions of her own potential—circumstances that were common in an era that, according to Albert Reynolds, generated a pervasive sense of "hopelessness" in the absence of opportunity and change (interview, 2006). Playing in a showband offered an antidote to what amounted to a social poverty born of economic deprivation and offered Beirne a glimpse of the broader possibilities as a young person.

Mildred Beirne was also lucky to have found employment as a musician, given that performance, generally, was traditionally the domain of men. Dating back to the preceding era of Irish dance bands and orchestras, women seldom appeared on stage. The few who did might be found at the piano or, more often, featured as the "girl singer." And as vocalists, their roles were often minimal: they usually alternated with a male vocalist, singing a song or a set of songs sandwiched between longer sets of instrumental dance music. By the 1960s, the new showband industry was still profoundly male dominated—from musicians, managers, and agents to the dance hall owners and record producers. What was different for this generation of aspiring Irish women performers was the changing attitude generally in Ireland regarding the role of women in the workforce by the early 1960s. Moreover, women showband singers could observe and emulate the performance practices and images of successful women artists elsewhere. Some Irish women showband singers looked towards Britain, for example, and the new generation of female pop stars there. Others were inspired by the women country music stars in the United States, who also served as models for Irish women as they joined showbands and sought to establish themselves as artists.

As such, the number of women in showbands steadily increased through the 1960s and into the 1970s. Breaking down the barriers to the stage, these artists necessarily developed strategies—personal, musical, performative—that enabled them to function in a male-dominated showband music world and, for some, to eventually move into positions of leadership, a dynamic that had been all but unheard of prior to the 1960s. At the same time, women showband players came to better understand their lives as musicians and stage artists and, in doing so, increasingly articulate boundaries and how they wished to be treated and perceived.

Challenging the Conventions

From the start, women showband players were faced with navigating their dual identities of being female and being a performing artist and, as such, straddled a liminal social space. Some developed a hyperfeminine persona in their presentation and image: their clothing, makeup, hairstyles, and comportment were largely viewed as the epitome of Irish femininity and up-to-date fashion. Others embraced a somewhat more conservative feminine image, one that resonated with rural expectations of womanhood. No matter the image, women in showbands on both sides of the border challenged the conventional roles of wife and mother in the private spheres of home and family while navigating the unfamiliar public domain of the masculine: on stage and in view.

This contradiction almost always came at a cost. Women showband artists universally contended with near-constant logistical challenges when touring in what had been an almost exclusively male circuit. They often navigated demeaning acts of disempowerment at the hands of their fellow band members and suffered from a lack of personal and musical agency. Many contended with some level of sexual harassment or, even worse, outright abuse by bandmates as well as audience members. Some also report significant financial exploitation at the hands of managers, agents, and record companies. On top of this were the ongoing challenges of how women artists maintained a sense of artistic self and their own identity both on- and offstage.

To this end, women showband artists developed an array of strategies that addressed many of the challenges of stage life. Almost all cultivated expertise in one specific music genre, embracing, for example, the image, repertoire, performance practice, and musical style of English pop icons or American country singers. Some were lucky to be befriended by their mentors and learn crucial business and artistic practices as well as how to best navigate an often sexist environment. For most, the images of already successful British and American women performers offered a vision of what was possible and modeled how independent and outspoken women could break free from the limitations imposed by gender. With these tools—and no small dose of courage—women showband artists developed stage personas designed to please their audiences while also insisting on being heard on their own terms.

Economic Change, Labor, and Gender

G. J. Barker-Benfield (1992, xxiv) demonstrates that with national economic change comes new definitions of male and female activity. Ireland's expanding economy in the mid-1960s was no exception, given the increased work opportunities for women. According to a 1973 report by Ireland's Economic and Social Research Institute, Irish industries that had traditionally employed women—textiles, clothing, and food—experienced significant growth in workers between 1961 and 1966. Women workers also swelled the ranks of Ireland's new and growing service industry (Walsh 1971, as cited in Russell, McGinnity, and O'Connell, 2017). By 1966, Irish women made up 25 percent of the total labor force and 35 percent of the nonagricultural labor force. Despite these increases, robustly traditional attitudes regarding gender roles skewed conservative, with a majority of male workers believing that women should earn a lower minimum wage than their male counterparts and that the increasing numbers of women in the workforce posed a threat to the "correct discharge of the duties of mother and wife" (Walsh and O'Toole 1973, 81, as cited in Russell, McGinnity, and O'Connell 2017, 400). These attitudes were not limited to men: 20 percent of Irish women similarly expressed overall disapproval of married women's employment. This stance was clearly evidenced in overall wages: a 1972 report by the Commission of the Status of Women documents an institutionalized pay gap for teachers and civil service workers whereby women workers received wages that were 20 percent lower than their male counterparts and Irish trade union agreements sanctioned pay rates for women workers at a fraction of what male workers received for the same work (Russell, McGinnity, and O'Connell 2017, 113).

Following the trend of Irish women entering the workforce in larger numbers were women artists who increasingly joined showbands. While their numbers were unquestionably small compared to those of men in the showband circuit, their status in the band shifted from the underutilized adornments of the "girl singers" in dance bands and orchestras to a more central role, both onstage and in their band's hierarchy. By the early 1970s, women performers had so successfully established themselves that a handful went on to lead their own bands with great success.

But these developments were gradual and, like most processes involving the politics and social dynamics of gender, cannot be viewed in absolute terms. Jazz scholar Sherry Tucker (2000, 2) writes that the stories that she collected regarding all-women jazz and swing bands "were far too complex to fit neatly into the heroic pattern [she] had anticipated." Like Tucker, I often heard contradictory stories. Some, like Mexicans Showband vocalist Tina

Figure 7.1 Tina (Quinn) Tully, ca. 1970. (Photo courtesy of Tina Tully.)

Tully, recall the showband era as a progressive moment in a male dominated industry when women could nevertheless share the stage and be seen as equals to their male bandmates: "It was [a male world], it was. But, sure, I loved that. I did. . . . Because they respected me, and that's one thing that's needed in a band like that" (interview, 2008).

More often, I was told very different narratives that bitterly recalled chronic objectification and marginalization of women as equal members of the band, particularly with respect to their musical expertise and performance skills. These dynamics reinforced the long-entrenched stereotypes and expectations of women performers as strictly ornamental. Recalls vocalist Sandy Kelly, "The male singers in those bands always saw the woman [singers], for the most part . . . [as] a window dressing. The woman was expected to dress sexy. Wear a short skirt, or, at those times you were showing your belly and stuff like that, wear platforms [shoes]" (interview, 2008).

Further complicating the perception and treatment of women in showbands was the fact that many grew into excellent singers and, in smaller numbers, instrumentalists and, as such, were able to draw increasingly larger audiences based on their musical and performance skills alone. In doing so, women showband musicians challenged the concept of their presence as mere "window dressing" and embodied what Sherry Tucker (1999, 75) argues is the "classic paradox of what it means to cross the gender division of labor." Tucker draws on an oral history with the late Vi Wilson, bassist in the Darlings of Rhythm, a post–World War II era all-women American jazz band. Wilson recalled the widely held assumption from male musicians that "woman musician, she can't play," a conundrum that women musicians cannot win. Writes Tucker (1999, 75), "Women know that what they do is considered a 'man's job,' and . . . they also know that if they do the job well, they will be said to be good 'for girls,' or that they 'play like men.'" Like their jazz counterparts across the Atlantic, Irish women showband artists routinely demonstrated that they could indeed play and sing and did so with great confidence and expertise. As they grew professionally, they developed more performance skills, further challenging these long-entrenched and damaging assumptions.

Supporting the efforts of women showband artists were their very receptive audiences, particularly the scores of young Irish women whose ambitions and desires matched their own. Historian Caitríona Clear argues that the stage was set in the years just after World War II when Irish women were rethinking what they wanted for themselves. By the early 1960s, Irish women were experiencing a changing set of expectations, including choosing to work rather than marry and thus heralding a "coming of age of a generation of women who wanted to change their lives" (Clear 2004, 136, 145). At this time, too, emigration slowed as newly created jobs put money into the pockets of young Irish women, resulting in their growing presence in public spaces, most notably, the dance halls. What these women typically encountered was an all-male showband, but increasingly, they may also have danced to those that featured a woman as a prominent band member.

Ultimately, a number of women vocalists made their mark in the showband world, including, among others, Eileen Kelly, Karen Black, and Maisie McDaniel, all of whom fronted various iterations of the Nevada Showband; Mary Lou Coleman (the Harvest), Belle Crowe (the Melotones), Muriel Day (Dave Glover Band), Amy Hayden (the Hoedowners), Terry Mahon (Jim Farley Showband), Patricia Pender (the Crackaways), Eileen Reid (the Cadets), Eleanor Toner (Hilton Showband), Penny Trent (the Millionaires, the Skyrockets), Tina Tully (the Mexicans), Carole Wallace (New Blues), and, somewhat later, the Irish pop trio Maxi, Dick, and Twink. Still other Irish women performers started out in the showband world but, by the mid-1960s,

Figure 7.2 Jim Farley Showband with Terry Mahon (vocals). (Photo from Jimmy Higgins collection.)

turned to country music: Philomena Begley, Sandy Kelly, Susan McCann, Maisie McDaniel, Nita Norry, and Margo O'Donnell, to name a few. A handful but nevertheless notable number of women performed in showbands as instrumentalists, including electric bassist Patsy Fayne of the Exciters Showband (and later Paddywagon) and the members of the Mayo-based Granada Girls Showband (bassist/Hawai'ian guitarist Anne Coleman, Stephanie O'Connor on mandolin and saxophone, accordion/Cordovox player Mary Morris, saxophonist Kathleen Maxwell, and Mildred Beirne on drums).

Starting Out: "Showband Looking for Girl Singer"

Like many of their male counterparts, the typical woman showband musician was often a teenager, as young as thirteen, at the time of joining a band.

She often had prior experience as an amateur singer, perhaps as part of a choir or local singing group, and may also have been an avid dancer who was already well familiar with dance halls. Some were literally born into the world of commercial music and performance, such as vocalist Sandy Kelly (née Philomena Ellis), who first appeared onstage as an infant in her family's fit-up, Dusky's Road Show: "I was carried on stage as a baby. For the parts in plays. And then from once I could walk, I was doing everything from Shirley Temple to assisting the magician, to [playing] child parts in the plays. It was a magical childhood!" (interview, 2008).

Other women found their way into showbands through responding to an ad placed in the local newspaper that specifically targeted a female vocalist. These typically required a photograph and then an audition, as was the case with vocalist Muriel Day (née Galway), who, at the age of eighteen, answered an ad placed by the Belfast-based Dave Glover Showband:

> [Dave Glover] had an ad in the newspaper, looking for a girl singer. And I sent him a photo and a letter with my [singing] experience. But Dave didn't even answer my letter, because he didn't like my photograph.
>
> [At the time], I was singing with a little [skiffle] band called the Saints. And in the meantime, Dave couldn't get a singer, and he was talking to this guy [who] said, "There's a wee girl called Muriel Galway and she's quite good." And Dave said, "I seem to know that name," but he said, "Where would I hear her?" So he came up to hear me. . . . And someone said, "Dave Glover's here to see you." And I said, "I don't want to see Mr. Glover. He was very rude to me, he didn't reply to my letter." So I didn't want to talk to him.
>
> But eventually I auditioned for him. I sang my first song and then the rest of the band would do their thing and then he'd get me up again. Sang the same three songs all night because that's all I knew. (Interview, 2008)

As the showband industry grew, bandleaders often kept an eye on developments in the larger music industry, both in Ireland and England, in an effort to recruit band members. Vocalist Tina Tully, for example, entered and won a local talent contest in 1964 in England, where she was working at the time. Her accomplishment was reported in the local papers back in her native Greystones, County Wicklow. There, Tommy Hayden, then the manager of the Mexicans, read of her success and sent her a telegram, asking her to join the band, which she did the following week (Tully, interview, 2008).

And still other women singers came into the showband world by simply being in the right place at the right time. Eileen Reid, for example, was at a Dublin dance in 1960 that featured the Blue Clavons, a well-known showband. Her friends urged her to take to the stage and sing a handful of songs;

Figure 7.3 *Left to right*: Tom Costello (Cadets showband manager), Jimmy Day, Jas Fagan, Paul McCartney, Eileen Reid, John Lennon, Brendan O'Connell, and Pat Murphy, Noel McGann. November 7, 1963. (Photo courtesy of Eileen Reid.)

she was a hit, and shortly thereafter, she joined the Melody Makers Showband. Reid went on to become the lead singer with the Cadets, the first showband to feature a female lead vocalist (Power 1990, 326). With her trademark blond beehive hairdo, Reid's remarkable career included being the only female showband singer to have a number-one hit in the 1960s with "Fallen Star" (Pye Records, 1964). This was followed by the 1965 hit "Jealous Heart," which made the British charts for one week, a rare accomplishment at the time.

School and church choirs also produced many women showband singers. In 1967, for example, members of the trio, Maxi, Dick, and Twink, were singing in their school choir when they heard of an opportunity to audition as back-up singers for the recently established Pye Records in Dublin. Maxi McCoubrey recalls,

> We would be backing the early, early showband records, and you never knew who they were, you just were told what to sing. So you'd come in and then they'd say, "Sing this," "Sing that," "Sing the other." Sometimes they'd be there, the band guys, sometimes they wouldn't, you'd just [do] overdubs. So every song that you can hear in the late '60s to the '70, we would've been on it, singing *ooh-pa-pas* and all of that." (Interview, 2009)

Eileen Kelly (whose stage name was "Kelley") also entered the showband world having been a member of her school choir in Cork City. After a stint as vocalist in a semiprofessional showband, Kelly replaced the popular Maisie McDaniel in the Nevada Showband in 1964.[2] While she was delighted to move into the very public and glamourous world of full-time performance and travel, Kelly was not allowed to sign her first agreement with showband manager George O'Reilly, who insisted on adhering to traditional expectations set for Irish women at the time. Instead, her father and her then fiancé signed her first contract:

> George O'Reilly actually brought [my father] to Dublin, and he told him that he was going to give me a three-year contract and what was involved moneywise. But the two of them, my father and [my fiancé] both signed the contract. They agreed with George. I think George was afraid that my boyfriend might kick up, and that he might say, "We'll leave in the middle of whatever." [George] showed [my father] what was involved and that I'd maybe put so much money away and all that for the marriage. And my father agreed then (E. Kelly, interview, 2008).

Eileen Kelly's experience underscores the expanded role of the showband manager who, like bandleaders, often exerted a strong hand in selecting and molding the image of the band and, in particular, that of the women singers. George O'Reilly spent considerable time developing and marketing Kelly's persona as both a singer in the Nevada Showband and as a fashion pop icon, encouraging her to look toward London fashions and pop stars such as Petula Clark and Twiggy:

> [The band] needed somebody who was, I suppose, glamorous. . . . There was a dressmaker associated with George O'Reilly's office. She made some stuff for me, and it was very elegant, very nicely done, very beautifully cut. Although [George] generally left it to this woman, he'd say, "Well, maybe if you wore something darker, that would kind of fit in with what the lads are wearing," and then if he saw something on you that he liked, he'd also admire it and say, something like, "Hmm, that does become you."
>
> George knew everybody! He was in touch with everything that went on in the business. And he could pick up a phone and ring anybody, the model agencies, you know. He had all the media onboard, so I was always going to the hairdressers, going from the hairdressers to lunch with the press, going from lunch, maybe to dinner with the press. Going from dinner, then maybe to have photographs taken with the band or without the band. I was always going, going, going (E. Kelly, interview, 2008).

Vocalist Muriel Day received similar guidance from bandleader Dave Glover, whom she would eventually marry. She recalls that she learned

Figure 7.4 Muriel Day with the Dave Glover Band, ca. 1967. (Photo courtesy of Muriel Day.)

much about musicianship and performance from him: "[Dave] taught me all sorts of stage presence because I didn't have any. He taught me to relax, first of all. And how to use the microphone at the correct distance so that it wouldn't distort. How I could take it off the stand and walk around, if I wanted to, rather than be standing still. Just, presence" (interview, 2008).

Out on the Road: The Delights and Challenges of Touring

Like the men in their showbands, women artists well remember the pleasure of singing and making music, the elation of performance, and the adulation of fans, as well as the exhaustion and tedium of near-constant travel. Unlike their male bandmates, however, women showband artists faced additional physical, psychological, and emotional challenges of being on the road. That the nature of performance meant that these women were also constantly in the public eye added layers of logistical and interpersonal complications to their working and private lives.

A universal concern of women showband artists was that very few dance halls and virtually no marquees provided changing facilities for them. Dance hall proprietors more often than not assumed that showbands were strictly male in their constitution and failed to accommodate women musicians. This mindset, recalls some women performers, went hand in hand with the dance hall owners' larger concerns of profits over the well-being and professional treatment of the visiting women musicians:

MAXI MCCOUBREY: The proprietors were making an awful lot of money but my complaint was that they didn't put anything back in. . . . I was offered one dressing room that actually had a stream running through it—a kind of outside shed where beer crates were stored. It was freezing cold. The stream flowed through it! You weren't treated like a human being. You travelled five hours sometimes to get to these places. When you got there, they just wanted to make the money fast. They didn't stop to think that if they made the punters and the artistes more comfortable, maybe the business would have lasted longer. It was all about a quick buck. (Quoted in Power 1990, 337)

MARGO O'DONNELL: When I came onto the showband scene, it was totally a male orientated world. Like there was no dressing rooms for a girl, there was no facilities for a girl, it was just man, man, man, man. And they didn't really accept us, and you had to fight all the harder. . . . If we were on the marquee, we changed in the barn, we changed in fields. There was nothing there for the women. (Interview, 2008)

EILEEN KELLY: I'll give you an example of what happened to me when we arrived at a gig. It was lashing, lashing, lashing, pelting rain. So we arrived in with our mini-bus. But we got stuck halfway between the marquee and the gate. And now, in this lashings of rain, in a field that's all muck and mud, and for somebody like me, who's wearing white boots and maybe a mini-skirt . . . the hair's all done, the makeup's all done, and you've got to get in there to get on that stage. So I was lifted. I was carried in and just plonked onto the stage. The place was packed with people, so we got the gig done and then we got back out and back on the road. . . . Oh, yeah, you had to put up with the good and you had to put up with the bad. (Interview, 2008)

There were other challenges, both explicit and implicit, that came with working in a man's world, not least of which was the frequent denigration that women showband performers experienced at the hands of their male bandmates. For some, there was a pervasive sense that at least some of these men simply resented their presence in the band. Margo O'Donnell recalls initially needing to prove herself as a bona fide singer before being accepted into the showband world. Once there, she discovered that her opinion was rarely, if ever, taken into account with regard to band performances or recordings, despite, as O'Donnell notes, that she was "the voice that would sell the product" (interview, 2009). Similarly, Eileen Reid recalls the strong and clearly expressed opinions by members of the Cadets when she was hired as lead singer: "When the boys found out, they nearly had a fit . . . [they] felt uneasy

Figure 7.5 Eileen Reid and the Cadets. Publicity poster, ca. 1970. (Photo courtesy of Eileen Reid.)

about having a female in the band. . . . I ended up marrying one of them, Jimmy Day, the one who definitely didn't want me in the beginning. He said he had nothing against me. He just didn't want me in the band" (quoted in Power 1990, 326). Once in the band, Reid found that musical decisions were strictly the domain of the male band members and managers. She points out that she had little agency in terms of repertoire choice and that she, like other women singers at the time, "had to do what the men in the band told them":

> None of [the women] had the say. The boys would say, "Here's two or three country numbers. We're going to do them. You learn them." I was being paid and that was it. I wasn't going to rock any boat.
>
> I love Barbra Streisand, and I wanted to do "Second Hand Rose." Could you imagine doing that in the ballrooms? And I brought that down, and they rehearsed it and all. And our manager, Tom Costello, says, "No, I don't think that song is [going to work]. They couldn't really dance to it." Really. It was nearly a show stopper. But I loved it. I used to love Streisand, but I said, "I don't mind." So they dropped it. (Interview, 2018)

There was also the very real threat of physical assault from male audience members as well as bandmates. All of the women I spoke with recalled the need for vigilance before and after shows and kept an eye out for bizarre or aggressive behavior by male fans. Some also reported sexual harassment by band members, including one woman who, under the condition of anonymity, recalled being literally chased around the dressing room by a male colleague: "He'd be trying to get me to kiss. And . . . the first time we stayed over [after a gig], him banging on my bedroom door, and stuff like that."

Onstage, many showband women report incidents of being mauled by fans rushing the stage. More than once, I heard about women performers literally being grabbed at while performing and hauled off the stage by an audience member. Eileen Kelly vividly remembers these frightening moments:

> There were times when it could be quite dangerous because when we'd have a certain gang of guys around the stage or whatever and I was pulled off the stage a couple of times and the lads just had to drop the instruments and get me back up there. Pulled off the stage. That's very, very frightening, you know? There'd be a certain amount of mauling going on. The lads immediately dropped the instruments and that, but you know, it's a pretty frightening thing, all right.
>
> But that happened a few times, but the lads just made sure it never happened again. They were always on the lookout for it and they'd just get the instruments and they'd say, "OK, ladies and gentlemen, sorry about that. We just had an incident here at the stage, but we're going to continue now." . . . The show must go on, oh, yeah. (Interview, 2008)

Offstage, the dynamics of women showband artists moving into what had been a nearly total male work domain resulted in women forced into positions of subservience and passivity. Sandy Kelly recalls that some of her bandmates in Fairways appeared to be threatened by her success with the release of her first hit single, a cover of Cliff Richard's, "Come Back Billy Joe," in 1977. She found that, in general, her bandmates did not welcome her musical ideas. Ultimately, she found it easier to communicate suggestions about repertoire and performance through her husband, Mike Kelly, who played bass and managed the group (Kelly, interview, 2008). This expectation of feminine docility extended to onstage demeanor: Sandy Kelly recalls that women showband artists "were expected to stand there and wait your turn, and come and sing whenever it was your turn. And smile and look cute. While the guy got out there and [got to] be Elvis and the leader and, you know, basically, 'get drunk, get laid, get paid.' Which they did every night, you know" (interview, 2008).

That male showband musicians were frequently promiscuous is well documented and many men I interviewed candidly acknowledged their own and their bandmates' sexual liaisons and extramarital relationships while on the road. Some wives of showband musicians—all of whom insisted on anonymity—spoke of the pain and humiliation caused by the widespread and public knowledge of their husbands' infidelities. A handful of showband players have gone public on this issue, notably Gerry Anderson, in his memoir, *Heads: A Day in the Life* (2008), in which he chronicles his and his bandmates' musical, sexual, and substance-fueled adventures in the early 1970s showband scene. Similarly, vocalist Dickie Rock of the Miami Showband details in his memoir, *Dickie Rock: Always Me* (2007), the fact of his extramarital relationships, one of which resulted in the 1974 birth of a daughter.

But promiscuity is strictly equal opportunity and by no means limited to male showband artists, recalls Sandy Kelly. "Some of the girl singers in bands did the same. . . . I used to hear stories and obviously I'm not going to name names, but they lived like the guys did" (Kelly, interview, 2008). And in 2015, Eileen Reid went public about her own multiple affairs over twenty years as a showband star (Brady 2015). Rather than suggesting "loose" or inappropriate behavior, it is perhaps more constructive to understand promiscuity among stage performers generally as a common byproduct of adulation and fame. For this reason, promiscuity by women showband artists while on the road is more equitably seen through the lens of gender parity, if not potentially a type of resistance to gendered expectations of women's behavior.

The Pleasure of Performance

Despite the challenges, women singers and instrumentalists report many moments of happiness associated with playing in a showband. Not only was there financial security from the substantial income they often earned, but showband women also found artistic, creative, and intellectual satisfaction. Philomena Begley, for example, recalls the satisfaction derived from performing: "I just loved getting on the stage and I just loved entertaining the people and, especially in concerts and cabaret and that. I would always get down on the floor and go around the audience, have a bit of *craic* and chat to them. Sit on their knee, do all the things and embarrass everybody . . . I was never one for sitting in the dressing room waiting for, you know, the big introduction" (interview, 2008).

Some made the best of the many hours they spent traveling together to gigs. Maxi McCoubrey, who has since gone on to become a radio presenter and producer, recalls the value of sharing a van with her male bandmates and having the opportunity to observe male culture: "I'm very interested in the psychology of people. So I would look on the different personalities and I would feed from the different conversations they would have and the thoughts they would have. They would knock me sideways at . . . how men think because women think so totally differently" (interview, 2009). Beyond that, McCoubrey recalls the constant social stimulation, the camaraderie of her bandmates, and her delight in connecting with the audiences: "It was a great meeting place for people and to this day, it's people I met there that remember you all the time. And part of my audience on radio are people who

Figure 7.6 Kelley, ca. 1963. (Photo courtesy of Eileen Kelly.)

say 'I remember you in the marquee in Drumlish,' and I go, 'Yeah, I remember it too'" (interview, 2009).

Other women point to the admiration of their fans and the opportunities that came with a life of performance.

> MURIEL DAY: I just loved it. . . . If you were a popular showband, when you got on the stage there were maybe 1,500, 2,000 people, and they were all standing close up to the stage, as close as they could get. All standing. And when you came on, you could have played for half an hour and nobody would have danced. They were just standing there applauding. That's magic! (Interview, 2009)

> EILEEN KELLY: My life opened up unbelievably when I came into this business. I met so many people and I did so many things and I was at all these receptions and dinners and pubs. I was a playgirl and a nocturnal animal. I was out and about at all the parties and all the dos. I really lived! (Interview, 2008)

In addition to the excitement of performance, women artists embraced the opportunity of playing in a showband as an excellent—and in some instances, the only—source of income available to them. The wages that even an amateur or semiprofessional could earn in a six-day week of shows allowed performers to support themselves and their families and, in the process, establish unprecedented levels of independence. In 1962, for example, Mildred Beirne was delighted to earn a single pound from her first job with the Granada Girls Showband. Her pay increased over time to six or seven pounds per night, and by 1965, she was earning, as a full-time band member, nearly fifty pounds per week, which she recalls as quite generous and which she spent almost entirely on supporting her mother and herself (Beirne, interview, 2006).

Women could earn substantially more playing in a showband than they might from jobs that were typically available to them, notably in the growing service industry, as clerks/typists, and in textiles, clothing, and agricultural sectors. As the new lead singer in the Dave Glover Band, Muriel Day performed seven shows weekly during the summer of 1960 in the County Antrim seaside resort town of Portrush as well as a Sunday show in Dublin. Day recalls that her starting weekly pay was ten pounds; her brother, in comparison, worked as a painter/decorator and was earning between seven and eight pounds per week, which was considered a reasonable salary (Day, interview, 2009). As a teenager and at the start of her musical career, Muriel Day's showband wages were objectively substantial.

That said, Muriel Day's wages were nothing close to those paid to her male colleagues in the Dave Glover Band. This became apparent when, some months later, Day's mother confronted Glover about her daughter's work conditions and pay:

> And she said, "What are you paying your boys?" And [Glover] said, "Twenty-five pounds." And she said "What are you paying my daughter?" At the time he was only paying me about ten pounds. (This is at the very beginning, and I got more as time went by.) So my mother says, "My daughter's not worth what your boys are worth, is that right?" He said, "They're musicians." And she said, "OK, that's no problem." And he said, "What do you mean, that's no problem?" And she said, "She's been offered twenty-five pounds to stay in Belfast as a resident [in another band]." Which I was, but I didn't want to go to that band; I didn't like that band. So he said, "OK, I'll give her twenty-five pounds a week." So it was because of my mother I got the money. And I thought, she should have been my manager! (Day, interview, 2009)

In contrast to the Dave Glover Band, the earliest showbands adopted what was known as the co-op band model, that is, the income from a gig was shared equally among band members after deducting expenses such as

Figure 7.7 The Keynotes Showband, ca. 1964. (Photo courtesy of Margo O'Donnell.)

sound equipment, petrol, uniforms, and the like. By the late 1960s, showbands increasingly began to move away from the co-op structure; instead, bandleaders or managers paid each band member a weekly wage, explains Muriel Day: "When I worked with Dave Glover, whether we worked two nights or six night, we got pay at the end of the week. . . . He did everything by the book. He took, you know, PAYE,[3] he took insurance, he took tax, he took

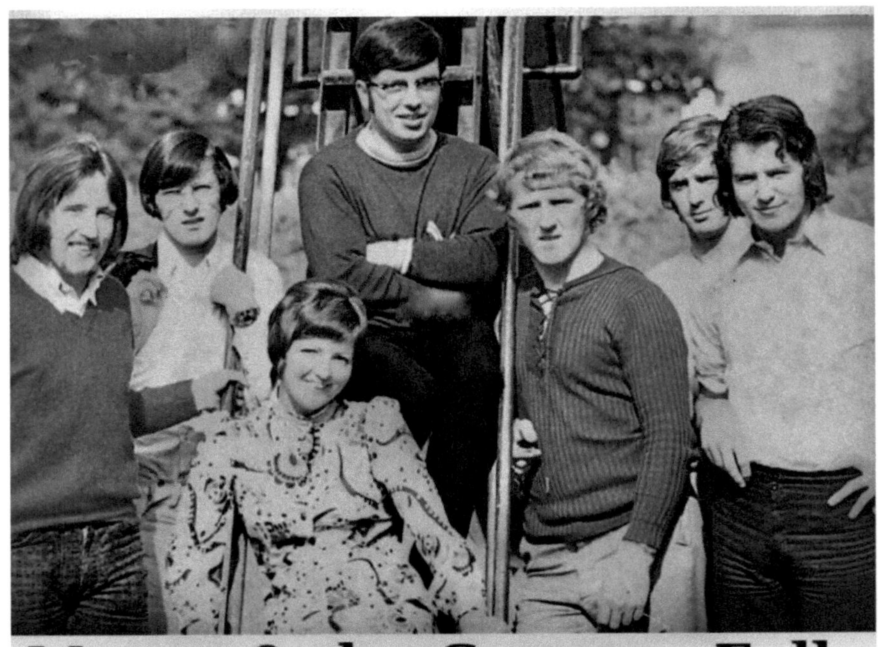

Figure 7.8 Margo and the Country Folk, 1972. (Photo courtesy of Margo O'Donnell.)

everything off it. And then at the end of it, whatever money we had [earned], we had no problem with the government" (interview, 2009).

While this type of arrangement was certainly convenient for band members, it arguably was not set up for an equitable distribution of profits and perhaps more importantly, put bandleaders and managers in positions of greater control, in contrast to the more egalitarian coop approach of the earlier showbands. By the 1970s, managers increasingly persuaded lead singers to either form new bands or rename the group to highlight the bandleader or lead vocalist. The reward for the bands was membership in a loose network of similarly involved managers as well as better promotion and guaranteed engagements. What was lost, argues Paul Maguire (2013b) was "the independence that had been the hallmark of the early showbands."

Such was the case with Margo O'Donnell. One of the first women to front a showband, O'Donnell began singing at age thirteen in 1964 with the Donegal-based Keynotes Showband. As they became better known, the Keynotes expanded beyond Donegal to venues elsewhere in Ulster, eventually touring Scotland and England. Despite the growing popularity of the band

and O'Donnell's delight working with a group of musicians whom she describes as akin to older brothers, she was compelled to leave the group when a Dublin promoter offered her significantly more money fronting a new band:

> I was sixteen when my father died [in 1968]. So we didn't have any money. But we were no worse than anybody else because nobody had a lot. I was offered in late '69, £100 a week and a car to take me everywhere. I knew I could look after the rest of [my family]. So I left the Keynotes . . . they knew that I had to go because of the family, but it broke my heart. . . . I moved to Dublin and then to Galway [and] I formed Margo and the Country Folk. (Interview, 2008)

"A Handful of Glamour": Balancing Gender and the Stage

Virtually every woman showband artist I spoke with saw herself first as a performing artist who happened to be female. This self-understanding contrasts with the dominant perception by audiences, bandmates, agents, and managers: that women performers are seen first as female and secondly, as musicians/performers (Davies 2001, 301–2). With society placing such an emphasis on femininity, sexuality, and appearance, the musical and performance competence of these artists, not to mention the many years they devote to developing these skills, are all but erased. Among countless examples of this from the Irish showband world is a December 1966 article published in the *Dancing Gazette* that features a photograph of Eileen Kelly held aloft by her new bandmates in the Big Eight and captioned "a handful of glamour."[4] The article describes Kelly first as "blond" and second as the "featured vocalist" formerly with the Nevada Showband. Kelly's many publicity photos further privilege appearance over musical skills as they present her as more of a playful fashion icon than a working musician.

In negotiating her role as lead singer, Kelly's strategy entailed a certain degree of accommodation and conformity, rather than an insistence on space to be both a woman and a performing artist: "When it's male-dominated like it was, you can still be yourself but you can give a little, as well. I was very good at becoming one of the boys" (interview, 2008). Like other women performers at the time, Kelly's approach of simply fitting in may have allowed her to flourish professionally but, in doing so, reinforced the very system that limited the role of women in the showband industry in the first place.[5]

Kelly's navigation of a feminine image in an otherwise masculine context generated its own narrative among fans and the press. The title of a *Dancing Gazette* article, for example, "Why Eileen Never Married (But She Says Yes to New Band)," neatly articulates the common assumption of the options available to Irish women: a woman can marry and have children, or she can work, but not both. So deeply ingrained was this assumption that a 1971

Figure 7.9 Kelley with the Nevada Showband, ca. 1965. (Photo courtesy of Eileen Kelly.)

survey (based on the 1966 Irish Census) documented that 34 percent of Irish women age fifteen to sixty-four held jobs but that, significantly, 75 percent of these working women were single and only six percent were married (Walsh 1971, cited in Russell, McGinnity, and O'Connell 2017, 398).

It is well worth noting the variety of motherhood and marital statuses among Irish women showband artists. While many did marry and have children, others chose not to and opted instead for the professional challenges, excitement, and hard work of stage careers. In living a life beyond what at the time typically defined womanhood—that is, as wife and mother—women showband artists directed their energies toward cultivating professional competence in the workplace by mastering the requisite musical and professional skills. Some simply rejected the option of marriage. Kelley, for example, had been dating one of her Nevada Showband bandmates. She recalls a moment of clarity while on tour in England:

> We were looking in a jeweler's window and he said to me, "If you were to pick a ring there, which one would you pick?" Now, this wasn't planned a sort of engagement or anything, so I picked a big rock. And he said, "Look, I have the money in my pocket, let's do it." And I kind of went into, I suppose, a little

shock because I didn't expect that. But it wasn't until then that I realized I just didn't want to get married. No, I don't know how that can make sense to anybody. So that was one of my almost-marriages that didn't happen. No regrets. (Interview, 2008)

Other women in the showband industry ultimately decided against marriage, given their responsibilities as the major breadwinner for their families and the lucrative reality of performing in a showband. Margo O'Donnell, for example, had always believed that she would marry and have children:

> And that was always my dream. But when I was put into the music business and my father died, I couldn't leave it because we didn't have any other earnings coming in. . . . So the lot sort of fell on me. And then I was very involved with a guy from home. We were going to get married. I was willing, very willing, to give up the music. I wasn't going to continue in the music if I got married. But then I would see my family and I would think but I can't leave just now. (Interview, 2008)

Of those showband women who chose to marry, some did so with a fellow band member, bandleader, or, in some instances, band manager. Some of this was a response to the logistics of life on the road: that they were away from home so often meant that the chances of meeting and marrying somebody outside of the showband world were slim. Recalls Eileen Reid: "You couldn't have a [long-term] relationship with anyone. I mean . . . you'd never see them" (quoted in Power 1990, 333).

The lives of showband women were further complicated by pregnancy and child-rearing. In Ireland at the time, there was general disapproval of a pregnant woman appearing on stage and many women were pressured by their husbands and extended families to immediately retire from performing upon discovering that they were pregnant. Some never returned to the stage; others took a lengthy break from performance, returning only after their children were grown. And still others, like Philomena Begley, found ways to perform during pregnancy and after, successfully balancing the demands of child-rearing with stage careers:

> I had my three children. I was dead-on the stage 'til they were nearly born, the three of them. . . . I never really had any problems with the children and looking after them because I had someone in to look after them when they were smaller, you know, if we were away.
>
> The children never came home from school at any time and nobody there. Always someone there. And their dinner was always ready, got their breakfast in the morning before they left for school. And I would always make it a point to go home when I would play anywhere around [home], especially when it was within distance . . . and I would very seldom ever stay over when the children were small. (Interview, 2008)

Figure 7.10 *Left to right*: Tom Costello, Eileen Reid, Roy Orbison, and Jimmy Day, ca. 1967. (Photo credit Tony O'Malley; photo courtesy of Eileen Reid.)

Singing Pop: Representations of Ireland at Eurovision

Like their male counterparts, women showband singers chose and then specialized in the musical style that most appealed to them and thus carved out a performance niche within the band. Those who preferred contemporary pop, for example, were most often inspired by and modeled their stage performances after such British singers as Petula Clark, Lulu (who toured with the Hollies in the 1960s), and Cilla Black. By the mid- to late 1960s, Motown, an American record label that specialized in soul, R&B, and pop styles, was also inspirational, as were, in particular, the Motown girl groups. Muriel Day, who was well known for her renditions of contemporary pop songs and ballads, was inspired by the music, vocal skills, and stage sensibilities of British pop superstar Dusty Springfield: "I loved the Dusty Springfield ballads. . . . I did all that stuff. But I really loved good heavy ballads. It was really great. It was all Top of the Pops sort things, you know, at the time" (interview, 2008).

In 1969, Day was the first woman and the first singer from Northern Ireland to represent the Republic of Ireland in the international Eurovision

Figure 7.11 Muriel Day performing at Eurovision, 1969. (Screen grab from YouTube.)

competition, where she placed seventh out of a field of sixteen. Her stage costume in the competition was a bright-green minidress with a capelike top that fell loosely from her shoulders to the upper thigh, at once modest yet revealing. Her three backup singers, the Lindsays, wore floor-length dresses: teal from the waist down and light blue from the waist up, evoking shades of green Irish landscapes and blue skies. Thus equating "the Emerald Isle" with all things modern and frisky, Day sang Michael Reade's, "The Wages of Love." Combining insistent musical perkiness and high-energy enthusiasm with dour lyrics, "The Wages of Love" cautions that while love is wondrous, "when you fall in love, you pay / the wages of love" and that "there will be bridges to be crossed / And there'll be teardrops to be lost / You will have to pay the cost / Just wait and see."

Performed with showy arm and hand gestures that were characteristic of Dusty Springfield's stage presence, Muriel Day's rendition of "The Wages of Love" contains the melodrama of the "pop aria," a song type popularized by Springfield in the 1960s. Musicologist Annie Randall (2008, 71) describes the pop aria as "a short-lived rarefied genre laden with musical and emotional bombast that can only be described as histrionic and shamelessly manipulative." While mirroring the aesthetic style of Dusty Springfield through the emotionalism of "The Wages of Love," Muriel Day's performance at Eurovision semiotically located a modern and united Ireland with the pop sensibilities of contemporary Europe.[6]

Singing Country: "I [Chose to Give] My Wedding Dress Away"

While some women showband artists cast their gaze toward Britain for pop songs and fashion inspiration, others looked to the United States and specifically to the Nashville country music industry. Starting with Kitty Wells and her 1952 breakout hit, "It Wasn't God Who Made Honky Tonk Angels," a new wave of female singers emerged as headline performers, including Jean Shepard, Patsy Cline, and, by the early 1970s, Dolly Parton. These artists rejected the historical personas long attached to country woman stars such as the 1930s/1940s singing cowgirl or the supposedly simpleminded "hayseeds" and "rubes"—country singers who framed their comedy routines with razor-sharp critiques of social norms. Instead, country music stars, such as Patsy Cline, embraced an image of urban sophistication (Bufwack 1998). This, along with the apparent independence, success, and sheer grit of many American women country artists, in turn inspired a number of Irish women showband singers, some of whom would move on to front their own country bands.[7]

That country music appealed to many women showband performers as well as their fans is unsurprising as it has long addressed multiple images of femininity through its inclusion of women as both performers and the subjects of songs. Country music scholar Bill Malone (2003, 13) writes that these feminine images range from the "rough and tough old ladies who are so mean that even the Devil won't take them" to the decidedly more dominant image of women as virtuous—"the principal quality that men hoped to find in their women." Many country songs, therefore, present women as lovers, wives, sisters, and, of course, mothers—that is, woman as nurturing, down to earth, and authentic, whose role it is to reinforce family values.

For all their formulaic patterns and tropes, American country songs rely on subtle (and not so subtle) imagery and symbols whose meanings become increasingly convoluted upon crossing the Atlantic to Ireland. Irish audiences had long responded to the familiar sound of country music as well as the many universal themes of found and lost love, family and home, rural life, and other narratives common to both the American South and rural Ireland. Other country songs contain themes that resonate with Irish audiences for reasons that are specific to local expectations and lived experience. Nowhere is the significance of culturally specific reception and meaning making clearer than with the enormous embrace by fans of Eileen Reid and the Cadet's 1964 showband hit, "I Gave My Wedding Dress Away."

Written by American songwriters Hy Heath and Fred Rose and popularized in 1963 by the American country star Kitty Wells, "I Gave My Wedding Dress Away," according to music writer Georgia Christgau (2016, 223), "takes its urgency from a tormented family dynamic straight out of the traditional Appalachian music playbook." Recorded in 1964, the Cadets' version adopts a country feel with its loping, slow two-step rhythm and standard country-western instrumentation, including prominent harmonica. Eileen Reid's lead vocals are characteristically unornamented and reminiscent of a country vocal style while a chorus offers background "oohs" and "aaws," reflecting more of a pop music sensibility.

In the annals of showband history, Eileen Reid's "I Gave My Wedding Dress Away" gets a prominent spot thanks to her performance strategy of appearing in a full wedding dress each time she performed the song. Well in keeping with the original tradition of integrating dramatic components into the "show," the appearance of Eileen Reid in a full wedding dress became something of a national obsession.[8] The first time she performed the song in full wedding regalia was in the Arcadia ballroom in Bray; according to Vincent Power (1990, 325), "Three thousand people shouted for more. She had to sing it six times." All this was very good for Eileen Reid and the Cadets as "I Gave My Wedding Dress Away" clearly hit a nerve with Irish audiences and sent it to fourth place on the Irish charts.

The song tells of a woman who selflessly raises her younger sister after "mother went away" and whose constant sacrifices, at the least, raise questions of an unhealthy codependency ("Everything I've ever wanted, she's always wanted too / And maybe giving in to her was not the thing to do . . ."). The song's protagonist was to be married the next day, but she recognizes her younger sister's desire ("I saw the love light in her eyes, the day she met my Jim") and allows the sister to take her place at the marriage altar with the fickle Jim, whose own utterly passive role in this drama is never questioned nor criticized. While the song reinforces the stereotype of woman as nurturer, it also casts her as martyr, if not enabler:

> My baby sister wanted him,
> and so she took my place.
> It's worth a broken heart,
> to see the smile upon her face.
> I've cared for her since Mother went away,
> so I gave my wedding dress away.

"I Gave My Wedding Dress Away" clearly resonated with Irish audiences through the familiar figure of the unwed Irish woman who was single by choice or, in this peculiar case, "orchestrates her own jilting" (Christgau 2016, 223). From the 1920s to the 1950s, Ireland's marriage rate was the lowest of any country that kept these types of records. In the 1930s alone, 29 percent of men and 24 percent of women were "permanently single," with 74 percent of men in the twenty-five to thirty-four age group remaining single in 1936 alone (Ryan 2007, 143). By the 1950s and 1960s, there remained "an abnormal reluctance to marry in Ireland," writes Diarmaid Ferriter (2004, 495)—this, despite improving marriage rates throughout the rest of Europe at the time.

While marriage remained the standard expectation for Irish women during the 1940s and 1950s, the fact that a notable percentage of an entire generation—and statistically significant number—of women decided to neither emigrate nor marry and remain celibate can be seen, argues historian Caitríona Clear, as an empowered choice. With little economic incentive for marriage during these years, given the high rates of unemployment and poorly paid work in Ireland, women rejected what Irish writer Mary Frances Keating describes as "a life of drudgery and hardship" and "inability to control the behaviour of a spouse" (Keating, quoted in Clear 2004, 142). In short, writes Clear, "Women were rejecting men—not the other way around" (141).

Aside from its saga of truly twisted notions of gendered familial responsibility, "I Gave My Wedding Dress Away" presented to Irish audiences what was, by then, the familiar figure of the unmarried woman, but one whose sacrifice clearly reflected her own agency. The fact is that she gave her wedding dress away, but she also *chose* to do so. The song resonated with audiences and especially Irish women who understood the lyrics as an empowered decision to not marry and, in doing so, defied the cultural expectations of the times.

Kicking Down Doors

Country music profoundly resonated with many Irish women showband singers, to the point that some were spurred on by the careers and personal lives of specific American women country stars. Sandy Kelly, for example, was inspired by the Nashville legend Patsy Cline, who, like Kelly, was also a contralto (the lowest female vocal range), a rarity among women singers and one that allowed Kelly to render Patsy Cline songs in their original keys. By 1973, Kelly had left the showband world to front a country band: "In a way, turning to country music, for me, was a savior because I regained my own voice. And being myself" (interview, 2008). In 1989, Sandy Kelly's cover of Patsy Cline's signature hit "Crazy" was Ireland's biggest-selling record that year.

Sandy Kelly was further encouraged by Patsy Cline's strength and independence in determining how she managed her career and how she navigated her place in the largely male-dominated country music industry:

> Patsy Cline was feisty, and cocky and, you know, a woman before her time. I mean, she didn't knock on the door of country music . . . she kicked the doors down! And when women were window dressing, she was one of the female artists of her time that men were [playing] support to her.
>
> For me, as an artist, [sometimes] she'd be there in my mannerisms. I'd put my hand on my hip and say something that I would never say, but it was good, because it'd give me an edge. (Interview 2008)

Taking a lesson from Patsy Cline's insistence on controlling her place in the music industry, Kelly found her own gumption during a final major confrontation with the other lead singer in her band:

> We were doing six nights a week all over the country. . . . And I remember one night saying to him, "You know what, you're right, there isn't room for both of us in this band." And I could see relief in him. And I said "But guess what, I'm not leaving." And he said, "What do you mean?" I said "There isn't room for two of us," I said, "but I'm not leaving, you're leaving." And sure enough, shortly after that, he left. (Interview, 2008)

Like Kelly, Margo O'Donnell found that American country music offered a better avenue for self-expression. She too drew from the modeled strength of some women country stars, made all the more powerful because O'Donnell's background paralleled that of some these singers, two of whom would become her mentors—Nashville icons Jean Shepard and Dolly Parton:

> When I left Donegal and when I did hit the big time, people would . . . see where I came from, they would say, "How in the hell did you get out of there?" And yet the first time that I went to Dolly [Parton]'s in East Tennessee, I said, "God, how did she get out?" I became very friendly with her dad. He was a wonderful man, and he would talk to me about them times and how hungry Dolly was to get out and do something with herself.
>
> But you know the greatest thing that I found about Dolly? When Dolly said she was going to do something, it was done. So I'm very like that, and I think that there's a bit of that kind of tie with the women in the music business. It grounds you more. People can hear it in your voice. (Interview, 2008)

O'Donnell was also inspired by Patsy Cline, both as a singer and as a professional in the music industry: "It was just the quality, the depth, the actual ache [of Patsy Cline's voice]. It was [as] if she was aching the notes. And I never tried to sing like anybody, I just sang my own way. But she was my icon.

Patsy was a strong woman, she really was. And she was able to stand up for herself" (interview, 2008).

Rather than emulate Patsy Cline onstage, Margo O'Donnell retained her own performance style, which evoked the girl-next-door sensibility, including modest stage outfits and her trademark voice that exuded strength and warmth. Her image combined her working-class background with her Donegal roots; as such, O'Donnell projected an Irish rural identity shared by many of her fans. Her career as one of Ireland's most popular Country and Irish singers could itself be rendered the subject of country song. O'Donnell recorded over forty albums between the mid-1960s and the 1980s. Her records sold well; indeed, in the 1970s, by her own account, she was selling more records in Ireland than were the Beatles. Unlike the Beatles, however, O'Donnell never saw a single royalty, and she believes that agents, managers, and record producers pocketed the profits: "My life was totally and utterly controlled by gangsters in the music business here. . . . They thought we [women] were second class citizens. They thought we had no brains. Honest to God, they really thought that it was empty in there and they could do anything they wanted with us. But I'm afraid that's not true" (interview, 2008).

In 1978, O'Donnell's former manager sold thirty of her master tapes, without her knowledge or permission, to a Belfast-based producer. The producer then released them for his own profit including scratch (practice) tracks that were never meant to be heard by the public. O'Donnell took the Belfast producer to court and eventually won the fight to have her master tapes returned: "I just had to know my own worth. When I heard the judge['s decision] that day in court, I cried. But I knew [the tapes] were mine. But I feel as if he raped me. . . . I felt that he had taken my inside out of me and kicked me along the path of life. And I was not in control of it" (ibid.).

Few showband artists were paid royalties for their recordings. Ireland's popular music industry was all but unregulated, with nonexistent or vaguely worded contracts the norm. Most musicians, men and women, were subject to questionable business practices, and the absence of written records that documented real income and expenses made it virtually impossible to track profits. The subsequent sale and re-release of O'Donnell's master tapes and scratch tracks was a particularly pernicious act that severed her from her voice, the ultimate symbolic silencing.

It is tempting to equate the preference of country music by these successful women singers with notions of tradition and conservatism. Such an interpretation would cohere neatly with historian Anne McClintock's (1995, 358–59) argument of "the temporal anomaly within nationalism—veering between nostalgia for the past and the impatient, sloughing off of the past": McClintock further notes that "women are represented as the atavistic and authentic body of national tradition (inert, backward-looking and natural), embodying nationalism's conservative principle of continuity. Men by contrast, represent the progressive agent of national modernity (forward thrusting, potent and historic) embodying nationalism's progressive, or revolutionary principle of discontinuity."

While performers such as Margo O'Donnell, Philomena Begley, Sandy Kelly, and others sang country songs that celebrated rural aesthetics, home, locality, community, and family, these women were looking anywhere but backward. Rather, they were radical in their insistence that, unlike their predecessors, they were not to be seen as ornamental nor as "window dressing" and, instead, fully capable and in charge of fronting their own bands and doing so on their own terms. It was radical to challenge the music industry in a hugely public, civil act, as did Margo O'Donnell, by insisting that it was she and nobody else who owned her voice and her music. For Sandy Kelly, it was radical to stand firm and insist on her place as leader of a band. And ultimately, it was radical to simply reject the notion of the girl singer altogether—that is, a performing artist who is first defined by her gender and then by her skills. As Philomena Begley notes, "I just am a singer . . . I would just go out, I would sing, I was just another singer" (interview, 2008).

"We Were So Different!": The Granada Girls Showband

Just as women vocalists pushed the boundaries of social acceptance, so too did the very few women who found their way into showbands as instrumentalists. While a woman singer might also play guitar or tambourine, instrumental performance remained almost exclusively the purview of male band members. One exception was Mildred Beirne's all-women five piece, the Granada Girls Showband. Beginning in 1962, this semiprofessional showband performed six and even seven nights a week locally and regionally, with an occasional trip to Northern Ireland. The manager, agent, and bandleader was musician and arranger Leo Beirne, whom Mildred would later marry. Leo Beirne taught the band members—all of whom were teenagers at the time—the music, did the booking, drove them to jobs, and served as music director.

Beirne was apparently a strict taskmaster: he demanded unblemished behavior when in the public eye, forbidding the young women to leave the stage during breaks or socialize after the show. He insisted on an absolutely conservative stage appearance and had the women wear matching slacks rather than dresses on stage for the sake of propriety. In contrast to the glamourous femininity presented by many other women showband artists, the

Figure 7.12 The Granada Girls Showband, 1962. (Photo courtesy of Mildred Beirne.)

publicity photographs of the Granada Girls Showband present the members as young, girlish, and cheerful but masterfully doing what most audience members perceived as the onstage performance work of men.

Leo Beirne taught the band members well, insisting on absolute musical precision. And by all reports, the Granada Girls Showband played well. So good, in fact, that patrons who might have initially been drawn to the exotic appeal of an all-girl band were surprised at what they heard, recalls Mildred Beirne: "I'd say that they were taken aback a bit, you know? They couldn't believe that five women could be as good as we were. I suppose they came thinking that the band mightn't be as good. And instead of that, it was wonderful. . . . They treated us just like queens. We were the belle of the ball. They could not get enough of us!" (interview, 2007).

The members of the Granada Girls Showband clearly recognized their audiences' assumptions regarding gender and stage performance. Despite mastering their instruments, their harmony vocals, and their stage performance skills, they were nevertheless trapped in what musicologist Christina Baade (2008, 117) describes as the "false binary of male competence and female incompetence." While Irish audiences appreciated the novelty of an all-women's band, they were often skeptical of their musical abilities. If women showband vocalists blurred gender codes simply by moving onto the stage, then the Granada Girls as competent instrumentalists and dance musicians further vexed these boundaries.

Playing in a showband offered women artists professional prospects that were all but unheard of in generations past. Moreover, as Mildred Beirne points out, taking to the stage also introduced them to the pleasure of performance, a state of mind that arguably transcends gender. And, perhaps most importantly, the experience enlarged their worldview and offered a broadened lifestyle without having to emigrate. For Mildred Beirne, it allowed for a personal and emotional mobility, one that offered possibilities well beyond the parochial and familiar: "You were taken from nothing to the most wonderful things that could happen to you. You were out every night, playing to all those wonderful dancers on the floor. And like to be on the stage, the people on the dance floor thought we were like angels. And we felt it. And they always made us so welcome and so good and that we were so different" (interview, 2007).

For many showband women, there was delight in the mastery of musical and stage performance skills, and, in the end, some measure of personal empowerment that accompanied that expertise. For most, performing in a showband was also fundamentally a job that saw substantial income and, with it, financial security—rewards nevertheless tempered by challenges that ranged from routine indignities to outright exploitation. As pioneers in Ireland's fledgling popular music industry, women showband players served as models by insisting on their place both on- and offstage. In doing so, they effectively challenged and ultimately reshaped existing gendered boundaries at a time when Ireland's popular music industry was just taking shape.

Notes

1. For many Irish women in the 1950s, chronic unemployment was exacerbated by the lasting effects of the 1932 Marriage Ban, a law that required compulsory retirement of female teachers upon marriage and that was later extended to the entire Civil Service. The marriage ban was repealed among teachers in 1958, but according to Diarmaid Ferriter (2004, 327–28; 496), there was "still an ethos predicated on the idea that a woman working was acceptable in terms of economic necessity, but intolerable in the context of them having independent career ambitions."

2. Maisie McDaniel, in turn, went on to sing with the Fendermen.

3. In Northern Ireland, the taxes owed by workers are regularly deducted by employers via the PAYE, or (pay-as-you-earn), system.

4. In 1971, Brendan Bowyer and Tom Dunphy formed the Big Eight after the Royal Showband split up. The Big Eight spent half the year performing in Las Vegas and the other half on the showband circuit in Ireland.

5. Eileen Kelly's observation underscores musicologist Susan McClary's (1991, 20–21) argument that because music is dependent on the conferral of social meaning, participation often results in "unwittingly reproducing the ideologies that inform various levels of . . . discourse" and, in particular, notions of gender.

6. Muriel Day's success in Eurovision raised the visibility of Irish women singers, especially those from Northern Ireland, and arguably paved the way for the following year's first-place Eurovision winner, Dana (Dana Rosemary Scallon), from Derry.

7. So popular was country music at the time that women showband singers were sometimes pressured to enlarge their repertoire in this direction. Eileen Kelly, for example, recalls being urged by her manager, George O'Reilly, to capitalize on the growing audiences for country songs despite Kelly's very strong preference for pop songs and ballads: "I never liked country and western, honestly. And I think when George brought me into the band, I think he probably hoped that maybe that's the role that I would take. But I didn't take it; I went into the pop" (interview, 2008).

8. Eileen Reid wore the famed wedding dress on stage six nights a week for nearly a year. When the dress became quite worn and dirty and Reid refused to continue wearing it, the Cadets capitalized on its retirement by holding a raffle of the dress with the proceeds donated to a charity. In this brilliant publicity stunt, the band sold thousands of tickets for several months to many hopeful, soon-to-be-brides. The winner was a married, middle-aged man, who had been given the winning ticket. Apparently, the winner was more interested in the cash prize of fifty pounds and ultimately threw the dress away (Reid, interview, 2018).

8

Hucklebucking across the Waters

Irish Showbands in Diaspora

> Everybody has an uncle in America, an Uncle Tommy in England. In those times, families were ten and twelve in the family. And the majority of them would go [abroad], and one or two of them might stay at home and get the [farm]. And invariably, one would get lost somewhere, you'd never hear of Uncle Peter for a while. . . . Then they'd all go to the Irish Center, that was the common denominator, the Dance Hall.
>
> *Jimmy Higgins, interview, 2007*

In 1964, when he was just seventeen, trumpeter Jimmy Higgins left his home in Galway for England. Already a seasoned performer with the Tuam-based Paramount Showband, Higgins was offered a job as the bandleader of the International Showband, which was in residence at the Astoria (later known as the Carousel) in Plymouth Grove, Manchester. Upon arrival, Higgins found a large community of immigrant Irish who, over several decades, had left Ireland in search of steady employment in the post–World War II years. In contrast to earlier eras of Irish immigration, a majority of this wave of émigrés went to Britain while a smaller, but still significant number of Irish arrived in the United States, settling in New York, Boston, Philadelphia, Chicago, and other cities.

In both Britain and in the United States, the new arrivals were welcomed into a long-established network of Irish-owned businesses and social institutions. After a day's work, they flocked to Irish-owned or operated dance halls to socialize. They also came to dance. Stepping into dance halls throughout Britain, the new arrivals found a familiar sonic landscape as they danced to groups on tour from Ireland and to music played by local ensembles of immigrant Irish musicians, such as Jimmy Higgins with the International Showband. Whether on tour or in residence, showbands provided an antidote to the inevitable homesickness experienced by émigrés in Britain and those in the United States and reinforced a sense of Irish identity for their displaced audiences.

This was anything but a straightforward process. Showbands abroad were immersed in layers of cultural hybridity: they performed primarily covers of British and American pop and rock 'n' roll to Irish audiences in the context of Irish dance halls, which were, themselves, located in British and American spaces. Despite these dislocations of space and place, diasporic showbands remained recognizably Irish in terms of repertoire and performance practice: they played in a familiar style and included well-known Irish popular songs as well as sets of ceílí dance music. They incorporated into their performances frequent allusions to Irish localities and regional affiliations. They also functioned as messengers between the diasporic communities scattered throughout Britain and the United States as well as between these audiences and their families and friends back home in Ireland.

As such, Irish showbands abroad served as sonic bridges between the Ireland left behind and the new culture and pace of British and American cities. In these ways, showbands neatly underscore Glenda Norquay and Gerry Smyth's argument that diasporic Irish culture is best understood in terms of the "Atlantic Archipelago," which, given the historical transnational realities of Irish immigration, allows us to better "hear voices talking 'across' borders and not only to or through an English [or American] centre" (Norquay and Smyth 2002). Through touring diasporic communities and relying on performance strategies that spoke directly to their audiences' desires and needs, showbands abroad reinforced Irish identity among displaced audiences while connecting families and friends across borders and time.

There were differences, both subtle and otherwise, in the reception and dynamics of showbands situated abroad in Britain versus those in the United States. Showband musicians often looked toward Britain for inspiration and more often than not, their success depended on how they compared with British popular culture. This was unsurprising considering Ireland's centuries-long engagement with and physical proximity to Britain. Irish populations in the northern and eastern Irish counties could hear pop music via BBC radio broadcasts; sit-down dance bands prior to the showband era relied on sheet music arrangements published in London and exported to Ireland. Moreover, many musicians saw, heard, and then modeled their performance style on their British counterparts (M. O'Hanlon, interview with Paul Maguire, 2007).

Looking toward Britain in these ways, was, in part, a byproduct of what former Taoiseach Albert Reynolds recalled as generations of Ireland's "over-reliance" on Britain for trade and business generally (interview, 2006). This historical imbalance reinforced Britain as a de facto economic center with Ireland on the periphery, an inherently unstable position that played out not only in business and trade, but also in terms of establishing some level of cultural—and, in this case, musical—expectation and approval. A March 1956 article in the *Irish Press* alludes to this aspirational understanding of Britain as the standard bearer among Irish popular dance musicians:

> It is a fair indication of the worth of the men and girls who play and sing in Irish bands, and of the bands themselves, that from among those who started their careers in those bands, have come young men now leading bands in fashionable London nightclubs, instrumentalists who are playing with the principle British bands, and vocalists who have become famous on the stage, on radio and on television; that visiting bandleaders and artists have spoken of Irish in the very highest terms; and that when Irish bands tour Britain, they are given, invariably, a tremendous reception. (10)

The dominance of the British music industry among Irish musicians remained firmly in place at the height of the showband era. With reference to his 1969 hit, "Make Me an Island," the late showband star Joe Dolan recalled that it wasn't enough for the song to be popular in Ireland; its success in Ireland relied on British validation, proven by rising on the British charts: "When 'Make Me an Island' came out first, it climbed up to number five in Ireland and then went back down again. But then, when it went to number three in England, suddenly it's number one here [in Ireland]! So we were always in a situation in Ireland that we were dedicated followers of fashion. If it happened overseas, then it had to be good" (Joe Dolan, quoted in Gillan 2007).

Showbands in Britain: Navigating the Center from the Periphery

Margo O'Donnell and the Keynotes Showband initially performed throughout their native Donegal but, as they became better known, expanded to venues in Northern Ireland and, eventually, to Irish immigrant audiences in Britain, recalls O'Donnell: "We would tour Scotland and England because of the great immigration that was there at the time. And you'd see more people from home over there than at home!" (interview, 2009). Between 1946 and 1961, half a million Irish—nearly 17 percent of the population—left Ireland. Irish immigration had skyrocketed by the early 1950s: historian Enda Delaney (2007, 16) estimates that four out of five Irish migrants "went across the water" until the early 1970s (see also Barrett 1999). Two-thirds of immigrants during these years left largely rural regions of Ireland and settled in the urban, industrial centers of England and Scotland. Many emigrants were quite young, with an estimated 40 percent being between the ages of ten and nineteen (G. O'Hanlon 2004, 72, 76).[1]

Unlike the waves of nineteenth-century Irish immigrants who settled in the United States, the majority of mid-twentieth-century Irish émigrés went instead to England. Many factors explain this shift, including the ease of postwar travel between Britain and Ireland and the similarity of British urban culture to that of Ireland. Arguably, the most significant "pull factor" was the postwar labor shortage in Britain, starting in the mid- to late 1940s. British companies offered incentives to prospective Irish workers, such as funding the cost of their travel. In 1946, for example, thousands of Irish men were recruited for coal mining in Britain; the following year, nearly three thousand Irish women traveled to Britain for training in nursing (Delaney 2007, 48). Apart from the pragmatic nature of these schemes, one of the strongest pulls for young Irish to Britain was the image of experiencing the modern world, one that, according to Delaney, "offered glimpses of a different way of life based on material wellbeing, a consumer-based social scene organized around popular activities such as dancing and going to the cinema, and most importantly, a vision of a future that centered on the fulfillment of individual aspirations" (21).

As such, Irish immigrants settled throughout England and Scotland, primarily in Glasgow, Manchester, Birmingham, Bristol, Coventry, Liverpool, Luton, Leeds, Newcastle, and in London (Camden Town, Paddington, Kilburn, Acton, Notting Hill, Holloway, and elsewhere). Smaller towns like Swindon and Gloucester also boasted large populations of new Irish. People from specific parts of Ireland tended to settle nearby each other, recalls Jimmy Higgins (2007, 118): "Tribalism was a big thing. You would find a lot of Mayo and Galway people around Manchester and Leeds while the Dublin people seemed to head for Liverpool and Birmingham. . . . As for Scotland, sure it's full of Donegal people."

Young Irish men found work in industry and postwar demolition and construction; women worked in the service sector, factories, and professional services such as nursing (Travers 1995; see also G. O'Hanlon 2004, 76). Much of this work—particularly the heavy labor jobs taken on by young men—was relatively well paid. Many held down a second job as well, earning as much as twenty to twenty-five pounds per week with overtime—excellent pay compared to what they might earn in similar jobs in Ireland. Music scholar Reg Hall (1995, 4) writes that with low overhead expenses and even after remittances that were regularly sent home to support their families, the bulk of these wages—at least for Irish men —was spent on leisure, "drinking, a flutter on the horses with a street bookie, and a visit to a dance hall."

Indeed, both Irish men and women visited the Irish dance halls. In London alone, three catered specifically to Irish immigrant audiences in the years before and during World War II: the Garryowen Club, the Pride of Erin Club, and St. Patrick's Club in Bayswater (R. Hall 1995, 10). By the mid-1950s, a proliferation of new London dance halls responded to growing audiences and demand and included the Buffalo in Kentish Town, the Angel in Islington, the Shamrock Club at the Elephant and Castle, and the Innisfree Club in Ealing Broadway. Dance halls catering to the new Irish arrivals also thrived outside of London—the Astoria in Manchester and the Harp and Shamrock in Birmingham. There were also the large ballrooms owned by the British-owned Mecca chain, including London's Hammersmith Palais and smaller Irish centers and clubs, such as the Blarney, the Shamrock, the Emerald, the Glacamara, and the Banba in Coventry. While most of these were Irish-owned, English dance hall owners also sought to cash in on the demand and lined up Irish showbands at large venues such as the London Palladium. Whether Irish- or English-owned, these dance halls offered new arrivals a place to socialize, create and extend networks, exchange information about work opportunities and places to live, and, in many cases, meet their future spouses.

A well-known figure in the Irish dance hall scene during these years was the promoter Bill Fuller. Born in County Kerry in 1917, Fuller immigrated to London as a teenager in search of construction work. Jailed during the London Blitz for refusing to join the British army, Fuller was advised by a fellow inmate that England would have to rebuild after the war "and that the only ones who could rebuild it would be the Irish" (R. O'Hanlon 2008, 6). Thus inspired, Fuller went on to develop a successful construction business, eventually amassing a small fortune initially from post–World War II demolition work. So prolific was Bill Fuller with this work that it was said, "What Hitler didn't knock down, Bill Fuller did" (Scanlon 2008).

In 1937, when he was just twenty years old, Fuller took over the Buffalo (later known as the Electric Ballroom). What started as a notoriously rough and run-down Irish ballroom on Camden High Street, the Buffalo had developed into a central attraction for London's Irish immigrants by the late 1950s. Fuller himself would go on to become known as a major showband and entertainment promoter: his string of Irish dance halls in London and elsewhere in England, as well as in Ireland and the United States, would become highly sought-after venues on the showband circuit.

"The Musical Tour of Ireland": Repertoire, Nostalgia, and Modernity

One of Fuller's best-known Irish dance halls was the Astoria in Manchester, the venue that featured Jimmy Higgins's resident ensemble, the International

Showband. The band was kept busy there, performing five to six hours per night, six nights a week, in addition to frequently tours of England and Germany. The showband got their name thanks to their membership, which included musicians from the United States, England, and Ireland. Despite this, the International Showband claimed a local Irish affiliation, a practice well in keeping with other showbands that catered to Irish diasporic audiences:

> All the bands would have the tag. You were the Bangor Six from Kerry, Margo and the Keynotes from Donegal, Pete Brown, the Rye Blues, from County Mayo. You'd have a band from Cork maybe.... And that'd be big business. Keeping them all happy. And then [emigrants from Donegal] would be saying, "You haven't brought a band from Donegal in a while." . . . So I being the leader, from Galway, I'd say, "the International, from Galway!" (Higgins, interview, 2007)

In addition to the emotional reinforcement of belonging via referencing a particular place in Ireland, showbands that performed to diasporic audiences were utilitarian in that they served as messengers. Those on tour from Ireland, for example, happily took messages and greetings from individuals abroad back home to Ireland, further facilitating communication across time and distance. Showbands in residence, like the International, were similarly helpful as they often served as messengers between the many Irish immigrant communities scattered throughout England and Scotland.[2] Jimmy Higgins recalls that when his band was planning to travel to a gig in another city, he would put the word out to his audiences, offering them the opportunity to connect with friends and relatives:

> What we used to do as well when we'd be going on tour is say, "We're going to visit Leeds and Manchester if you have any sisters or brothers [there]." They'd be coming up to us with requests: "When you're in Birmingham, play this for my sister." . . . And people would be coming up after the dance writing them on cigarette packs and everything, saying, "Play this for my brother Johnny!"
>
> We'd even put an ad in the paper saying [where] we're going next week and people would write in requests. It was like PR for us, like public relations, I suppose. But you knew what it meant to them. It just meant a lot. (Interview, 2007)

Given the many number of Irish clubs and dance halls in England and Scotland, touring showbands could book a performance every evening in a different venue throughout Britain for two or three weeks or more. Touring was an exciting prospect and musicians took great delight in the crowds of immigrant Irish who came to see the visiting showband. Drummer Des Hopkins frequently toured Britain with his County Mayo–based showband: "That band was extremely big in England because there was so many emigrants from Mayo. And because they were a Mayo band, they used to draw massive crowds in halls in London, and Birmingham, and Manchester, so I quite enjoyed them" (interview, 2007). In London, the best-known showbands could easily sell out the largest venues. A 1962 engagement featuring the Royal Showband at the Hammersmith Palais, for example, attracted an estimated audience of seven thousand, setting a new record for this ever-popular group. That night, a riot ensued and the police resorted to fire hoses to disperse the crowd. Remembers Brendan Bowyer,

> It was a mass of people in a ballroom, wall-to-wall. You could walk across the people without falling down, from the stage. And there were a lot of people locked out that night too. I had friends that didn't get in, that were caught, and there was a whole lot shoved off into cells. (Interview, 1992)

As profitable as touring was, equally important was the fact that traveling and playing for diasporic audiences offered the musicians an opportunity to experience new places and expand their world view. Mildred Beirne recalls the hard work of touring as well as the benefits of seeing the world beyond her own parish:

> We liked it because I suppose it was so far away from home. It was an adventure. Like when we were kids, we always heard of the border. . . . The weekend in England would have been tough. You'd be playing Friday, Saturday, Sunday afternoons, Sunday night, and back again [home] Monday. And you'd be playing Monday night at home someplace in Ireland. So it was hard going . . . but it was great. It was great! (Interview, 2007)

Needless to say, dance hall owners and operators in Britain were interested in hiring musicians who could attract large audiences. Musicians on tour therefore needed to be able to read—and then cater to—their audiences' emotional needs as much as their aesthetic sensibilities. To this end, showband players adjusted their repertoire to address their displaced audiences' inevitable homesickness and nostalgia. While showbands in Ireland might play one or two Irish popular songs and an old-time waltz, those performing for diasporic audiences added considerably more specifically Irish material to an evening's performance. Jimmy Higgins recalls one strategy put into play by the International Showband:

> We invented what we called "The Musical Tour of Ireland." And what we did was we got each guy in the band to sing a different song. We'd go into "The Homes of Donegal" and then "The Boys from the County Mayo" and then "Molly Malone." Then after that, "The Boys from the County Armagh." . . . When you'd come to their song, there'd be a "Yahoo!" But the trouble was, you

> couldn't fit in all the songs, so they'd be coming up, giving out to you: "You never played a Kilkenny song." "You never played one for Waterford!"
>
> But we'd wind it up with a song called "If We Only Had Ol' Ireland Over Here." And we'd say, "We'll include in this now everybody who we didn't sing a song for their County," and that's the one that would get them. It'd really get emotional, yeah. (Interview, 2007)

The effect was palpable: a single song could swiftly define the reality of the diasporic experience for audiences and performers both, recalls Margo O'Donnell: "In London, I would go out and I would sing an Irish ballad and I would have everyone from Ireland around the stage, crying. And that time they couldn't just as easily hop on a plane and come home" (O'Donnell, interview, 2009).

"The Girl from Donegal"

This profound connection to place was also heard in the repertoire of Irish solo singers who shared the British touring circuit during these years. Among the best-known of these was Bridie Gallagher, aka "the Girl from Donegal." As one of Ireland's first internationally renowned vocalists, Gallagher recorded on such labels as Beltona, Decca, London Records (US), Emerald Records, and Pye Records between 1956 and 1962—recordings that were cherished by immigrant Irish audiences, particularly in Britain. In Camden Town, for example, writes Reg Hall, pubs such as the Bedford Arms featured Bridie Gallagher recordings as a sort of audio backdrop: "If the barmaid had the time, she would put a pile of Bridie Gallagher records on the auto-change, until the live music was due to start" (R. Hall 1995, 8). Performing with just one or two supporting musicians, Gallagher's live shows routinely packed the larger London ballrooms on weekends and smaller dance halls midweek: "At Manor House, the density of the crowd once stopped dancing altogether, and a promoter in Ireland, speaking in the late 1960s, said 'Bridie Gallagher was unbelievably big—easily as big as any of the showbands'" (Hall 1995, 14).

Like the touring showbands, many of the songs performed by Gallagher addressed themes that resonated with the Irish immigrant experience. Some evoked an idealized Ireland ("If We Only Had Ol' Ireland Over Here," "The Homes of Donegal"), while others lamented leaving Ireland in the first place ("At the Close of an Irish Day"). Still others nostalgically located specific Irish counties ("Moonlight in Mayo," "Boys of the County Armagh"), towns ("Killarney and You," "The Rose of Tralee"), and smaller Irish locales ("Lovely Inishowen"). Some of Bridie Gallagher's songs spoke to the dangers of emigration, such as the possibility of contracting a fatal case of tuberculosis ("Noreen Bawn"). Still others tapped into feelings of ambivalence that surrounded emigration, given, on the one hand, the excitement of starting a new life with new friends and sure employment while, on the other hand, coming to terms with the responsibility of sending remittances to support family in Ireland. Most poignant were songs that spoke to the sorrow of leaving family and loved ones ("Goodbye, Johnny Dear") and were commonly performed by both the showbands and Bridie Gallagher and that were, undoubtably, the most resonant for their audiences.

Showbands and Céilí Dancing

Unsurprisingly, Irish diasporic audiences delighted in dancing to music that specifically located the Ireland they left behind. Before the advent of showbands, touring sit-down dance orchestras in the 1950s responded with sets of contemporary ballroom dance music until halfway through the evening, when the band took a break. At that point, they were replaced with a duo or trio who took to the stage to perform a set or two of céilí dance music. So popular was ceílí dancing among diasporic audiences during these years that some enterprising Irish promoters offered both styles for the price of a single admission. For example, Cork-born John Byrne's ballroom, the Galtymore in Cricklewood, London, consisted of two separate halls, one that was devoted to céilí dancing and the other to modern, ballroom dancing. Dancers could freely move between the two halls and dance genres. This combination proved so successful that Byrne, who would become one of London's most illustrious Irish dance hall promoters, was able to open the equally popular venue, the Hibernian on Fulham Road (R. Hall 1995, 11).

A decade later, Irish showbands on tour in Britain similarly adapted their repertoire for diasporic audiences, replacing as much as 30 percent of pop covers with Irish music and song. Depending on the makeup of the group, certain showbands were better equipped to handle this dual repertoire. The musicians in the Dixies Showband, for example, were also excellent traditional instrumentalists and could easily supply high energy céilí dance music, all wrapped up with their signature ribald humor, recalls lead singer Brendan O'Brien:

> Brendan O'Brien: Well, there was a huge emphasis on the céilí. Our bass player, Chris O'Mahoney, was a really, really good box [accordion] player so he'd play the "Walls of Limerick" and the "Siege of Ennis."
>
> RSM: And you'd have people getting up and dancing?
>
> Brendan O'Brien: Yeah, yeah. And [drummer] Joe [McCarthy] would be doing the comedy, of course, and the swearing in between and getting away with it. He could tell a multitude to F-off and he'd get a round of applause! (Interview, 2006)

Figure 8.1 Poster of the Dixies Showband, no date. (Collection of Jimmy Higgins.)

Unique performance practices aside, even a showband as popular as the Dixies calculated and adapted the Irish content of their shows when performing for immigrant audiences in Britain. By dancing the "Siege of Ennis," the "Walls of Limerick," and other céilí dances between sets of jive dancing, the musicians and dancers created a space that reflected the hybrid nature of the immigrant experience as well as the interplay between popular British dance music and Irish traditional culture.

At the same time, it was this very hybridity that spurred the perception in England that Irish showband music was, at heart, conservative. This was in stark contrast to the reputation of showbands back home in Ireland where, until the late 1960s, they were viewed as modern and cutting edge. In England, however, the Beatles and Beat bands dominated the radio waves and recording industry by 1964. And while Jimmy Higgins's International Showband was still in high demand at Irish dance halls, he soon came to realize that it could not compete with the Beat bands and their new sound, particularly in the English-owned venues:

> The trend at that time [was the Beatles]. Beat bands [were] at [their] heyday: four-piece rhythm 'n' blues bands. And the most they'd have, they might have

> keyboards, or they might have a sax player. But the Showband had about seven or eight people with a brass section, so we looked about twice as big. And when we went into the English scene playing the English clubs, we didn't really fit in at all. We'd wear suits and doing the step and we were kind of playing the Top 20. . . . We probably had the wrong image for the younger set. We were more geared for the cabaret or the working man's club scene. (Interview, 2007)

For the immigrant working-class Irish audiences, the evenings of showband music at the dance halls nevertheless continued to fill crucial needs. While migration opened up employment opportunities and a sense of possibility, life in Britain could be bleak for the new arrivals. A January 26, 1963, article in the *Connacht Tribune*, entitled "The Hardships That Some of Our Emigrants Endure," points to the possibility of exploitation of young immigrant Irish by employers and details the material difficulties that many encountered: "In Britain, where conditions of overcrowding in lodgings are a major cause of complaint, many of our people, especially girls, have to endure conditions that they had not expected."

Many émigrés lived in inexpensive bedsits or hostels that did not permit them to remain there during the day. Indeed, some bedsits rented out beds to day workers and then the same bed to those who worked night shifts. This mattered little during their workweek, which was often six days. But, on Sundays, many young Irish simply needed a physical place to go. Jimmy Higgins recalls that they might have attended Mass in the morning and then, perhaps, the cinema and, eventually, would have arrived at a local Irish dance hall. These Sunday afternoon tea dances, as they were called, provided the emigrant Irish with an activity between 3:00 and 6:00 p.m. as well as the comfort of a familiar social atmosphere, sandwiches, and plenty of restorative tea:

> The Irish guys and girls were living in digs [bedsits], so it wasn't like an apartment, you couldn't hang around it. You got up, went out to work at nine o'clock in the morning, don't come back till the evening. . . . At that time, there was no drinking in the Irish clubs and the halls there. But there was these tea bars, and you'd go in for a cup of tea, and there'd be piles of [ham] sandwiches, tomato sandwiches. (Higgins, interview, 2007)

The audience danced to whatever showband was playing on Sunday afternoons. Many would then attend yet another Sunday evening dance, where they could also hear the weekly news from home, recalls Jimmy Higgins: "The MC would take the microphone and he'd announce, 'Now we have the latest football results from Ireland.' And there'd be total silence. Everybody'd be listening to see, how did your team do? . . . It was one of the most important things of the week, the keeping in touch with home" (ibid.).

Part II: Hucklebucking across the Atlantic: Showbands in New York City

Staying in touch with home was even more difficult for the Irish who immigrated to the United States, a move that was marked by a strong sense of finality. Whereas Irish immigrants to England could and did reverse migrate—returning to Ireland both temporarily and permanently with relative ease—those who came to the United States did so with the understanding that they probably would not be returning often, if at all, given the distance and considerable expense. Recalls the late County Longford fiddler Paddy Reynolds, who immigrated to New York City in 1948: "I remember when people were coming to America. It 'twas the same as if somebody had died, leaving forever, gone. Come here for good" (interview, 1992). Linda Almeida points out that given these circumstances, Irish immigrants during these years had no choice but to work "very hard to make their stay in the United States successful" (Almeida 2004, 209).

In contrast to earlier waves of Irish immigration, far fewer Irish opted to come to the United States in the post–World War II years. Of the 531,255 Irish who left Ireland between 1941 and 1961, only 68,151—or just under 13 percent—chose the United States over Britain (Almeida 2004, 208). Of these, 48,362 arrived between 1951 and 1960, an increase spurred by endemic unemployment in Ireland as well as the passage of the United States' Immigration and Nationality Act of 1952—the McCarran-Walter Act. Favoring white, English-speaking immigrants, the McCarran-Walter Act allowed for unrestricted immigration from the Western Hemisphere and gave preference to individuals with relatives who were already citizens of the United States. Thanks to the earlier waves of immigration, many new arrivals from Ireland were able to draw on these existing relationships.

In 1946, Pan American Airlines introduced transatlantic flights from Ireland to the United States. Initially very expensive, these flights were largely out of reach for most young Irish immigrants who had, until the late 1950s, made the journey by ship. On April 28, 1958, Aerlínte Éireann (later renamed Aer Lingus) operated its first transatlantic service from Shannon Airport to New York. The easing immigration laws, coupled with increasingly affordable air travel costs, resulted in a slight uptick of Irish immigration to the United States, a trend that was further enhanced by travel incentives. For example, a February 2, 1957, advertisement in New York City's *Irish Echo* by the airline TWA describes a transportation revolution already in progress, one that was encouraging and optimistic: "Bring your family and friends over now! Save with TWA Immigrant Fares until March 31st! On TWA, you can buy tickets here. Prepay their fare from Ireland to any part of the U.S.

TWA delivers tickets and whatever expense money you wish to send, without charge! A TWA Passenger Service Representative meets your Family or friends on arrival at New York. Helps them through US Customs and Immigration formalities. Bring them now. Pay later."

Another "pull" factor that further stimulated immigration to the United States was the lure of widely available and comparatively well-paid work. Musician Matty Connolly left his home in Scotstown, County Monaghan, in 1960. He recalls that, by then, he could also have found work in Ireland thanks to its improving economy, but instead, chose New York: "You could make a living in Ireland, but you could make a much better living in the United States, dollars and cents-wise. I came in 1960. I started working as a construction worker those years and I was getting about three times the wages here that I would get on the other side. That in itself tells you right there that this was the place to be!" (interview, 1988).

Like their counterparts in Britain, the newly arrived Irish in the United States were typically young, single, and unattached; at least half were women. Many came to the United States after first immigrating to and living for a time in Britain. Having already lived outside of Ireland and often in large cities, this new cohort was relatively cosmopolitan and worldly compared to those who came directly from rural Ireland.[3] Once in the United States, the majority of immigrants worked in blue-collar jobs, much of it unionized. Irish men joined the carpenters union and found plenty of work in construction. They also worked in warehouses or as dockworkers after joining the International Longshoremen's Association. Still others found union jobs as city utility workers and in other trades. Irish women worked in the service industry, as clerical staff in offices, store clerks, and domestics (nannies and maids). New arrivals from Ireland often worked a variety of jobs until landing more secure, long-term trades that could ultimately support themselves and, eventually, their families. Flutist Jack Coen, for example, immigrated to New York City from Galway in 1949. He eventually joined the Electricians Union after a series of miscellaneous jobs: "I worked washing dishes for a while, a couple of months. And then I moved out to [New] Jersey and went loading trucks. And then I came back to New York, got a job on the railroad, so I stayed there. I worked in the rail department . . . and then I went into line gang, transmission lines. [I worked there for] thirty-four years. It 'twas good enough, I guess" (interview, 1992).

Along with the promise of well-paid work, many young Irish chose cities in the United States in response to the allure of urban life and the adventure of living in a new place. Martin Mulhaire arrived in New York City in 1958 from Eyrecourt, County Galway. An outstanding traditional button accordionist, Mulhaire was a member of the Galway-based Tulla Céilí Band, which, at the time, was on tour in the United States and booked to perform at Carnegie Hall. Recalls Mulhaire: "I had never heard of Carnegie Hall, it didn't mean anything to me! This was an opportunity to see the US!" (interview, 1985).

After that performance, Mulhaire's excitement about the United States was the decisive factor in his decision to stay:

> I always had a fascination with the US as most European people have. We're very influenced by the music, by the styles, and just by hearing about the US. And just to be here and see place names that you'd heard of . . . and never thought you'd be there. It was very fascinating for me and I just fell in love with the country. I decided, well, I think it's time to make a change and I decided I would stay here. I was twenty-one! (Interview, 1985)

Irish émigrés settled primarily in American cities, including Boston, Philadelphia, Chicago, St. Louis, and San Francisco, and helped reenergize already established immigrant and Irish American communities.[4] New York City was the destination for a majority, and, between 1958 and 1961, became home to nearly one-third of the total number of Irish émigrés (Almeida 2004, 207). These numbers remained high and mirrored national immigration trends but eventually tapered by the end of the 1960s. For example, in 1950, there was a total of 144,808 Irish born in New York City; by 1960, this figure dropped to 114,008 and by 1970, to 68,778, as a result of changing immigration laws.[5]

In New York, Irish immigrants settled in Queens and Brooklyn as well as the Willis Avenue section of the Bronx (dubbed the "Thirty-Third Irish County"), and in parts of Manhattan, specifically Yorkville on the Upper East Side. Within these areas, the newly arrived Irish mixed with the largely working- and middle-class immigrants and second-generation Irish Americans who had established businesses, forged networks, and created community infrastructures. Frank Holt, a former president of the New Jersey Gaelic League, was born in the Bronx in 1933. He remembers the response of New York's Irish community to this newest wave of Irish émigrés: "Anything that we could do, we would certainly do for these people. Like get them jobs, come by the house to get a good feed. When they were homesick and lonesome, we'd talk to them" (interview, 1992). In addition to finding housing, jobs, and other support, they also found ample opportunity to socialize at the many establishments that catered to the Irish—pubs, social clubs and fraternal organizations—and of course, Irish ball rooms.

New York City had long been home to a number of dance halls and other Irish social institutions, including the New Shamrock Dance Hall, located at the Peter Stuyvesant Hotel at West 86th Street and Central Park West. In the years following World War II, additional Irish dance halls opened or expanded to accommodate the newest wave of Irish. Manhattan's Upper East Side—from Fifty-Ninth Street to Eighty-Sixth Street between Lexington and Madison Avenues—was home to many of the best-known venues, including Jaeger House on Eighty-Fifth Street; Yorkville Casino (aka Turn Hall) on Eighty-Sixth Street; the New Tuxedo Ballroom (located one story below the Yorkville Casino); the (Old) Tuxedo Ballroom on Fifty-Ninth Street; the Caravan also on Fifty-Ninth Street; and Palm Gardens on West Fifty-Second Street. The Bronx boasted several major Irish dance halls, including the Star of Munster on Willis Avenue and the Red Mill on Jerome Avenue. In Queens, the Tower View Ballroom in Woodside was a popular spot for dances as were many smaller venues in Rockaway, which as home to a substantial number of Irish immigrants, was known as the "Irish Riviera" (see Noonan 1992).

"All Roads Lead to the City Center"

This was sort of an enclosed environment. The people that were there were mostly Irish born. So it was like a home away from home.

Martin Mulhaire, interview, 1988

The most popular New York City Irish dance venue was the City Center Ballroom, which, between 1955 and 1963, was, by all accounts, a dancing and social mecca. Banner advertisements in the *Irish Echo* routinely announced who was performing at City Center in any given week, trumpeting that "All Roads Lead to the City Center!" This was literally the case, as City Center was located in the center of Manhattan on West Fifty-Fifth Street between Sixth and Seventh Avenues and was easily accessible by the many subway lines that connect New York City's outer boroughs to and converge in midtown Manhattan. A new arrival who lived in one of the many Irish neighborhoods in Queens, the Bronx, Brooklyn, or Staten Island could easily arrive at City Center by hopping on any number of subway or bus lines—public transportation that very well might have been operated by a fellow Irish immigrant, notes music arranger/saxophonist Brendan Ward. "It was a mass of Irish people and they all knew each other. At that time, remember too that the bus driver—if you were waiting for a bus—was probably Irish also. The man who drove the train was probably Irish" (interview, 1992).

City Center was owned and operated by Bill Fuller, who by the mid-1950s, had expanded his entertainment empire beyond England and Ireland, eventually owning or managing an estimated nineteen ballrooms throughout the

United States.[6] His entrepreneurial sensibilities often found him mentoring musicians in the earliest stages of their careers and convincing some to push beyond their own self-doubt. Brendan Ward, for example, left his position in Mick Delahunty's Orchestra to immigrate to New York in 1955. Almost immediately, Ward was contacted by Bill Fuller. Having just opened the refurbished City Center as the premier Irish ballroom in New York on September 15, 1955, Fuller offered Ward the position of leader of what would become City Center's renowned resident dance orchestra. Ward was initially hesitant. "[Bill Fuller] said, 'You're a leader, from tomorrow on.' And I said, 'Bill, I just can't.' He said, 'You have to get a band together. I know you're capable of doing it. I will help you get a band'" (interview, 1992).

Brendan Ward went on to do exactly that. From 1955 to 1963, he conducted the Brendan Ward Orchestra, a twelve-piece ensemble that featured many of New York City's finest instrumentalists (both Irish and otherwise). Ward also wrote the iconic arrangements that he had developed while working for Mick Delahunty—dance numbers that reframed Irish songs for big band instrumentation. Ward enjoyed the regular and well-paid work in a highly visible venue that attracted other recent émigrés. And thanks to his longtime work with the Mick Delahunty Orchestra, audiences at City Center knew him and his music well: "In City Center, these people would come up and say, 'I remember you with Mick playing in Arklow or in Dublin or whatever, down in Clonmel or up in Sligo.' So it was good for Bill Fuller that I was instantly kind of known by people who came in here from all parts of the country. And it was good for me, by the way" (Ward, interview, 1992).

A seemingly inexhaustible producer, agent, and manager, Bill Fuller reputedly commuted an average of six thousand miles a week between his many properties.[7] He organized tours of Irish dance orchestras, céilí bands, and, later, showbands, both at his ballrooms and elsewhere, freely shifting from venue to venue the many house musicians who worked for him. Accordionist Paddy Noonan, for example, provided céilí dance music at City Center from 1956 to 1965. He recalls being sent to play evenings at Fuller's other ballrooms in San Francisco, Los Angeles, Boston, Pittsburgh, and abroad, in Toronto, London, and Manchester (interview, 1992).

Bill Fuller also routinely served as sponsor to Irish musicians, both those on tour from Ireland as well as those who wished to immigrate to New York, including Martin Mulhaire:

> At that time, I met Bill Fuller. . . . So along with playing Carnegie Hall, we played in his ballroom, the City Center Ballroom. And when he heard that I had an interest in staying here, he said, "Well, you're going to need somebody

> to claim you here. Somebody to help you." So he said, "If I can help, I will." Which he did. And he employed me to play the Irish section of the dances [at City Center Ballroom]. (Mulhaire, interview, 1988)

Weekends at City Center

By the late 1950s, a Friday or Saturday evening could find up to two thousand young Irish flocking to City Center for dancing that began at 8:00 or 9:00 p.m. and went until 2:00 a.m. or later. The venue's allure was well known beyond New York City, recalls Paddy Noonan: "We're a people that like to stick together. City Center, you'd go there on a Friday night, you'd probably meet seven or eight people that you knew from home [Ireland], that came out that week. . . . If you lived in Cleveland, on a long weekend, you'd pile into a car and drive to New York. People from Boston would come down, because they'd meet one hundred people that they knew in Ireland" (interview, 1992).

Audiences at City Center tended to dress formally. While alcohol was available (unlike the dance halls in Ireland at the time), the emphasis was less on drinking and more on socializing and dancing, recalls Martin Mulhaire:

> People came to dance. It was a large dance floor and tables and so forth, and people just came to dance to the music. The crowd at the time, they were Irish immigrants, really, because immigration at that time was wide open. People were coming in at a rate of five or six thousand a year. So they naturally went towards the places where they would meet people that had come before them. So while the flow of immigrants were coming, the dance hall scene was really booming here. (Interview, 1988)

Like the majority of music and dance venues in New York City at the time, City Center was a union hall under the jurisdiction of Local 802, Associated Musicians of Greater New York. Union regulations demanded that for every forty-five minutes musicians played, they were given a fifteen-minute break. At the interval, a solo accordionist or a trio consisting of an accordionist, drums, and piano player took over the stage and provided Irish traditional music for céilí dancing. This structure satisfied union regulations and audiences enjoyed the near-continuous music and dance.[8] Fuller was able to offer well-paid work to many of the outstanding traditional Irish musicians in New York at the time—Paddy Reynolds, Andy McGann, Louis Quinn, Joe Burke, among others—who, night after night, provided music for standard céilí dances such as the "Walls of Limerick," "A Stack of Barley," "Highland Fling," and a polka or two. The trio concluded with a set of old-time Irish waltzes, which held wide appeal, according to Brendan Ward: "The waltzes, the whole ballroom would get out! It was an easy dance. Irish people seemed to like to waltz" (interview, 1992).

Figure 8.2 Martin Mulhaire, ca. 1980. (Photo courtesy of Martin Mulhaire.)

Irish traditional musicians who were nimble and could play popular American dance music were rewarded with additional jobs and added income streams. The late fiddler/bandleader Louis Quinn emigrated from County Armagh to New York City in 1936. There, he organized both the Louis Quinn Orchestra and the smaller ensemble, the Shamrock Minstrels, groups that, given their instrumentation and facility with repertoire, could provide both American popular music as well as Irish tunes and songs. Thanks to their musical versatility, Quinn and his bandmates were able to find more consistent work: "The American music was in demand and so was the Irish music, that's why I got so many jobs at that time because I leaned a bit towards the Irish dancing. . . . And you'd usually be called because of the fact that you were able to play the traditional Irish and popular music together" (Quinn, interview, 1990).

Among the dancing audiences, there existed different levels of experience and appreciation of céilí dance and music. Some émigrés had enjoyed céilí dancing prior to leaving Ireland, while others might have been largely unfamiliar with it. Still others may have chosen not to attend ceílís back home given the perception that this style was old fashioned and out of touch

Figure 8.3 Louis E. Quinn and His Shamrock Minstrels, ca. 1955. Lad O'Beirne (seated, fiddle) next to Louis E. Quinn (standing). (Photo courtesy of Sean Quinn.)

with youth. However, as new arrivals in New York, these same immigrants may have found new meaning and significance in ceílí dancing because of its sonic and kinesthetic evocation of Ireland. And for many, ceílí dancing was a palliative that eased feelings of homesickness while underscoring nostalgic memories. Sets of céilí dance music at a City Center evening were therefore not only expected but mandatory. Recalls Brendan Ward: "Because it was an Irish ballroom and [Bill Fuller] was catering to Irish people, 100 percent, 1,200 people wanted céilí [dancing]. They enjoyed it!" (interview, 1992).

Showbands on Tour in the United States

Beginning in 1958, a handful of the top showbands in Ireland began touring the United States, both during the Lenten season and beyond. American tours were initially limited to the best-known professional showbands, unlike the lesser-known professional and semiprofessional groups that more often toured Britain. Even for the top professional bands, touring the United States was typically not as lucrative as touring Britain or simply performing in Ireland. Steve O'Hara, a music writer for the Irish publication, *Top Ten Weekly*, noted this in a February 17, 1967, article: "While reports reveal that there is good money to be made across the water [in Britain], America is nothing more than a well-paid and highly enjoyable holiday."

That said, touring the United States did come with the all-important factors of prestige and publicity. Showband engagements were routinely advertised beginning with their imminent departure for or return from a United States tour. A March 1, 1963, advertisement in the *Connacht Tribune,* for example, was typical in its exhortation for readers to not miss "the greatest St. Patrick's Night Dance in all Ireland," featuring a performance by The Capitol Showband in Tooreen Hall in Knock, County Mayo: "Look out for THE CAPITOLS HALF-HOUR on Telefís Éireann—before their grand tour of the US. Their new show is the most brilliant yet."

In 1958, Bill Fuller brought over the Clipper Carlton on a multicity tour, a very successful project that reputedly took Fuller only one month to organize. Recalls drummer Mickey O'Hanlon, "We went out for St. Patrick's Day in '58 and we sailed on the Queen Mary.... And we played New York and we did Boston, Philadelphia, and I think we did San Francisco too and a whole stack of places like that. And jayse, we couldn't believe it! The first sighting of New York City, just driving into New York, seeing the skyline, I'll never forget that. I thought that was brilliant" (interview, 2007).

The Clippers' second tour was organized in 1960 by Harry McGuirk, a well-known Irish radio personality in New York City and the manager/promoter at the Jaeger House. Their first performance was at St. Nicholas Arena, a boxing venue in Manhattan at 69 West Sixty-Sixth Street. It was an unqualified success, recalls O'Hanlon:

> The fee into a dance in those days was $2 or something, not too bad. But he had no fee up on the poster and he charged them something like $5. About two people objected. The rest just paid and walked in. And there was seven or eight thousand at it. And your man [McGuirk] was paying our way out and putting us up and all; he had expected about two thousand. And he came down and said he had made his money in one night. We done some big business in America in them days! (O'Hanlon, interview, 2007)

The Clippers' performances challenged the stereotypes about Ireland and Irish music at the time. For many Irish immigrants who had arrived in the United States before World War II, Ireland was remembered as a provincial, isolated place, untouched by the realities of modern life, a perception reinforced by the American media. Mickey O'Hanlon, for example, recalls an interview with two American journalists who met the Clipper Carlton when the Queen Mary docked in New York City in 1958:

> These two newspaper men came on the boat.... And the boys said [in an American accent]: "You're the Irish band over from Ireland? You're a céilí band of course?"
>
> I said, "No, we're not a céilí band. We're a modern type band."

Figure 8.4 The Clipper Carlton and the Queen Mary, 1962. *From left to right*: Mick O'Hanlon, Fergus O'Hagan, Victor Fleming, Terry Logue, Dom Shearer, Art O'Hagan, Billy McFadden, and Hugo Quinn. (Collection of Jimmy Higgins.)

"Yeah, well, that figures, a modern céilí band."

"No, we don't play céilí music."

"You don't play céilí music? You're from Ireland, crossroad dances, and all that?"

"No, there's none of that there now. Ireland's just like every other country now. It's all modernised, not fully modernised, but they follow music and [Elvis] Presley's very big in Ireland."

"Presley? In Ireland? Jeez, are you kiddin'?"

"No. Kids love Presley over there."

"What about the old thatched cottages?"

"There's thatched cottages but the Irish people now are living in modern bungalows, they're going to the films, they love Presley films, they're listening to the big American bands."

Well, they twisted that story 'round: "The Saints in Heaven Preserve Us!" was the headline. "What has happened to our Irish heritage? Gone are the crossroad dances, gone are the thatched cottages. Instead we are informed by two members of this Irish band that . . ."

And it done us a lot of harm. Oh jayse, aye. There were people writing into us and saying "How dare you go over there and slag Ireland?" We were trying to build Ireland up. But there [are] ones in America don't want to hear of Ireland being modern. They're out there fifty years or forty years and they want to call it "the oul' sod" and they don't want to hear about anything modern. (O'Hanlon, interview, 2007)

The Clippers' tour was followed in 1960 by the Royal Showband, who performed at City Center as part of their first American tour during the Lenten season. Brendan Bowyer recalls performing their standard rock 'n' roll numbers as well as classic Irish songs such as "Boolavogue" and "The Croppy Boy," but soon realized that Irish immigrant audiences wanted to hear more of the latter. Like Jimmy Higgins's "Musical Tour of Ireland," Bowyer came up with a similar performance strategy: "I actually have a song for every county in Ireland. I do! And that would have been the aim in those days, to make sure we would cover [the Counties]. You can do 'The Rose of Tralee' for Kerry, 'Galway Bay.' Especially the rural—Mayo, Galway, Kerry, Cork, the western seaboard. Donegal. Sure, Dublin and they all have 'Molly Malone' and so on. There's a song for every one" (interview, 2006).

For many showbands on tour in the United States, reframing their repertoire this way was crucial. When Jimmy Higgins and the International Showband came to New York City, they quickly discovered that performing covers of Top 20 from the American charts was perceived as derivative and inauthentic:

> The first night we played, we died the death. People were saying like, "Jesus, what are you guys doing?"... Learning all the American charts! We wanted to really impress them with the American charts! We were playing City Center, and we thought, we're nearly on Broadway. Let's play all the big ballad numbers, the big show-stoppers. (*Laughs.*)
>
> [But] they wanted to hear us play music that they remember being played when they left Ireland twenty years previously. They wanted to be reminded of Ireland. They didn't want to hear the latest Bobby Darin tune [because] they could go down the road and hear Tony Bennett, or Cliff Brown, or any of these guys and go into the real thing. They didn't want a yellow-pack version of it.[9] (Higgins, interview, 2007)

Similar to the demands of their immigrant and Irish American audiences, touring showbands often did not live up to the expectations of media critics. In 1966, for example, the Royal Showband made their debut performance at New York City's Carnegie Hall. A *New York Times* review of their performance a few days later described an audience of about one thousand listeners, noting the "ethnic appeal" of the band's Irish rebel and "sentimental" songs but gently concludes that while "one does not wish to be inhospitable to the Irish visitors . . . the pop competition from Britain and the United States is perhaps keener than they imagine" (Shelton 1966). In contrast to their reception back in Ireland, touring showbands in the United States were perceived centrally as Irish groups that played popular Irish music. Anything else was heard as strictly derivative.

By the late 1960s, showbands of all stripes—not just the top-tier groups—were able to tour the United States, thanks to the increasingly affordable transatlantic flights. At that point, however, Irish establishments seemed to have met their saturation point, as opined by Dan Kiely to a journalist writing for *Top Ten Weekly*:

> This is the opinion of Kerry-born, 24-year old ballroom owner Dan Kiely, who is on a short visit to Ireland.
>
> When I talked with Dan in Dublin this week, he told me: "I think that if 12 showbands went to the States during Lent or in the Autumn, it would work out better for all concerned. As it is, they are crowding the American scene."
>
> Dan was the first Irish ballroom proprietor in New York to bring out the Freshmen from Ballymena.
>
> "Don't get me wrong," said Dan. "Showbands are very popular in America, and will be for a while to come. But I still believe that some control should be put on the numbers coming in." (*Top Ten Weekly*, February 25, 1967)

Dancing at the Red Mill: The Majestic Showband

Like their counterparts in England, showbands made up of immigrants increasingly became fixtures at the many Irish-owned dance halls and pubs in New York, Boston, Chicago, and other urban centers. One of the best-known New York showbands was the Majestics, formed in 1963, and led by Matty Connolly, who had recently arrived from County Monaghan. Upon arriving in New York, Connolly found work as a guitarist and vocalist in the Mickey Carton Band and the John O'Neill Band, both of which were the house bands at the Jaeger House. There, Connolly met Martin Mulhaire, who had been hired to play sets of céilí dances and old-time waltzes on button accordion. The timing of their meeting coincided with Mulhaire having just followed through on a long time dream:

> Always loved the guitar, listening to the American Forces Network. It was mostly Country and Western music that was transmitted to Europe—Hank Williams and Hank Snow and people like that. So I just loved listening to guitar. I had never seen a guitar actually until I came [to New York]. Nobody played guitars. Nobody had them in Ireland. So when I came here, I decided, well, I just had to buy a guitar and I had seen a picture of Dion on an album playing this beautiful looking guitar with a carved tailpiece. I didn't know what it was, so I wrote to Gibson and I asked them to send me a catalog. So they sent me a catalog. It was called a Gibson J200.
>
> Now I couldn't play a note. I said, well if I never play, I'll just have this and I'll hang it on the wall and it's such a beautiful looking guitar. That's all I need.

> Just to look at it! So, I went to a place in town, I think Eddie Bell. I told him what I was looking for, and he says, "Just hold on!" He went in the back and took out this guitar. A blond J200 guitar. And he says "It's for sale." So this one was, I think, $350. About three weeks pay at that time, anyway. Which was a lot of money. So I purchased my J200 and came home on the subway train and was very, very happy. And I didn't even know how to tune the damn thing! But I had a J200. One of my ambitions! (Interview, 1988)

Mulhaire bought a chord book, learned to play his J200, moved on to the electric guitar, and joined the Majestic Showband. The group included Martin Mulhaire and Matty's brother, Peter Connolly, on electric guitars; Matty Connolly on electric bass; Connolly's sister, Mary, on vocals; Connolly's brother-in-law, Arthur Sherry, on saxophone; and Johnny Hanley on drums. Like the showbands back home, the members of the Majestics wore matching outfits—sometimes blue blazers with white pants, white shoes, and ties and, at other times, black trousers, ties, and checked jackets. Recalls Mulhaire, "We looked like a fleet!"

As the Red Mill's house band, the Majestics, performed every Friday, Saturday, and Sunday night from 9:00 p.m. to 2:00 a.m. They were also in near constant demand for private events, often playing two weddings on some Saturdays, followed by their standard evening set at the Red Mill. The Majestics were able to maintain this punishing schedule because, like other showbands in Ireland, they spread out the work of lead vocals between four members of the band, each of whom specialized in a particular song style. Matty Connolly also attributes their longevity as a band to clean living: "No member of the band done a lot of drinking. We weren't teetotalers, but we didn't abuse the drink either. For that reason, we were able to stay in the game" (Connolly, interview, 1988).

The Red Mill featured a large dance space with tables lined around the room's periphery, a spot-lit stage, and a crystal ball chandelier. Weekend performances there routinely drew large crowds of Irish immigrants who were eager to socialize and dance to a diverse repertoire:

> In the earlier part of the night, you played mostly the older music and slower music, and maybe the waltzes and that, which the older people liked. They would dance to all the new songs . . . foxtrots, quicksteps, slow waltzes, slow foxtrots, words that have gone by the wayside. We played a lot of country 'n' western and the modern music of the day, which was a lot of the Beatles and Rolling Stones. [They] were very popular in them days. And then as the younger people came in, you moved more into the say, the Top 40 type music.
>
> You played for three quarters of an hour and then somebody else would do a totally Irish set, like a "Siege of Ennis" or "A Stack of Barley." At that time, there was a fiddle player, Andy McGann, who played in the Red Mill. Andy

Figure 8.5 The Majestic Showband, ca. 1963. *Left to right*: Matty Connolly, Martin Mulhaire, Johnny Hanley, Mary Connolly, Arthur Sherry, and Pete Connolly. (Photo credit Matthews Photo Studio, Woodside, Queens, NY; photo courtesy of Matty Connolly.)

> McGann, Tommy Goodwin, and Cyrilla Parsons was the pianist who played with them.
>
> If you wished, you could go sit down at a table, just listen to the music and talk. If you felt like dancing, you just got up and danced. If you wanted to meet people, or meet different girls or guys, you just asked them to dance. It was a social gathering place. And you also met people from all parts of Ireland. . . . That was the scene and it was a lot of fun (M. Mulhaire, interviews, 1985 and 1988, Flushing, NY).

The Ambivalence of Heritage

While a majority of audiences at the Red Mill appreciated the short intervals of céilí dances and old-time waltzes, more than this might have been too much, recalls both Matty Connolly and Martin Mulhaire. This was particularly true by the 1960s and pointed to a sort of threshold of this era in the United States when ethnicity was celebrated only up to a certain point and not beyond. In fact, Irish ethnic identity among immigrants in New York City during these years was anything but straightforward. At one extreme was a minority of recent Irish immigrants and second generation Irish Americans—those who preferred traditional music and song and enjoyed an evening of céilí dancing, most often sponsored by one of the various arms of the Gaelic League (Holt, interview, 1992).[10] At the other extreme were those with no interest in Irish traditional music and dance and sought instead, contemporary Irish American and American popular music. Among these were younger immigrants who may have had little prior exposure to traditional Irish music and who had danced exclusively to showbands back in Ireland. The majority of patrons however had eclectic tastes that encompassed some of both.

New York–based Irish musicians, bandleaders, and producers were well aware of this range of taste and displays of Irishness. Fiddler Paddy Reynolds recalls having to "read" his audiences and tailor his performances to their tastes, most often playing an even split of American popular and Irish dance music "to suit the blend of the people that would be there" (interview, 1992). Reading their audiences in terms of perceived levels of "Irishness" extended also to those in the Irish American media and entertainment worlds. The late Dorothy Hayden Cudahy was a well-known personality in New York City's Irish American community, who, from 1943 to 1990, hosted the weekly WEVD-FM radio show, *Irish Memories*.[11] Regarding how she curated the content of this long running program, Cudahy recalled:

> I put on a show the way I thought an Irish American show would go over in New York. If they were a real Irish audience, you could play what we'd call a "heavier" song, a real Irish song. So you had your jigs there, because it's familiar to everybody. The most familiar music in the world is jig-time, you understand?. . . So then you always ended with the hornpipe, you end with a smash! (Interview, 1992)

Some Irish immigrants in the 1960s rejected elements of Irish traditional culture altogether. Some felt that Irish music itself did not reflect their contemporary lives in the United States. For others, traditional music was a source of deeply rooted cultural ambivalence, in part a result of years of historical political oppression, believes Martin Mulhaire.

> That goes back deep into our heritage of British occupation. When the British came to Ireland, they tried to destroy everything that was Irish and what they couldn't destroy, they tried to make you feel ashamed of. They abolished the language, they weren't allowed to fly green flags, you weren't allowed to play music. The music was played, but it was played sort of underground. It wasn't mainstream. . . . The[y] tried to [stop the Irish] from playing the music, but they still played. Along with that came a kind of reserve where they kept it to themselves and they didn't play for other people or they felt ashamed to play for other people. (Mulhaire, interview, 1985)

Figure 8.6 Andy McGann (*left*) and Paddy Reynolds (*right*), New York City, ca. 1970. (Photo courtesy of Mary Reynolds Tielve.)

Along with this lingering trauma of colonial repression, there also existed a profound class dimension associated with Irish traditional culture, argues folk singer Tommy Makem. "Irish music was thought of as peasant music and had come from times and places when people were very poor and almost ashamed of their music" (Makem, interview, 1992). This association of traditional culture and class affiliation was widespread: flutist Jack Coen recalled that in Ireland, "they used to call it 'diddley-diddley' music. Irish traditional music was something that they figured was associated with the poor, the poor people. And they didn't want to be associated for that reason. Everybody wanted to associate with the rich and they want to be, do what they did. In the big dance halls, they all wanted to be associated with that" (interview, 1992). This ambivalence was especially strong among young people who left Ireland in the years after World War II. For them, showband music, rather than Irish traditional music, better reflected the life left behind in Ireland, one that engaged with the popular American moment and set aside memories of an impoverished and colonized past.

The heyday of showbands and dance halls waned in the United States beginning in the late 1960s, with demographic changes accounting for much of this decline. The once single young Irish men and women who had constituted showband audiences were now married and starting their families and had less time and interest in a night out dancing. Moreover, immigration from Ireland decreased to a trickle and then essentially ended as a result of the Immigration and Nationality Act of 1965. Signed into law by then President Lyndon B. Johnson on October 3, 1965, the Act was, in part, an effort to bring US immigration policy into line with other antidiscrimination measures. The Act essentially eliminated the national-origin quota system that had, up to that point, favored immigrants from northern and western European countries (Gjelten 2015). It also had far reaching consequences for almost every sector of New York's Irish community, recalls Matty Connolly. "[The Act] killed the Irish dance hall scene, it killed the bar scene, it killed the [Irish] football scene in Gaelic Park. It killed it for a lot of Irish people here in New York. And it certainly killed it for the bands" (interview, 1988).

"If We Only Had Ol' Ireland over Here"

Showbands in Britain and the United States served as vehicles that, for thousands of immigrant Irish, helped connect the Ireland left behind with their new lives abroad. Flexible and inventive, showbands mirrored the experiences of their audiences and affirmed the complicated realities and emotions of displacement, while, at the same time, reading and responding to their audiences' changing sensibilities as to what constituted "Irishness." By providing audiences with the sounds and cultural affiliation from home while also engaging with the contemporary realities of a modern, urban life abroad, showbands provided a respite from the isolation and homesickness that only an immigrant can know. In doing so, they served as a musical bridge that connected Irish emigrants and linked the old life with the new.

Notes

1. That so many emigrants were so young had historical precedence. The late button accordionist, Tom Doherty (b. 1913) was only fourteen years old when he left his home in Mountcharles, County Donegal, in 1927: "You had to go [to school] until you were fourteen. And the day after I finished school, I landed in England, stole away. Stole away, because there was nothing at home. It was a big family . . . a lot of children. So there weren't very much to be got at home and there were no work to be got either. And there weren't very much to eat sometimes there. We were poor people" (interview, 1991).

2. In this way, showbands became an integral component of an important Irish migrant network that relied, argues Delaney (2007, 25), on "norms of reciprocity and obligations towards family and friends as well as the basic needs of companionship."

3. See Gedutis (2004, 169).

4. See Gedutis (2004) on the Irish immigrant community and music and dance scene in Boston and Miller (1996) on the same in New York from the 1930s through the 1970s.

5. US Census Bureau Reports, 1860–1980; *Public Use Sample*, New York, NY, 1990.

6. Fuller's ballroom empire included the Keyman's Club in Chicago, the New State Ballroom in Boston, and the Carousel in San Francisco, which later, in 1968, was leased to rock promoter Bill Graham and famously renamed Fillmore West.

7. In 1966, Fuller broke into the entertainment industry in Las Vegas, where he successfully booked the Royal Showband for the first of their many appearances and eventual residency. Fuller's business acumen was legendary as recounted by his friend and fellow promoter, Frank Murray: "I remember Bill telling me about the day someone offered to introduce him to Elvis Presley. He turned around and said: 'Fuck Elvis, I want to meet the Colonel [Elvis's manager]!'" (Murray quoted in Scanlon 2008).

8. New York musicians were required to join Local 802 in order to play in Union halls. Among other advantages of union membership, Irish musicians benefited from a regulation concerning "stand-ins," which required that the venue hire an equivalent number of union musicians when a nonunion band from outside of the United States was booked to play. Fiddler Paddy Reynolds explains:

> PR: [If] it was a twelve-piece band, there had to be twelve pieces [union players] employed to sit along the wall with their instruments. . . . And many a one of those I brought my fiddle and sat down and never played a tune all night, but got paid the same as they did. That was the good thing about the union.
>
> RSM: Weren't you bored doing that?
>
> PR: No, goddamnit! When I got that check, it cured everything! Are you kidding? When we'd get our check, we'd go somewhere else and enjoy a good *seisiún*! (Interview, 1992)

9. Yellow Pack was a brand of groceries launched in 1980 throughout Britain and Ireland. In Ireland, the term, "yellow pack," came to refer to generic, inexpensive, and sometimes poor-quality products.

10. The various branches of the Gaelic League all sponsored regular céilí dances. These included the Philo-Celtic Society, founded in 1876, in Manhattan; the Bronx Gaelic League, founded in 1940; St. Brendan's in Brooklyn; St. Elizabeth's in Washington Heights; the Gaelic Society in the West 50s in Manhattan; and the New Jersey Gaelic League, founded in 1958 (Holt, interview, 1992).

11. Dorothy Hayden Cudahy inherited *Irish Memories* from her father, James Hayden, who had hosted the program on WEVD-FM starting in 1928. Sixty years later, in 1988, Dorothy Hayden Cudahy had the distinct honor of being the first female Grand Marshall of New York City's Saint Patrick's Day Parade, leading 200,000 marchers in the nation's largest and oldest Saint Patrick's Day celebration.

9

The End of the Showband Era

Early in the morning of July 31, 1975, on their way home from a dance at the Castle Ballroom in Banbridge, County Down, five musicians in the Miami Showband were stopped at a roadblock set up by members of the Ulster Volunteer Force, a loyalist paramilitary group. During a short confrontation, three musicians—Fran O'Toole, Brian McCoy, and Tony Geraghty—were shot to death. A prematurely exploded bomb placed by the UVF in the Miami's vehicle killed two UVF men (Harris Boyle and Wesley Somerville) and critically injured two additional musicians, Stephen Travers and Des McAlea (aka Des Lee).[1] The Miami Showband massacre, as it came to be known, was stunning in its violence. For many, it was particularly traumatic because the showband world had long been viewed as apolitical, happy-go-lucky revelry, recalls Fr. Brian D'Arcy:

> It changed. It really was the day like [song writer] Don McLean [wrote] "The day the music died" . . . because up until then, there was an innocence and naivete and a wonderful fluidity about the scene and that fellows could go up and down the north and were untouchables. . . . They were bringing happiness to so many people, north and south and the whole thing just began to fade ever so quickly after that. (Interview, 2007)

Adding to this was a host of more predictable factors that had been steadily building toward the inevitable demise of the showbands by the mid-1970s.

Primary among them was the shift of performance venues from entirely dry dance halls to new discos and pubs that sold alcohol along with live music and dancing. At the same time, Ireland was experiencing a resurgence of cultural nationalism, driven in no small part by "the Troubles" in Northern Ireland, all of which set the stage for the ascendance of specifically Irish music—both rock and traditional dance music and folk song—to national and international stages. Coupled with this was the even more predictable shift of a changing audience demographic: young people were largely uninterested in dancing to their parents' popular music and looked to the new, hip sounds and relatable song lyrics as performed by Beat bands, Irish pop, and Irish rock groups.

The Troubles

While the Miami Showband massacre linked the political and sectarian violence of the Northern Ireland conflict with what had been an almost entirely apolitical showband world, it came neither out of the blue nor in isolation. The exchange of working musicians to and from Northern Ireland had been largely trouble free and seamless for decades. With the beginning of the Troubles in 1968, however, tensions mounted on the roads to and from Northern Irish dance halls. Northern Irish showbands in particular were routinely stopped and searched at the border by the Ulster Special Constabulary, also known as the B-Specials—Protestant militia groups that were widely viewed as defenders of Northern Irish unionism. Gene Turbett, trumpeter in the Omagh-based Melody Aces, recalls the often explicit sectarian dynamic during these road block searches:

> It was always scary. They had guns, rifles and all. And they would have been pointing them at you all the time [while searching the van] and the lights of the bus were shining on you and standing with your hands up while they took all the gear out. . . . They wouldn't have wanted you to be playing down there [in the Republic], because they didn't like the Republic of Ireland, you understand. They would say, "What are you doing playing down there, could you not find enough work up here?"
>
> If it was on a Sunday night, for instance, some of the boys [in the band] might be carrying rosary beads, or a prayer book in their pocket, in their overcoat. [The B Specials on patrol] would have known then. I seen them actually taking a prayer book out of a pocket and throwing it on the road. It was a tough old time then, to be honest, very tough. (Interview, 2007)

The stress of performing in Northern Ireland in the years leading up to the Miami Showband massacre was also palpable among musicians on tour from Ireland. The Dixies vocalist Brendan O'Brien recalls a bomb scare at a dance in Arboe, County Tyrone, during Christmas week in 1973 that required three thousand audience members to evacuate the dance hall at 2:00 a.m. Later that night, as the Dixies drove back to Cork from the dance, they were ambushed and robbed of their collective pay—over £2,000 (O'Brien, interview, 2006). While it was well known that showbands were paid in cash and therefore vulnerable to being robbed, Jimmy Higgins recalls a more sinister motive when his showband, the Big Time, was similarly ambushed after a job in Banbridge, Northern Ireland, exactly one week before the Miami Showband massacre:

> We played in Banbridge Hall. [After the gig], we were flagged down. Now I'd always fall asleep. And I was just leaning against the window, and I just woke up like that. And there was a guy outside with his face right up against the window. And his face all blackened up. And I got the fright of my life. He did it deliberately, just to frighten me. And it was pitch dark, and he says to Brendan [Mulhaire]: "Can I see what's in the back, the boot of the car." So Brendan got out to open the back. And as he did, a car started to report from a distance, and because it was so dark, it was lighting it up. And your man said, "You're OK, go on." So we went on.
>
> So I often wonder, was it a dry run? . . . They were looking for a name, and we were nobody. But then when they did get the Miami the following week, they asked them, "Now which of you is Dickie Rock?" Now Dickie Rock had left the band about two or three years before that. So that shows you how much their research was. (Interview, 2007)

Throughout the years of political instability in Northern Ireland, Protestant and Catholic dance audiences generally mixed easily and without incident in the shared social spaces of dance halls. That said, inevitable tensions permeated some dances in the North, recalls County Leitrim saxophonist Mick Wood: "I used to be kind of scared going down the North, all right. I used to prefer playing back here in the south of Ireland because [the Northern Irish audiences] were always on edge, even in the dance halls, you know?" (interview, 2007).

In the wake of the Miami Showband massacre, the Northern Irish dance hall scene effectively shut down. Ballrooms closed and dancing was curtailed. Paddy Cole's County Monaghan based-showband was particularly affected because the group relied primarily on work in the large ballrooms in the North:

> Everything died in the North after that for a while. Everything closed down, ballrooms . . . certainly that was like the death knell for us all. And suddenly we were trying to get scramble dates down South in places that didn't really mean an awful lot. Well, we had a meeting with the band, and we said, "It's either we

> fold the band or we decide to go back up North." And we were the first band to go back up North after the Miami [massacre]. And we got great receptions everywhere, from all different communities, because they loved the bands, they loved the dancing. (Cole, interview, 2007)

The Drink

While the Miami Showband massacre marked the beginning of a psychological and emotional end to the showband era, musicians, managers, dance hall owners, and promoters point to an equally insidious cause: "It was the drink that killed it," recalls Dublin-based agent George O'Reilly (interview, 2008). Indeed, the reputation of showbands as innocent fun had much to do with the fact that, for decades, the main venues—dance halls, parish halls, marquees, and ballrooms—had all been alcohol free with patrons limited to mineral water, soft drinks, and tea. By the early 1970s, however, pub owners saw the commercial potential of luring dancers away from the dance halls. Some renovated their pubs into cabarets, lounge bars, and the quintessentially Irish phenomenon known as the "singing pub." They installed dance floors, hung disco balls, and hired smaller pop bands ("combos"). Patrons could now drink while enjoying the live music and dance. For the showband musicians, the often challenging working conditions steadily deteriorated. Jimmy Higgins recalls performing one night at a pub that had turned into a disco: "I felt this thing flying past [me]. And I got a slap of beer on the jaw. Some guy had been drinking [and] when he finished the old glass, he just threw it up at the stage! And there was a dreg of beer in the bottom, and I got the splash across the face. . . . You think, hello, am I really enjoying this? In the space of about two years, [the showband scene] just died completely" (interview, 2007).

Former Taoiseach Albert Reynolds contends that ultimately, ballrooms could compete neither with these changing drinking trends nor existing licensing structures: "The pubs started to put on entertainment. . . . And to me, that was the start of the showbands going down the hill. Because [young people] went in and they were being entertained and they were drinking at the same time. The ballrooms had no bars. Never! Had none. And the license was against them having them too" (interview, 2006). Concerns about licensing and the shift of revenue from dance halls to pubs even made it to the floor of the Dáil Éireann, such as this 1975 debate regarding the Restricted Licenses Conversion Fund Bill. Argued TD Tom Enright,

> The Minister should also consider allocating a certain amount of this money for a survey as to why public dance halls and marquees are suffering a serious loss of revenue. The attendance at these places has been dropping, and bars and

singing lounges have taken over from them. People might wonder what was the relevance of that to this Bill, but many young people. . . who used to attend dances without having consumed large quantities of alcohol, no longer attend them. They are going into bars and lounges and stay there until closing time. I believe this is caused by the glamorisation on television of drink, and of the fun and games in bars and lounges. (Enright 1975)

Along with an explicit condemnation of the role of mass media, the clear subtext here of attendant social and moral decay parallels similar anxieties expressed some twenty years earlier in 1955 with the emergence of the earliest showbands. This discourse, in turn, echoes the stance two decades before that, in 1935, by the Church, by the state, and by the Gaelic League, with regard to the moral dangers posed by jazz and dance bands on Irish youth, ultimately giving rise to the Dance Halls Act of 1935. This neatly episodic resistance by the Church, state, and other cultural institutions underscores the ongoing, cyclical tensions between dominant Irish institutions and popular culture throughout most of the twentieth century. Beyond that and in combination with other factors, it also contributed to the inevitable demise of the showband era.

The Music

By the late 1960s, the perception of showbands by fans as cutting edge was beginning to fade. Irish youth started turning their attentions to the new sounds of Beat bands—smaller groups that emerged first in Britain and captured the new sounds of rock 'n' roll and R&B. Beat bands focused less on covers and more on original songs, earning the praise as "poor but honest" by *Top Ten Weekly* columnist Joe Kennedy (1967, 6): "They may not make much money but they are playing the music they like—the hell if nobody wants to listen to it." While this was no doubt true for the less well-known Beat bands, some, like the Beatles, enjoyed a quick ascent to international popularity and all its rewards. Their success contributed in no small part to the beginning of the end for showbands, recalls Melody Aces trumpeter Gene Turbett:

> The Beatles came on the scene. As you would well know, they were all guitar bands, everybody in the band played guitars. Our lineup was more brass. . . . The Beatles were a younger band, so therefore their voices and all could suit the songs that they were singing, whereas we were getting older, and weren't able to sing the songs that the people would have wanted to hear then—"She Loves You (Yeah, Yeah, Yeah)" and all that. Wasn't up our street, that. Young folk going to dances then would have wanted to go to listen to younger people then. So gradually then, our bookings started to get thinner and lighter. (Interview, 2007)

Showbands were thus increasingly seen as conservative in both their music and performance style. In the same 1967 column, Joe Kennedy opined that showbands "are wary of expansion, of new ideas, of taking even calculated risks. They are reactionary, unprogressive, even—dare I say—unknowledgeable about current trends, songs, styles, about what's happening in contemporary music." And for the next generation of Irish pop and rock musicians, the showband sound was simply passé. Drummer/vocalist Don O'Connor was in his late teens when he joined the Limerick-based pop band, Reform, in 1968. While O'Connor appreciated the showbands and studied their performances, he had little interest in joining one:

> Showbands were not cool. There was a certain conservatism in the showband thing, you know, the people running them, the way they dressed.... They had given me wonderful enjoyment, and [on the] TV program, *The Showband Show,* which as a young teenager I watched religiously, watched what the drummers were doing and tried to sort of learn from them.... But [at] seventeen, eighteen, I was much more influenced by West Coast American groups and the Beatles, the Rolling Stones, the Kinks, which were groups as opposed to showbands. (Interview, 2006)

Irish pop bands, like Reform, made their way onto stages toward the end of the 1960s. Leaving behind the matching mohair suits and the variety approach to song repertoire, pop bands initially overlapped and competed with the showbands that dominated the popular Irish music industry. Don O'Connor recalls the struggle to get Reform into what was, by 1979, a shrinking ballroom circuit:

> The only way to do it was to break a group into the ballroom circuit. And it was not really done. You would have the occasional success—some folk group might have a hit record and they might do a guest spot in the ballrooms.... But in general, the ballrooms were where showbands played. So I figured, if a group could break into the ballroom circuit, they could make a lot of money, they could do really well and they would be a success. (Interview, 2006)

Reform mirrored the showbands in that they too played covers, but, unlike the showbands, focused on the less well-known songs rather than the hits of the day. Moreover, they did not aim to reproduce these covers note for note but, instead, took creative liberties with the material. Crucially, though, they also wrote what O'Connor describes as "good commercial original songs." In crafting new material that contained contemporary sounds and ideas, Reform and other Irish pop bands further eroded the staying power of showbands. Recalls Royal Showband singer Brendan Bowyer: "We were making so much money doing everybody else's stuff, that we neglected to do some original material. . . . I think we were overwhelmed with our own success. And we neglected to look farther than that" (interview, 1992).

Shifting Tastes and Blurring Lines: Irish Rock and the Folk Revival

Along with this generational shift in musical taste, another wave of Irish nationalism was sweeping Ireland and fueling renewed interest in cultural identity through the embrace of both popular and traditional music. Beginning in 1970, Horslips introduced the genre that would become known as Celtic rock, which combined rock instrumentation and original material with musical and lyrical elements that explicitly located Ireland. In doing so, Celtic rock essentially paralleled and updated the similar process of creative hybridity pioneered some four decades earlier by Mick Delahunty's Orchestra with their big band arrangements of Irish songs. At the same time, the earliest Irish rock musicians, such as Rory Gallagher, Thin Lizzy, Boomtown Rats, and others, began their ascent to national stages and, somewhat later, for Van Morrison and U2, to international stages.[2] With this growing affirmation of fans both inside and outside of Ireland, Celtic rock and Irish rock music updated Irish popular music and furthered the eclipse and eventual decline of the showbands.

Alongside the birth of Irish rock was the near simultaneous renewal of interest in Irish traditional music and song, a response to the same wave of Irish cultural nationalism. This "revival," as it came to be called, was, in part, kindled by the international success of the renowned Irish folk song quartet the Clancy Brothers and Tommy Makem, who made their mark initially not in Ireland but in the burgeoning folk circuit in the United States in the early 1960s.

Hailing from Carrick-on-Suir, County Tipperary, Paddy and Tom Clancy immigrated to New York City in 1951; their brother, Liam Clancy, joined them in 1956, as did Tommy Makem, who emigrated from Keady, County Armagh. Meeting for the first time in 1956 in the Bronx apartment of folklorist Kenny Goldstein, the quartet recorded their first album, *The Rising of the Moon* (Tradition Records). Well known for their full-throated singing, the quartet performed Irish folk songs, ballads, and rebel songs using guitar, banjo, tin whistle, and other traditional instruments. They also put to use their training as aspiring (and occasionally, working) actors in their dramatically staged presentations, all of which clearly resonated with their growing audiences. According to Tommy Makem, the quartet's meteoric success took them by surprise: "We just didn't give a damn. I mean, we weren't setting out to be singers. So we didn't care if this career took off or died a terrible death.

And I think that showed in the performances. And then after we started getting all these bookings, we decided, well, we'd better give this a serious look" (interview, 1992).

In Ireland, the Clancy Brothers and Tommy Makem were largely unknown until folk music collector and RTÉ radio broadcaster Ciarán Mac Mathúna returned from the United States in 1962 with their LP recordings in hand. The quartet skyrocketed to popularity in Ireland after Mac Mathúna played their recordings on his radio program, the timing of which coincided with the waxing popularity of the showbands. Indeed, the Clancy Brothers and Tommy Makem's trajectory in Ireland paralleled the success of the showbands in terms of aesthetics and performance strategies. On stage, for example, they were immensely charismatic and radiated professionalism through their highly choreographed performances. Makem recalls that they also drew on their earlier training in acting: "Having had the experience of theater, we would spend more time writing out a concert format, you know. . . . But we were very conscious that it wasn't a matter of getting up and singing a parcel of songs. There had to be form to it. It made it more palatable for people to listen to" (interview, 1992).

Like the showbands, the Clancy Brothers and Tommy Makem favored fastidiously matching stage attire that, in their case, quickly became iconic: Aran Island sweaters and West Ireland–style fishing caps. Their outfits evoked not the modern British and American fashion sensibilities of the showbands' mohair suits but rather a carefully crafted image of Irishness that located folk culture from the coastal Gaeltacht (Irish-speaking) regions of Ireland.

While the showbands aimed to get their audiences up and dancing, the Clancy Brothers and Tommy Makem focused on the performance of the songs, intentionally straightening out the often irregular rhythms heard in traditional unaccompanied Irish songs as sung by *sean-nós* (old-style) singers. The result was an added predictability that encouraged audiences to easily sing and clap along, recalls Makem: "It was very strict rhythmically. [The audiences] were getting the words very distinctly. All of us, because of our theatrical training, enunciated very well, and people didn't have trouble hearing what we were singing" (interview, 1992).

There were other parallels: when performing in Ireland, the Clancy Brothers and Tommy Makem initially made use of the same commercial performance circuit established by the showbands. They subscribed to a similar marketing strategy that quickly rocketed them, in just a few years, to international stardom—an unprecedented feat for an Irish folk ensemble, either in Ireland or the United States. Based on their chart hits, touring schedules, and

Figure 9.1 The Clancy Brothers and Tommy Makem. *Left to right*: Tommy Makem, Tom Clancy, Paddy Clancy, and Liam Clancy, 1967. From album cover, *The Best of the Clancy Brothers and Tommy Makem*. (Photo: Don Hunstein © Sony Music Entertainment.)

considerable earnings, the success of Clancy Brothers and Tommy Makem epitomized a moment in the 1960s, argues Méabh Ní Fhuarthháin (2011, 16), when the boundaries between folk and popular blurred and Irish folk music became pop music.

But unlike the showbands, the Clancy Brothers and Tommy Makem were unapologetically political both on and off stage and readily articulated a strongly Irish nationalist position, particularly with reference to the sectarian tensions in Northern Ireland. A 1968 review in *The Guardian* of a performance in Charlottetown, Prince Edward Island, Canada, for example, celebrates in mixed and somewhat muted terms, the effect of the quartet's explicit political position on the audience: "The group had a lot of success with the sing-along numbers, probably partly because of their infectious good humor and partly because nobody at last night's concert wanted to be typed as an 'English, Protestant teetotaler.' Everybody sang, maybe not very loudly, but sang." And while showbands focused on American and British popular song, the Clancy Brothers and Tommy Makem robustly embraced Ireland and Irish identity, all wrapped up in an outspoken political advocacy for a united Ireland. For these reasons, the quartet was spared the harsh critique aimed at showbands, despite their otherwise frank commercialism.

The growing popularity of Irish traditional music both contributed and spoke to a new trend of national identity and pride and set the stage for Ireland's eventual emergence into the global, "world music" market. Beginning in the early 1970s, traditional music "supergroups," such as Planxty, the Chieftains, the Boys of the Lough, the Bothy Band, and others, skyrocketed to international fame. Along with the founding of a spate of record labels in both Ireland and the United States, the revival of interest in Irish traditional music would come to redefine what constituted Irish music. Left behind were the showbands—increasingly out of tune culturally, politically, and musically with the times.

"Jiving Is as Irish as the Grass of Donegal": The Resilience of Dance Floor Memory

Showbands by name persisted throughout Ireland and in Irish diasporic communities into the 1990s. They retained varied repertoires of pop songs and Irish classics, featured different lead singers, and kept up with changing technologies. They maximized their commercial viability by offering something for everybody by moving seamlessly from covers of country songs, to pop arias, to rock 'n' roll numbers, to Irish rebel ballads, and to the occasional céilí dance. Indeed, the end of the showband era also saw the end to what had been a historical emphasis on variety in Irish popular entertainment.

Since the early 2000s, the exception to this are Irish wedding bands—an umbrella term describing a wide range of commercial groups that, in many ways, carry on the work of the showbands by providing dance music for social events. Like the showbands, contemporary Irish wedding bands perform a diverse repertoire and aim to get their audiences up and dancing. One such wedding band is the Cookstown, County Tyrone–based group the Coves, whose lead singer/guitarist is David Long, the son of the late Jim Long, lead vocalist in the 1970s showband Tuxedo Junction. The Coves provide their audiences with a range of Irish folk and country songs and instrumental music as well as music for jive dancing. They make a point of keeping their sound local by rendering American songs in their own local Irish accents rather than imitating an American accent. As David Long sees it, "Singing with an American accent doesn't help to sell it particularly well. Sometimes if you leave a little bit of your local twang in there, it helps a bit too, because it Irishifies it" (interview, 2023). In this way, the band takes their place in a historic and ongoing process of cultural translation by infusing imported repertoire with the familiar cadence of local accents, similar to the Clipper Carlton's treatment of *The Jolson Story* some seventy years earlier.

Further, in translating cultural memory into present-day practice, the Coves perform songs that trigger jive dancing, according to David Long: "The songs that [audiences] will jive to [include] American country songs, which have that kind of Irish two/four beat added to it and [are] usually sung by an Irish artist. . . . I think a lot of people in Ireland don't think of [John Denver's]'Country Roads' as being an American song. They consider it Irish. It's just what they've always done. It's as if jiving is as Irish as the grass in Donegal!" (interview, 2023).

The Coves also adhere to long-established expectations of Irish performance practice that is firmly lodged in their audience's collective memory. Dating back not only to the showband era but to the preceding dance band and orchestra years, the Coves, explains David Long, structure their dance tunes into sets of three:

> So it might involve a set of jives and then a rest and then a set of waltzes and then a rest. And then some bands would've done a set of foxtrots and then a slow dance set and then another jive set. . . . This is what the showbands used to do and this is what people were accustomed to. . . . I think there's an unwritten code in Ireland that this is how it's done and this is how you do it. And a lot of people who come from rural backgrounds seem to understand that. (Interview, 2023)

Showbands: Memory and Legacy

The lingering persistence of dance floor expectations is just one way that people recall the showband era. Many share nostalgic recollections of the joys of attending showband dances night after night while others retain stark condemnations of a music genre that some viewed as strictly imitative and crassly commercial. These wide-ranging perspectives include those who have historically enjoyed powerful access to the media and, significantly, those who have not and whose tastes and experiences so often go unrecognized and unrecorded. Taken together, these memories and resonances provide a democratic snapshot of a musical era and a social movement that ignited the imaginations of musicians and delighted dancers on both sides of the border.

Showbands both reflected and contributed to Ireland's changing social and economic landscapes from 1955 to 1975, informed the birth of Ireland's pop recording industry, set the stage for the emergence of Irish rock, and opened the doors for Irish women performers to ascend to local, national, and international stages. The showband world attracted a raft of entrepreneurs and musicians who quickly realized and benefited from the moneymaking potential of this scene. That said, as an industry, the showbands helped grow employment opportunities for workers on both sides of the border and inspired many working-class Irish to learn an instrument, form a band, and move beyond largely entrenched limitations of income and opportunity. In doing so, showbands democratized access to the stage and demonstrated that the pleasures of performance need not limited to a handful of stars but to any aspiring musician who was willing to put in the hard work.

Enjoying a good run of over two decades, showband musicians created a new world of popular entertainment that was quintessentially Irish. As such, the Irish showband world offered musicians and their audiences a renewed optimism about the possibilities of an enlarged life as well as new and different ways of thinking about their own potential and role in a changing world.

Notes

1. For a personal account of the Miami Showband massacre and its aftermath, see Stephen Travers's *The Miami Showband Massacre* (2007).

2. By the 1990s, the moniker, "Celtic rock" came to signify, particularly among Irish American showbands, any means of sonically updating Irish song and traditional music, explains Linda and Roisin Rutherford, members of the New York–based Rutherford Family Showband:

> LINDA: [We] take older types of music and put a rock 'n' roll beat to it. And so it becomes like a rock 'n' roll tune to an old Irish song. And with reels and jigs, instead of playing just [a] straight traditional beat, you start out like that and all of the sudden, the drums'll give a big crash and then you're in with like a disco beat!
>
> ROISIN: It'll explode! (Interview, 1991)

REFERENCES

Almeida, Linda Dowling. 2004. "'A Great Time to Be in America': The Irish in Post–Second World War New York City." In *Ireland in the 1950s: The Lost Decade*, edited by Dermot Keogh, Finbarr O'Shea, and Carmel Quinlan, 206–20. Cork: Mercier Press.

Anderson, Gerry. 2008. *Heads: A Day in the Life*. Dublin: Gill.

Austin, Valerie A. 1993. "The *Céilí* and the Public Dance Halls Act, 1935." *Eire-Ireland* 28 (3): 7–16.

Baade, Christina. 2008. "'The Battle of the Saxes': Gender, Dance Bands, and British Nationalism in the Second World War." In *Big Ears: Listening for Gender in Jazz Studies*, edited by Nichole T. Rustin and Sherry Tucker, 90–128. Durham, NC: Duke University Press.

Barker-Benfield, G. J. 1992. *The Culture of Sensibility: Sex and Society in 18th Century Britain*. Chicago: University of Chicago Press.

Barrett, Alan. 1999. "Irish Migration: Characteristics, Causes and Consequences." Discussion Paper 97, December 1999. Institute for the Study of Labor (Bonn). Accessed August 16, 2024. http://ftp.iza.org/dp97.pdf.

Beiner, Guy. 2013. "Disremembering 1798? An Archaeology of Social Forgetting and Remembrance in Ulster." *History and Memory* 25 (1): 9–50.

———. 2014. "Probing the Boundaries of Irish Memory: From Postmemory to Prememory and Back." *Irish Historical Studies* 39 (154): 296–307.

Bowen, Kurt. 1983. *Protestants in a Catholic State: Ireland's Privileged Minority*. Quebec, Canada: McGill-Queen's University Press.

Bradley, John. 2004. "Changing the Rules: Why the Failures of the 1950s Forced a Transition in Economic Policy-Making." In *The Lost Decade: Ireland in the 1950s*, edited by Dermot Keogh, Finbarr O'Shea, and Carmel Quinlan, 105–17. Cork: Mercier Press.

Brady, Sasha, 2015. "'I Was Unfaithful for Years'—Singer Eileen Reid Breaks Down on TV3 as She Admits Getting Pregnant during Affair." *Independent*, September 24, 2015.

www.independent.ie/life/family/family-features/i-was-unfaithful-for-years-singer-eileen-reid-breaks-down-on-tv3-as-she-admits-getting-pregnant-during-affair-31555152.html.
Brannigan, John. 2008. "'Ireland, and Black!': The Cultural Politics of Racial Figuration." In *Textual Practice* 22 (2): 229–48. London: Routledge.
———. 2024. "Blackface Minstrelsy, Irish Modernism, and the Histories of Irish Whiteness." In *Race in Irish Literature and Culture*, edited by Malcolm Sen and Julie McCormick Weng, 103–20. Cambridge: Cambridge University Press.
Bruce, Frank, and Archie Foley. 2000. *More Variety Days: Fairs, Fit-Ups, Music Hall, Variety Theatre, Clubs, Cruises, and Cabaret*. Edinburgh: Tod Press.
Bufwack, Mary A. 1998. "Girls with Guitars—And Fringes and Sequins and Rhinestones, Silk, Lace, and Leather." In *Reading Country Music*, edited by Cecilia Tichi, 153–79. Durham, NC: Duke University Press.
Byrne, Barbara. 1965. "this phenomenal showband business." *Development, Agriculture and Industry: The Journal of Ireland's Economic Progress*, no. 72 (June): 25–26.
Chan, Suzanna. 2005. "Some Notes on Deconstructing Ireland's Whiteness: Immigrants, Emigrants and the Perils of Jazz." *Variant* 22 (2): 20–21.
Christgau, Georgia. 2016. "Kitty Wells, Queen of Denial." In *Country Boys and Redneck Women: New Essays in Gender and Country Music*, edited by Diane Pecknold and Kristine M. McCusker, 211–30. Jackson: University Press of Mississippi.
Clayton-Lea, Tony, and Rogan Taylor. 1992. *Irish Rock. Where It's Come From, Where It's At, Where It's Going*. Dublin: Gill and Macmillan.
Clear, Catríona. 2004. "'Too Fond of Going': Female Emigration and Change for Women in Ireland, 1946–1961." In *Ireland in the 1950s: The Lost Decade*, 135–46. Cork: Mercier Press.
Cooney, John. 1999. *John Charles McQuaid: Ruler of Catholic Ireland*. Dublin: O'Brien Press.
Coughlan, John, 1965. "There's Profit in the World of 'Pop." *Development, Agriculture and Industry: The Journal of Ireland's Economic Progress*, no. 72 (June): 27–29.
Daly, Ann. 1959. "Mick Delahunty." *Irish Echo*, February 7, 1959.
Danaher, Deirdre. 1988. "*An Clár Abú*: Irish Music the Kilfenora Way." MA thesis, University College Cork.
Davies, Helen. 2001. "All Rock and Roll Is Homosocial: The Representation of Women in the British Rock Music Press." *Popular Music* 20 (3), "Gender and Sexuality" (October): 301–19.
Delaney, Enda. 2002. *Irish Emigration since 1921*. Studies in Irish Economic and Social History. Dundalk, Ireland: Dundalgen Press.
———. 2007. *The Irish in Post-War Britain*. London: Oxford University Press.
Edelman, Katherine. 1958. "Ireland, After Long Absence." In *The Capuchin Annual, 1958*, edited by Father Henry, OFM Cap., 51–55. Dublin: Irish Capuchin Franciscans.
Enright, Tom, TD. 1975. Dáil Éireann debate. *Restricted Licenses Conversion Fund Bill, Second Stage*, June 12, 1975. https://www.oireachtas.ie/en/debates/debate/dail/1975-06-12/50/, accessed August 23, 2024.
Evans, Damian. 2019. "'These Off-beat "Crazy Kids and Gals': Jazz in Ireland, 1918–1960." *Journal of the Society for Musicology in Ireland* 14: 3–30. https://jsmi.musicologyireland.ie/index.php/journal/issue/view/16.
Fehily, F. J. 1953. "Father Fehily on the Parish Hall." *The Furrow* 4 (1): 16, 22–24.
Ferriter, Diarmaid. 2004. *The Transformation of Ireland*. New York: Overlook Press.
Foley, Catherine. 2001. "Perceptions of Irish Step Dance: National, Global, and Local." In *Dance Research Journal* 33 (1): 34–45.

Garvin, Tom. 2004. *Preventing the Future: Why Was Ireland So Poor for So Long?* Dublin: Gill and Macmillan.
Gedutis, Susan. 2004. *See You at the Hall: Boston's Golden Era of Irish Music and Dance*. Boston: Northeastern University Press.
Gjelten, Tom. 2015. "The Immigration Act That Inadvertently Changed America." *Atlantic*, October 2, 2015. http://www.theatlantic.com/politics/archive/2015/10/immigration-act-1965/408409/.
Gillan, Patrick (Paddy). 2007. "Joe Dolan: Obituary." *Irish Times*, December 29, 2007.
Gilmore, Tom. 2009. *Larry Cunningham: A Showband Legend*. Dublin: Mentor Books.
Hall, Reg. 1995. "The Social Organisation of Traditional Music-Making: The Irish in London after the War." Ó Riada Memorial Lecture 10, Traditional Music Archive and Irish Traditional Music Society, University College Cork.
Hall, Stuart. 1981. "Notes on Deconstructing 'The Popular.'" In *People's History and Socialist Theory*, ed. Raphael Samuel, 227–40. London: Routledge & Kegan Paul.
Heffernan, David. 2001. *From a Whisper to a Scream: The Living History of Irish Rock*. Produced in association with RTÉ, distributed by Winstar TV & Video. WHE73125.
Higgins, Jimmy, 2007. *Are Ye the Band? A Memoir of the Showband Era*. Dublin: Mentor Books.
Hobsbawm, Eric. 1992. "Introduction: Inventing Traditions." In *The Invention of Tradition*, edited by Eric Hobsbawm and Terence Ranger, 1–14. Cambridge: Cambridge University Press.
Holohan, Carole. 2014. "More Than a Revival of Memories? 1960s Youth and the 1916 Rising." In *1916 in 1966: Commemorating the Easter Rising*, edited by Mary E. Daly and Margaret O'Callaghan, Royal Irish Academy, 174–98.
Holt, Eddie, "From 'Paddydom' to Punk." *Irish Times*, March 4, 2000. https://www.irishtimes.com/news/from-paddydom-to-punk-1.252257.
Horan, Monsignor James. 1992. *Memoirs, 1911–1986*. Edited by Father Micheál MacGréil. Dingle, Ireland: Brandon Book Publishers.
Ingman, Heather. 2007. *Twentieth-Century Fiction by Irish Women: Nation and Gender*. Farnham, UK: Ashgate.
Irish Federation of Musicians, Dublin and District Brand, Price List Minimum and Directory. 1955. Dublin: Ardiff.
Irwin, Collin. 2017. "Margaret Barry: Wild Irish Woman of the British Folk Scene." *The Guardian*, January 18, 2017. https://www.theguardian.com/music/2017/jan/18/margaret-barry-wild-irish-woman-of-the-british-folk-scene-celtic-connections.
Kennedy, Joe. 1967. "Showbands Are Looking at the British Scene with Aching Hearts." *Top Ten Weekly*, February 17, 1967, 6.
Keogh, Dermot. 1998. "Towards a Biography of an Archbishop." *Studies: An Irish Quarterly Review* 87 (348): 337–43.
———. 2004. "Introduction: The Vanishing Irish." In *Ireland—The Lost Decade in the 1950s*, edited by Dermot Keogh, Finbar O'Shea, and Carmel Quinn, 11–20. Cork: Mercier Press.
Lawler, Brian, and Adrian Scahill. 2013. "Céilí." In *Encyclopaedia of Music in Ireland*, edited by Harry White and Barra Boydell, 1: 181–84. Dublin: University College Dublin Press.
Lee, J. J. 1979. "Continuity and Change in Ireland, 1945–70." In *Ireland: 1945–70*, edited by J. J. Lee, 166–77. Dublin: Gill and MacMillan.
———. 1989. *Ireland 1912–1985, Politics and Society*. Cambridge: Cambridge University Press.
Lott, Eric. 1995. *Love and Theft: Blackface Minstrelsy and the American Working Class*. New York: Oxford University Press.

Lynch, J. 1960. *Díospóireachtaí Parlaiminte / Parliamentary Debates, Seanad Éireann* 52, May 18, 1960. https://www.oireachtas.ie/en/debates/debate/seanad/1960-05-18/6/, accessed August 20, 2024.
Maguire, Paul. 2012. "Conditions of Possibility: Changes in Popular Music Culture and the Development of Country & Irish Music," a dissertation, Faculty of Arts at the University of Ulster.
———. 2013. "Country and Irish." In *Encyclopaedia of Music in Ireland*, edited by Harry White and Barra Boydell, 1: 255–57. Dublin: University College Dublin Press.
Malone, Bill, 2003. *Flowers in the Wildwood: Women in Early Country Music, 1923–1939*. Notes to the CD. Trikont: Munich.
McClary, Susan, 1991. *Feminine Endings: Music, Gender, and Sexuality*. Minneapolis: University of Minnesota Press.
McClintock, Anne. 1995. *Imperial Leather: Race, Gender, and Sexuality in the Colonial Contest*. New York: Routledge.
McCormack, Jayne. 2015. "Sir James Galway: Flute Maestro Reflects on His Career." BBC News, Northern Ireland, March 9, 2015. https://www.bbc.com/news/uk-northern-ireland-31733453.
McLaughlin, Noel, and Martin McLoone. 2000. "Hybridity and National Musics: The Case of Irish Rock Music." *Popular Music* 19 (2): 181–99.
———. 2012. *Rock and Popular Music in Ireland: Before and After U2*. Dublin: Irish Academic Press.
Miller, Rebecca S. 1991. "Martin Mulhaire, Irish Traditional Button Accordionist." *Old Traditions—New Sounds*. Radio documentary archived at the World Music Archives, Wesleyan University, Middletown, CT.
———. 1992. "After All These Years It's Still the Hucklebuck." *Irish Echo*, August 12–18, 1992, 22.
———. 1996. "Irish Traditional and Popular Music in New York City: Identity and Social Change, 1930–1975." In *The New York Irish*, edited by Ronald H. Bayor and Timothy J. Meagher, 481–507; 692–95 (endnotes). Baltimore: Johns Hopkins University Press.
———. 2013. "Albert Reynolds"; "Brendan Bowyer"; "Capitol Showband"; "Dance Bands"; "Dickie Rock"; "The Dixies"; "Eileen Reid"; "The Hucklebuck"; "Miami Showband"; "Royal Showband"; "Showbands." Entries in *Encyclopaedia of Music in Ireland*, edited by Harry White and Barra Boydell. Dublin: University College Dublin Press.
Mooney, Reverend Michael L. 1953. "The Parish Hall." *The Furrow* 4 (1): 2–7.
Morrison, Van. 1997. "Van Morrison Interview." Interview by Paul Dunoyer, originally published in *Q Magazine*, April. Accessed online, August 25, 2024. https://www.pauldunoyer.com/van-morrison-interview-1997/.
———. 2012. "Van Morrison: 'Singing Is My Profession—There Is No Plan B.'" Interview by Don Was. *The Guardian*, October 1, 2012. http://www.guardian.co.uk/music/2012/oct/01/van-morrison-born-sing-interview.
———. 2015. "Van Morrison: 'People Who Say Others Are Difficult Are Usually Difficult Themselves.'" Interview by Robin Denselow. *The Guardian*, June 4, 2015. https://www.theguardian.com/music/2015/jun/04/van-morrison-people-who-say-others-difficult-are-difficult-themselves-lead-belly-lonnie-donegan.
Nelson, Brett. 2012. "The Real Definition of Entrepreneur and Why It Matters." *Forbes Magazine*, June 5, 2012. https://www.forbes.com/sites/%20brettnelson/%202012/%2006/%2005/%20the-real-definition-of-entrepreneur-and-why-it-matters/. Accessed August 26, 2024.
Ní Fhuartháin, Méabh. 2011. "Comhaltas Ceoltóirí Éireann: Shaping Tradition, 1951–1970." PhD diss., National University of Ireland, Galway.

———. 2013. "The Clancy Brothers and Tommy Makem." In *Encyclopaedia of Music in Ireland*, edited by Harry White and Barra Boydell, 1: 201–2. Dublin: University College Dublin Press.

Noonan, Paddy. 1992. *Irish Memories: Recollections of the Irish American Music Scene from the 1940s, 50s, and 60s*. Collector's Series, Garden City, NY: Copley Irish Records, a Division of Rego Irish Records and Tapes.

Norquay, Glenda, and Gerry Smyth. 2002. "Introduction: Crossing the Margins." In *Across the Margins: Cultural Identity and Change in the Atlantic Archipelago*, edited by Glenda Norquay and Gerry Smyth, 1–10. Manchester, UK: Manchester University Press.

Nott, James J. 2002. *Music for the People: Popular Music and Dance in Interwar Britain*. Oxford: Oxford University Press.

O'Brien, George. (1988) 1994. *Dancehall Days*. Belfast: Blackstaff Press.

Ó Gráda, Cormac. 2006. *Jewish Ireland in the Age of Joyce: A Socioeconomic History*. Princeton, NJ: Princeton University Press.

Ó hAllmhuráin, Gearóid. 2005. "Dancing on the Hobs of Hell: Rural Communities in Clare and the Dance Hall Act of 1935." *New Hibernia Review/Iris Éireannach Nua* 9 (4): 9–18.

———. 2016. *Flowing Tides: History and Memory in an Irish Soundscape*. New York: Oxford University Press.

O'Hanlon, Gerry. 2004. "Population Change in the 1950s: A Statistical Review." In *Ireland in the 1950s: The Lost Decade*, 72–79. Cork, Mercier Press.

O'Hanlon, Ray. 2008. "Impresario Bill Fuller Dies." *Irish Echo*, August 13–19, 2008, 6.

O'Hara, Steve. 1967. "Where Have All the Showbands Gone?" *Top Ten Weekly*, February 25, 1967.

O'Keefe, Finbar, 2002. *Goodnight, God Bless, and Safe Home: The Golden Showband Era*. Dublin: O'Brien Press.

O'Quigley, Senator John B. 1960. Seanad Éireann transcripts, May 18, 1960. Vol. 52. https://www.oireachtas.ie/en/debates/debate/seanad/1960-05-18/6/. Accessed September 2, 2024.

O'Reilly, Michael. 2015. *Dancehall Days: When Showbands Ruled The Stage*. Dublin: Gill and Macmillan.

O'Toole, Fintan. 1997. *The Ex-Isle of Erin: Images of a Global Ireland*. Dublin: New Island Books.

Portelli, Alessandro. 1991. "What Makes Oral History Different." In *The Death of Luigi Trastulli and Other Stories: Form and Meaning in Oral History*, 45–58. Albany: State University of New York Press.

Power, Vincent. 1990. *Send 'em Home Sweatin': The Showbands' Story*. Dublin: Kildanore Press.

Prendergast, Mark J. 1987. *Isle of Noises: Rock and Roll's Roots in Ireland*. New York: St. Martin's Press.

Randall, Annie. 2008. *Dusty!: Queen of the Postmods*. Cary, NC: Oxford University Press.

Reilly, Terry, 2006. *On a Wing and a Prayer: The Story of Knock Airport, Now Known as Ireland West Airport Knock*. Ballina, Ireland: Yew Plain Publishing.

Rock, Dickie. 2007. *Dickie Rock: Always Me*. Dublin: Merlin Publishing.

Rock, Mick. 1972. "String Bustin': Rory from Taste." *Rolling Stone*, May 25, 1972.

Rogin, Michael. 1994. "'Democracy and Burnt Cork': The End of Blackface, the Beginning of Civil Rights." *Representations*, no. 46 (Spring): 1–34.

Russell, Helen, Frances McGinnity, and Philip J. O'Connell. 2017. "Gender Equality in the Irish Labour Market 1966–2016: Unfinished Business?" *Economic and Society Review* 48 (4): 393–418.

Ryan, Louise. 2007. "'A Decent Girl Well Worth Helping': Women, Migration and Unwanted Pregnancy." In *Ireland Beyond Boundaries: Mapping Irish Studies in the Twenty-First Century*, edited by Liam Harte and Yvonne Whelan, 135–53. London: Pluto Press.

Scahill, Adrian. 2018. "'That Vulgar Strummer': The Piano and Traditional Music in the Gaelic Revival." In *Music Preferred: Essays in Musicology, Cultural History and Analysis in Honour of Harry White*, edited by Lorraine Byrne Bodley, 183–202. Vienna: Hollitzer.
Scanlon, Ann. 2008. "Bill Fuller: Irishman Whose Empire of Venues and Hotels Started in Camden." Obituary, *The Guardian*, September 8, 2008. http://www.guardian.co.uk/music/2008/sep/09/popandrock.musicindustry.
Shanagher, Sean. 2014. "Recreational Dance in Ireland 1940–1960: Politics and Pleasures." PhD diss., Dublin City University, Dublin.
Shelton, Robert. 1966. "Irish Pop Singers at Carnegie Hall." *New York Times*, October 3, 1966. https://www.nytimes.com/1966/10/03/archives/irish-pop-singers-at-carnegie-hall.html.
Smyth, Gerry. 2005. *Noisy Island: A Short History of Irish Popular Music*. Cork: Cork University Press.
Smyth, Gerry, and Sean Campbell. 2005. *Beautiful Day*. Cork: Cork University Press.
Smyth, Jim. 1993. "Dancing, Depravity, and All That Jazz: The Public Dance Halls Act of 1935." *History Ireland*, Summer.
Southall, Helen Vera. 2015. "Dance Bands in Chester: An Evolving Professional Network." PhD diss., University of Liverpool, Liverpool.
Stanley, Ruth. 2018. "'Jazzing the Soul of the Nation Away': The Hidden History of Jazz in Ireland and Northern Ireland During the Interwar Years." In *Music Preferred: Essays in Musicology, Cultural History and Analysis in Honour of Harry White*, edited by Lorraine Byrne Bodley, 231–50. Vienna: Hollitzer.
Staples, Jimmy. 1966. "Arranged by Jimmy Lally." *Crescendo*, June, pp. 9–11.
Sweeney, Joanne, 2017. "Fr. Brian D'Arcy: Ex-taoiseach Albert Reynolds Kick-Started My Writing Career." In *Irish News*, December 21, 2017. https://www.irishnews.com/arts/2017/12/21/news/fr-brian-d-arcy-ex-taoiseach-albert-reynolds-kick-started-my-writing-career-1215867/.
Swift, John P. 2012. *Striking a Chord: A Trade Union History of Musicians in Ireland*. Dublin: Watchword.
Thompson, Paul, with Joanna Bornat. 2017. *The Voice of the Past: Oral History*. 4th ed. New York: Oxford University Press.
Travers, Pauric. 1995. "'There Was Nothing for Me There': Irish Female Emigration, 1922–71." In *Irish Women and Irish Migration*, edited by Patrick O'Sullivan, 146–67. London: Leicester University Press.
Travers, Stephen, with Neil Fetherstonhaugh, 2007. *The Miami Showband Massacre: A Survivor's Search for the Truth*. Dublin: Hodder Headline Ireland.
Trotter, Mary. 2008. *Modern Irish Theatre*. Cambridge: Polity Press.
Tucker, Sherry. 1999. "Telling Performances: Jazz History Remembered and Remade by the Women in the Band." in *The Oral History Review* 26 (1): 67–84.
———. 2000. *Swing Shift: "All-Girl" Bands of the 1940s*. Durham, NC: Duke University Press.
Vallely, Fintan, ed. 2011. *The Companion to Irish Traditional Music*. 2nd ed. Cork: Cork University Press.
Waldron, Kieran. 2008. *The Archbishops of Tuam, 1700–2000*. Tuam, Ireland: Nordlaw Books.
Walsh, Brendan. 1971. "Aspects of Labour Supply and Demand with Special Reference to the Employment of Women in Ireland." In *Journal of the Statistical and Social Inquiry Society of Ireland*.
———. 1979. "Economic Growth and Development, 1945–70." In *Ireland: 1945–70*, edited by J. J. Lee, 27–37. Dublin: Gill and MacMillan.
Waters, John. 1994. *Race of Angels: The Genesis of U2*. London: Fourth Estate.

Whitaker, T. K. 1959. Archival papers, University College Dublin Archives, Catalogue Number P175/50.
White, Harry. 1996. "The Preservation of Music and Irish Cultural History." *International Review of the Aesthetics and Sociology of Music* 27 (2): 123–38.
White, Harry, and Barra Boydell. 2013. *The Encyclopaedia of Music in Ireland*. 2 vols. Dublin: University College–Dublin Press.

Interviews and Personal Communications

All interviews conducted by the author unless otherwise indicated.

Begley, Philomena, Pomeroy, County Tyrone, July 17, 2008.
Beirne, Mildred, Ballyhaunis, County Roscommon, July 29, 2007.
Bowyer, Aisling, Galway City, County Galway, July 29, 2006.
Bowyer, Brendan, Massapequa, New York, July 28, 1992.
———, Galway City, County Galway, July 29, 2006.
Bradley, William, Derry City, Northern Ireland, October 22, 2018.
Byrne, T. J., Carlow, County Carlow, July 23, 2007.
Carr, Eamon, Dublin, June 4, 2009.
Coade, Monica, Bray, County Wicklow, September 21, 2018.
Coade, Noel, Bray, County Wicklow, July 14, 2008.
Coade, Sharon, Bray, County Wicklow, September 21, 2018.
Coen, Jack, Bronx, New York, March 7, 1992.
Cole, Paddy, Dublin, July 19, 2007.
———, Ballsbridge, County Dublin, September 20, 2018.
Connolly, Matty, Richmond Hill, NY, June 12, 1988.
Coughlan, Michael, Waterford City, County Waterford, July 24, 2007.
Cudahy, Dorothy Hayden, Rego Park, New York, March 4, 1992.
D'Arcy, Father Brian, Enniskillen, County Fermanagh, August 4, 2007.
Day, Muriel, Belfast, Northern Ireland, July 18, 2009.
Delahunty, Mick, Jr., Clonmel, County Tipperary, November 22, 2018.
Doherty, Tom, Brooklyn, New York, October 8, 1991.
Doyle, John, Dublin, personal communication, February 10, 2006.
Duffy, Mary, Knock, County Mayo, July 10, 2009.
Fernandez, José (Joe), Howth, County Dublin, July 20, 2007.
Gallagher, Seamus, Falcarragh, County Donegal, July 21, 2008.
Garber, Ian (Henry), Isle of Wight, UK, September 4–5, 2018; personal communication, November 17, 2017.
Geary, Paddy, Tallow, County Waterford, December 20, 2018.
Harris, Máire, email communication, July 7, 2014.
Hayden, Anne, Greystones, County Wicklow, July 13, 2008.
Hayden, Tommy, Greystones, County Wicklow, July 13, 2008.
Higgins, Jimmy, Galway City, County Galway, July, 2007.
———, Renmore, County Galway, September 25, 2018.
Holt, Frank. Telephone interview, New York, June 29, 1992.
Hopkins, Desmond (Des), Clane, County Kildare, July 23, 2007.
Kearney, Bob, Cork, County Cork, July 27, 2007.
Kelly, Des, Galway City, County Galway, August 2, 2006.
Kelly, Eileen, Dublin, July 11, 2008.
Kelly, John, Knock, County Mayo, July 30, 2007.

Kelly, Sandy, Oldtown, North County, Dublin, July 12, 2008.
Killeen, Tony, Greystones, County Wicklow, July 13, 2008.
Knowles, Sonny, Dublin, June 5, 2009.
Lavin, Eileen, Knock, County Mayo, July 10, 2009.
Lennon, Charlie, Spiddal, County Galway, January 24, 2019.
Long, David, via Zoom, Cookstown, County Tyrone, September 11, 2023.
Lynch, Pat, Cork, County Cork, July 26, 2007.
Mac Gréil, Father Micheál, Westport, County Westport, July 23, 2008.
Maguire, Pat, Dublin, June 4, 2009.
Makem, Tommy, New York City, New York, April 4, 1992.
McCarthy, Claudette Colbert, Florham Park, New Jersey, January 8, 2019.
McCarthy, Joe, Cork City, County Cork, July 27, 2007.
McCoubrey, Maxi, Dublin, June 3, 2009.
McCullough, Henry, Ballymoney, County Antrim, Northern Ireland, July 19, 2007.
McDermott, Jim, Derry City, Northern Ireland, July 20, 2008.
———, Derry City, Northern Ireland, October 23, 2018.
McEvoy, Michael, Drumcondra, Dublin, September 22, 2018.
McIntyre, Gay, Derry City, Northern Ireland, July 20, 2008.
———, Derry City, Northern Ireland, October 22, 2018.
Moore, Ray, Omagh, County Tyrone, August 4, 2007.
Muldoon, Maxie, Rathmines, Dublin, June 4, 2009.
Mulhaire, Brendan, personal communication, Galway, August, 2006.
Mulhaire, Martin, Flushing, New York, October 4, 1985.
———. Flushing, New York, May 10, 1988.
Neary, Tom, Knock, County Mayo, July 23, 2008.
Noonan, Paddy, Garden City, New York, February 27, 1992.
O'Brien, Brendan, Salt Hill, County Galway, August 1, 2006.
O'Connor, Don, Limerick City, County Limerick, August 16, 2006.
O'Donnell, Margo, Castleblaney, County Monaghan, July 17, 2008.
———, Castleblaney, County Monaghan, June 7, 2009.
O'Hagan, Art, Strabane, County Tyrone, Northern Ireland, August 1, 2007.
O'Hanlon, Mick, interview with Paul Maguire, Strabane, County Tyrone, August 16, 2007.
O'Kelly, Leo, Dun Laoghaire, County Dublin, July 21, 2007.
O'Reilly, George, Howth, County Dublin, July 10, 2008.
O'Sullivan, Denis, Clonmel, County Tipperary, November 22, 2018.
Pennyfeather, Dave, Dublin, August 18, 2009.
Quigley, Johnny, Derry City, Northern Ireland, October 23, 2018.
Quinn, Louis, Flushing, New York, October 24, 1990.
Reid, Eileen, Dublin, September 14, 2018.
Reynolds, Albert, Dublin, August 10, 2006.
Reynolds, Jim, Longford Town, County Longford, July 15, 2008.
Reynolds, Paddy, Staten Island, New York, March 20, 1992.
Robinson, Billy, Ramelton, County Donegal, June 9, 2009.
Rock, Dickie, Dublin, August 9, 2006.
Rutherford, Linda, and Roisin Rutherford, East Durham, New York, August 23, 1991.
Scully, Barry, Dublin, August 7, 2006.
Sproule, Dáithí, Amherst, Massachusetts, August 24, 2009.
Stanley, Father Cathal, Portumna, County Galway, June 5, 2013.
Trotter, John, Derry City, County Derry, October 22, 2018.

Tully, Tina, Edenderry, County Offaly, July 14, 2008.
Turbett, Gene, Omagh, County Tyrone, August 4, 2007.
Ward, Brendan, New York City, New York, March 13, 1992.
Wood, Mick, Drumshanbo, County Leitrim, August 4, 2007.

Newspapers, Magazines, and Journals

Connacht Sentinel, May 27, 1930.
Connaught Tribune, October 29, 1955; June 21, 1958; January 26, 1963, March 1, 1963.
Dancing Gazette (Dublin). December, 1966.
Development: the Journal of Ireland's Economic Progress, no. 72 (June 1965).
Evening Herald, August 10, 1935; January 1, 1942.
Fermanagh Herald, March 4, 1944.
The Guardian, June 4, 2015.
The Guardian (Charlottetown, PEI, Canada), March 5, 1968.
Irish Examiner, May 2, 1951; April 24, 1958; January 17, 1959.
Irish Independent, February 24, 1941; January 23, 1950; September 6, 1960; July 1, 2011.
Irish Press, February 21, 1955; March 30/31, 1956; April 12, 1956.
The Liberator, August 18, 1925.
Leinster Leader, August 13, 1927.
Limerick Leader, February 6, 1957; November 15, 1958.
Longford Leader, September 25, 1926.
Meath Chronicle, October 7, 1950.
Sunday Independent, January 22, 1950.
Top Ten Weekly, (Dublin), February 17, 1967; February 25, 1967.
Waterford News and Star, January 1, 1960.
Western People, March, 1953.

Media: Radio Broadcasts, Podcasts, and Websites

Album of Irish Showbands. http://www.irishshowbandalbum.com. Accessed September 2, 2024.
Beirne, Francis K. Irish Bands Archive. www.irishshowbands.net. Accessed July 3, 2024.
Brendan Balfe's Dance Band Days. 2006. Programme One, RTÉ Radio One. Broadcast November 30, 2006.
Gallagher, Gerry. Irish-Showbands.com. https://www.irish-showbands.com/orchestras.htm. Accessed September 2, 2024.
Irish Statute Book, "Public Dance Halls Act, 1935." accessed February 4, 2019, http://www.irishstatutebook.ie/eli/1935/act/2/section/13/enacted/en/html.
King, Adele. Podcast interview with Eamonn Dunphy, 2007. Accessed July 2, 2018. http://www.rte.ie/podcasts/2007/pc/pod-v-dunphy-290907-44m59s.mp3.

INDEX

REBECCA S. MILLER is professor of music at Hampshire College, a public sector folklorist, and a traditional fiddler. She is the author of *Carriacou String Band Serenade: Performing Identity in the Eastern Caribbean.*

For Indiana University Press

Tony Brewer, *Artist and Book Designer*

Anna Garnai, *Editorial Assistant*

Sophia Hebert, *Assistant Acquisitions Editor*

Samantha Heffner, *Marketing and Publicity Manager*

Katie Huggins, *Production Manager*

Darja Malcolm-Clarke, *Project Manager/Editor*

Bethany Mowry, *Acquisitions Editor*

Dan Pyle, *Online Publishing Manager*

Michael Regoli, *Director of Publishing Operations*

Leyla Salamova, *Book Designer*